Advance praise for

CHILDREN'S RIGHTS AND EDUCATION

"The editors have assembled a thought-provoking and intellectually engaging collection of essays that demonstrate the benefits that flow from the adoption of a rights-based approach to education in a range of diverse social, cultural, linguistic, and religious contexts. This book deserves the attention of anyone genuinely concerned with the realisation of a child's right to education."

—*John Tobin, Professor, University of Melbourne, a leading children's rights expert*

"Be aware! Education and children's rights are taken seriously in this book. The topics, important and frequently controversial, are illuminated by research, expertise and passion—with particular emphasis on social justice, inclusion, evolving capacities, child agency, and best interests. A rigorous exploration and debate of critical issues is launched and encouraged. The reader is likely to strongly agree and disagree at numerous points—and to be stimulated to do more—all to the good in finding the way forward."

—*Stuart N. Hart; Deputy Director, International Institute for Child Rights and Development; Co-Director of Child Rights Education for Professionals (CRED-PRO)*

CHILDREN'S RIGHTS AND EDUCATION

Rethinking Childhood

Gaile S. Cannella
General Editor

Vol. 48

The Rethinking Childhood series is part of the Peter Lang Education list.
Every volume is peer reviewed and meets
the highest quality standards for content and production.

PETER LANG
New York • Washington, D.C./Baltimore • Bern
Frankfurt • Berlin • Brussels • Vienna • Oxford

CHILDREN'S RIGHTS AND EDUCATION

INTERNATIONAL PERSPECTIVES

EDITED BY
Beth Blue Swadener,
Laura Lundy,
Janette Habashi,
Natasha Blanchet-Cohen

PETER LANG
New York • Washington, D.C./Baltimore • Bern
Frankfurt • Berlin • Brussels • Vienna • Oxford

Library of Congress Cataloging-in-Publication Data

Children's rights and education: international perspectives / edited by
Beth Blue Swadener, Laura Lundy, Janette Habashi, Natasha Blanchet-Cohen.
pages cm. — (Rethinking childhood; v. 48)
Includes bibliographical references and index.
1. Right to education—Cross-cultural studies. 2. Children's rights—
Cross-cultural studies. 3. Comparative education. I. Swadener, Beth Blue.
LC213.C55 379.2'6—dc23 2013024275
ISBN 978-1-4331-2122-7 (hardcover)
ISBN 978-1-4331-2121-0 (paperback)
ISBN 978-1-4539-1158-7 (e-book)

Bibliographic information published by **Die Deutsche Nationalbibliothek**.
Die Deutsche Nationalbibliothek lists this publication in the "Deutsche
Nationalbibliografie"; detailed bibliographic data is available
on the Internet at http://dnb.d-nb.de/.

Cover image by Damian Charette; photograph by Bill Gibson.

The paper in this book meets the guidelines for permanence and durability
of the Committee on Production Guidelines for Book Longevity
of the Council of Library Resources.

Printed in the United States of America

*To educators and young people
working to realize children's rights.*

Contents

Acknowledgments

This volume represents a dialogue that the co-editors and contributors have been part of for several years, in part through our collaboration on the Children's Rights Learning Group of Una (a joint learning initiative on children and ethnic diversity). We have often speculated about how various social institutions—particularly those broadly related to education—would change if children's rights were an authentic priority. We thank all the children whose voices and perspectives helped inform the chapters in this volume—giving their views due weight is at the heart of our work. We also thank the contributing authors for raising critical issues and sharing diverse perspectives on children's rights, lives and education.

We want to thank Christopher Myers, Peter Lang Managing Director, who was very responsive and helpful, as well as our excellent copyeditor, Tom Bechtle. We also appreciated working closely with book series editor, Gaile S. Cannella and production editor, Sophie Appel. We benefited greatly from the assistance of student intern and editor, Nathalia Biscarra in formatting and reference checking. We thank Damian Charette for his cover art, that reminded us that children indeed dream the cosmos. Finally, we appreciate the support and patience of those who supported us throughout the book editing process.

Foreword

Kishore Singh

United Nations Special Rapporteur on the Right to Education

More than 20 years ago, the declaration adopted at the World Summit for Children (1990) stated that "There can be no task nobler than giving every child a better future." The Convention on the Rights of the Child, adopted the preceding year (1989), laid down a comprehensive framework for the rights of the child, including the right to education. Under the convention, which is the most universally ratified human rights instrument, states that parties have obligations to incorporate its provisions into domestic laws and policies and to ensure their implementation so that all children everywhere enjoy their right to education. At the same time as the World Summit for Children, the Education for All (EFA) agenda, launched at the World Conference on Education for All (1990) and moved forward by the World Education Forum (2000), expressed collective commitment by the international community to the realization of universal primary education of good quality as the right of every child—boys and girls alike.

However, in spite of progress over the past two decades within these international frameworks, there is an appalling gap between the commitments and the reality. Nearly 60 million children remain deprived of their fundamental right to education—including those belonging to economically and socially marginalized and vulnerable groups such as linguistic and ethnic minorities, immigrants, the handicapped, indigenous peoples, child victims of conflict in many countries, and street children. Millions of those living in poverty suffer educational deprivation and multiple disadvantages. Instead of receiving education, which is their fundamental right, children in many countries are engaged in child labor at an early age or—worse still—are lured into becoming child soldiers.

Thus, the right to education is not fully respected and is often least available to those who need it. Growing disparities in access to education are most worrying. Early childhood care and pre-school education, which, as an integral part of basic education, are the first essential steps in achieving EFA goals, are also scant. Ensuring equality of opportunity in education *in law and in fact* is a continuing challenge that almost all states face. While the right to quality education is the right of all children and a *core obligation* of all governments, many of the children who have access to education do not receive education of good quality, and there is widespread concern over poor learning achievements.

Therefore, at the 2010 Millennium Review Summit the international community made a renewed commitment "to provide equitable educational and learning opportunities for all children" and to ensure "quality education and profession through the school system" (United Nations General Assembly Resolution 65/1). Abiding concern about the impediments to realizing the rights of the child is also expressed in the United Nations Declaration on the Rule of Law (24 September 2012), which recognizes the importance of the rule of law for the protection of the rights of the child. The declaration commits governments to ensuring the best interests of the child in all actions, and the full implementation of the rights of the child.

A rights-based approach rather than a welfare approach should guide state action. Such an approach also enables us to understand better the concept of the "best interest" of the child and its multiple implications—to protect and promote the right to education of every child as an inalienable right; to inculcate in children universally recognized values of human rights and democratic principles, with a child-friendly pedagogical approach; and to nurture in them moral and ethical values and a love for learning. It also implies a school environment that is respectful of human rights and is conducive to preparing children for the responsibilities of freedom. Both the individual and the society are beneficiaries of the right to education, and the best interest of the child is also the best interest of a society, and its future.

The right to education is a primary responsibility of states. It is also a social responsibility—of community, of parents and families, of teachers, of schools, and of all stakeholders in education. It is incumbent upon public authorities to undertake affirmative action and positive measures in favor of children who remain deprived of their fundamental right to education because of historical injustice, social exclusion, marginalization, and poverty—in particular, extreme poverty. A child's right to education should be protected as a justiciable right and enforced in any situation involving its breach or violation. It is always useful to bear in mind the General Comment 5 on "General Measures of Implementation of the Convention on the Rights of the Child" (2003) elaborated by the Committee on the Rights of the Child, which states that "for rights to have meaning, effective remedies must be available to redress violations."

Collective reflections in this volume supported by empirical research on children's educational rights, and key issues addressing their more effective implementation in various geopolitical and cultural contexts enrich the understanding of human rights law. With its focus on a rights framework, the volume also shows how the right to education is a good example of the interdependence of all human rights, particularly the mutually reinforcing links between the right to education and cultural rights and the interface between the educational rights and religion rights and freedom in education.

A commendable feature of this volume is that it embraces a perspective inspired by social justice and equity as it applies to children's educational rights. This is of paramount importance in overcoming marginalization and exclusion in education, often grounded in historical and cultural patterns of a society. Education is a common global public good, and world leaders must safeguard this as such, preserving social interest in education. As this volume argues, education is a fundamental human right, not a product.

This volume will be very useful for policymakers in devising equitable and innovative approaches aimed at promoting and protecting the educational rights of children. It will also be beneficial to researchers and human rights defenders, as well as practitioners who safeguard and foster these rights. Educating every child is a noble cause that must receive unqualified support, especially since the right to education is not only a human right in itself but also essential for the exercise of all other human rights.

Introduction

Beth Blue Swadener, Laura Lundy,
Natasha Blanchet-Cohen, & Janette Habashi

> When asked about human rights, children inevitably say "show, don't tell" but they are very, very rarely asked. If we were to honestly and openly answer their questions, we would have to acknowledge that a great deal of change is needed to create space for human rights in education.
> —Katarina Tomaševski (2006, p. 140)

We all have stories about what has shaped our engagement with issues of children's lives and education rights. For Beth, doing research related to impacts of neoliberal policies, and volunteer work in sub-Saharan Africa, particularly with out-of-school children in Kenya, led to work on broader issues of children's rights. For Laura, a legal scholar and education researcher in Northern Ireland, understanding and advocating for the rights of children in this and other post-conflict settings has been a strong theme in her work. Janette has worked with Palestinian children in the West Bank and Jerusalem on projects related to their understanding of geopolitical issues and a journal project led by youth. Natasha has worked with diverse communities in Canada and focused on children's rights in Venezuela and Colombia; most recently, she has done research with young leaders of the Québec protests of the rapidly rising costs of education. Together, as colleagues and collaborators, we share a passion for social justice as it applies to children's rights and, as editors of this volume, to children's education rights.

This book engages with questions and possibilities related to children's lives, rights, and education. Contributors to this volume discuss, unpack, and share context-specific research from 10 countries on the impacts that children's rights do, can, and should have on children's experience of formal and informal education. Many of us have been in dialogue about intersections of issues, including roles that the UN Convention on the Rights of the Child (CRC) may play in the realm of education for all children, those in post-conflict and other challenging situations, cultural and theoretical tensions, as well as contradictions of universal policies often anchored in Western ideologies and linked to the neoliberal turn in education. We share a collective interest in how child rights–based framing of policy and practice might benefit children at the margins of dominant culture. While a tool for holding governments and communities accountable to the honoring of the protection, provision, and participation rights of children, the CRC is clearly interpreted and enacted in varied ways across differing cross-national contexts. This volume seeks to elucidate, complicate, and enrich such discussions and debates. Throughout, we emphasize the importance of children's experiences and voices in shedding light on how children's rights are—or should be—implemented.

What Are Children's Rights?

Human rights have been defined as rights that are "so fundamental to society's well-being and to people's chance of leading a fulfilling life that governments are obliged to respect them, and the international order has to protect them" (Feldman, 2002, pp. 34–35). Human rights, as set out in international legal frameworks such as the Universal Declaration of Human Rights, apply to all human beings, children included. However, in the latter part of the 20th century, there was increasing recognition that certain groups of people (including women, racial minorities, and children) were particularly vulnerable to human rights violations and, therefore, in need of additional, dedicated legal protections. The key statement of these rights in relation to children is the United Nations Convention on the Rights of the Child (CRC) (United Nations, 1989).

The CRC was adopted by the General Assembly of the United Nations in 1989 and came into force in September 1990. It is the most widely ratified and therefore internationally accepted statement of children's rights standards, with the United States now the major holdout among members of the UN. The CRC is a unique document whose coverage and scope "in recognising the rights of children and young people, and setting out how they are to be promoted and protected is unrivalled in terms of their comprehensive nature, national and international standing and relevance" (Kilkelly & Lundy, 2006, p. 335). It is a touchstone for children's rights throughout the world, providing benchmarks and standards across most aspects of children's lives that are widely supported, relevant, and easily understood. The value of a rights-based, as opposed to a needs- or welfare-based approach, lies not just in its universality or legitimacy, but also in the inherent "moral coinage" of rights, which allows rights holders to make claims for treatment that are not dependent on the goodwill or charity of those who can provide that help (Freeman, 2000). — *No consequences*

The CRC is legally binding in international law. The primary enforcement mechanism is a system of periodic reporting to the Committee on the Rights of the Child. Individual countries report on their progress in relation to the implementation of the CRC every 5 years (see www.ohchr.org). Then, states are required to reflect on their progress in implementing the CRC according to reporting guidelines, which specify the information that the state is required to submit (Article 44). In education, the committee asks for relevant and updated information in respect to

> laws, policies and their implementation, quality standards, financial and human resources, and any other measures to ensure the full enjoyment of the respective rights from early childhood to tertiary and vocational education and training, in particular by children in disadvantaged and vulnerable situations. (United Nations Committee on the Rights of the Child, 2010, p. 9)

Specific issues to be addressed by the states parties are: the right to education, including vocational training and guidance (Article 28); the aims of education (Article 29), with reference also to quality of education; the cultural rights of children belonging to indigenous and minority groups (Article 30); and education on human rights and civic education. The committee also welcomes submissions from other interested parties, including NGOs, many of whom work collaboratively to produce an alternative report often involving children meaningfully in the process of compilation. The committee conducts a hearing in which it questions state officials on their progress and takes evidence from other parties, at the end of which it publishes "concluding observations," reports about the individual state's progress in implementation. While the scope and depth of the reports are limited by the time and space available, the observations, along with the states parties' self-evaluations, provide rich insights into the state of children's rights and educational policy in each signatory state (Lundy, 2012). The observations also provide a benchmark for civil society to assess the fulfillment of education and advocate for change.

Why Education Rights and the CRC?

The right to education is one of the most widely accepted of all human rights provisions, having been a consistent feature of international human rights treaties since the establishment of the UN. It is regarded as "an indispensable means of realising other human rights" (UN, 2001, para. 1) and is, consequently, the only right that is administered compulsorily by the signatory nation-states. Children are required to receive an education, an obligation that recognizes not just the importance of education to society, but the fact that children cannot derive full enjoyment from their other rights unless they have benefitted from an education. It is this interconnectedness of educational rights with other rights in the CRC that makes a focus on educational rights especially important.

Also critical is that, while most human rights can be seen to be either socioeconomic or civil and political rights, the right to education is arguably both (Beiter, 2006). It places the burden on states to make provision for education, and that provision in itself enables the rights holder to engage and participate fully in society and therefore enjoy civil and political rights. The multifaceted nature of the right means that it cannot properly be described as a simple right "to" education in the way that there is a right to an adequate standard of living or to health care. Rather, it has become common to refer to it as collection of rights which, taken together, constitute rights *to*, *in*, and *through* education (Howe & Covell, 2005; Verhellen, 1993).

Prior to the CRC, the most comprehensive statement of the right to education was in the International Covenant on Economic, Social and Cultural Rights (ICESCR), Article 13, which places obligations on states to make elementary education widely available and to develop different forms of secondary education. However, the CRC makes provision for educational rights in a way that reflects more fully their complexity and significance. It contains the most detailed statement not just of the right to education (Article 28) but also the aims of education (Article 29): it expands on Article 13 of the ICESCR through an additional provision requiring states to encourage regular attendance at school and reduce dropout rates. It also addresses a significant aspect of children's rights "in" education by requiring states to take measures to ensure that school discipline is administered in a manner consistent with the child's human dignity and other CRC rights.

Likewise, Article 29 expands on the stated aims of education in Article 13 of the ICESCR: not only must education be directed to the development of the child's personality and respect for human rights and preparation for life in a free society in a "spirit of understanding, peace, tolerance, equality of sexes, and friendship among all peoples" (d), but it must also develop respect for the child's parents and culture as well as the country in which they are living, the country from which they originate, and for civilization different from his or her own (c), and to the development of the respect for the natural environment (e). Article 29 is also cross-referenced in Article 17, which encourages the media to disseminate information of social and cultural benefit to the child. Moreover—and this is perhaps most significant—all of the other rights in the CRC are enjoyed by the child wherever he or she is and, in particular, are not lost as the child enters a school gate (UN, 2001). For example, students enjoy their civil rights to freedom of conscience, privacy, and expression as well as protection from abuse and neglect and cruel, inhuman, and degrading treatment. Moreover, all of this must be provided without discrimination (Article 2), in giving his or her views due weight (Article 12), and considering his or her best interests (Article 3). While these provisions, like other human rights standards, are often worded very broadly, their remit and force is strengthened by the fact that they need to be applied collectively and interpreted teleologically, a process supported by the fact that the committee issues detailed General Comments expanding on their meaning—its first was on the aims of education in Article 29 (Kilkelly & Lundy, 2006).

Part of the value of the CRC for education researchers is that it provides a comprehensive set of standards that embrace most aspects of children's school lives and a language of rights and entitlement in which to frame the research, thus providing leverage to those who wish to bring about change (Lundy & McEvoy, 2012). Human rights place an emphasis on entitlement rather than need and enable those who hold rights to demand a response from those who have both the duty and the power to effect change. Rights are thus a key resource for those who lack power and are vulnerable. This is particularly true for children, who are often powerless in their interactions with adults, "being kept in an imposed and prolonged dependence which history and culture show to be neither inevitable nor essential" (Freeman, 2010, p. 16). In the context of research, this view has often resulted in ignoring children's views on the issues that affect them (Lundy & McEvoy, 2012). The past few decades, however, have seen a shift in thinking about children's agency and competence, including an emphasis on grassroots children's movements (Liebel et al., 2012) and an associated emphasis on the importance of engaging children of all ages in research (Habashi, 2008; Kirby, 2002), including in the early years (Lundy, McEvoy, & Byrne, 2011; MacNaughton & Smith, 2008; Swadener & Polakow, 2011).

Questions Engaged and Cross-cutting Themes

While cognizant of the critiques of human rights as universals that may be viewed as part of neoliberal policies or reflecting a Western bias, and challenges of implementation, this collection assumes that the CRC should make a difference in the way in which states choose to provide schooling to children living within their territories. That said, little is known about the extent to which the principles of the CRC are being implemented in practice, since empirical evidence of human rights implementation is generally scarce (Coomans, Grunfeld, & Kamminga, 2009) and particularly rare in the context of education (Tomaševski, 2006). Given that the primary worth of a rights framework lies ultimately in the ways in which its values are internalized and replicated within signatory states, as reflected in their laws, policies, and practices, this book aims to shed light on the efficacy and impact of the implementation of the CRC's right to education within a range of contexts.

Individual chapters in this volume compare the ways in which children's rights to formal and informal education are viewed and implemented in a variety of national and sociocultural contexts, with a view to providing insights into ways in which child rights–based policies and practices can impact access to education and enhance quality of life for children and society. Throughout the book, a focus is placed on understanding the opportunities and challenges for addressing children's right to participation and to educational inclusion. We consider the CRC framework as having value in the educational contexts reviewed as either shedding light on injustice or providing a springboard for rights holders and/or their advocates to hold government and other institutions to account. Authors bring internationally comparative policy perspectives from 10 national contexts and academic and practitioner perspectives, and draw from a range of interdisciplinary fields including education, law, and critical childhood studies.

When inviting contributors to the volume, we requested that they engage with the following issues and questions within their national or focal context.

- How are children's rights to education (as outlined in Article 29 and other articles) understood in particular national, state, or municipal contexts? What is the local discourse and understanding of children's rights?

- Drawing on their own work and that of others, what are some practices to help ensure that:

  1. children are facilitated to express their views on the issues that affect them and to influence decisions that are made?

  2. minoritized or "other" children's respect for their identity, language, and values are embraced?

  3. children's capacity is being built to claim their rights and that their views are given due weight?

  4. adults' capacity as duty-bearers to fulfill their obligations is strengthened?

- What more can be done to increase state accountability in fulfilling children's rights *to*, *in*, and *through* education, and to support the idea of children's rights among the public, parents, and teachers?

- In moving forward and addressing critiques of universal frameworks such as the CRC, what alternative discourses or framings may be helpful?

Several of the contributors have worked together on an international project, Una, a joint learning initiative focused on young children and ethnic diversity in post-conflict settings, as members of the Children's Rights Learning Group. This book extends our collaborative work on two working papers (Una, 2010, 2011) to include more focused discussion on how children's rights to education are unfolding in various geopolitical and cultural contexts, and opportunities for social and educational inclusion.

While each chapter focuses on a specific issue and context, several cross-cutting themes have been identified that can perhaps inform policymakers, educators, and researchers in the future. One contrast is in the choice of the method for understanding children's education rights. Most of these chapters point to the importance of breaking down national data on children's right to education in order to understand nuances and contradictions in how children are experiencing the right to education. In Cañete's chapter on the Philippines (Chapter 12), for example, his quantitative analysis of large data sets serves to show the high percentage of boys from the lower-income stratum not attending school, with lack of interest being the predominant reason for this. This growing disparity between boys' and girls' education is affecting the country's economic and social dynamics. In Chapter 4, on Roma children in northern Greece, Karagianni, Mitakidou, and Tressou's analysis of extensive interviews and other data serves to debunk prevalent stereotypes in the education system and wider society that Roma families are mainly welfare beneficiaries and uninvolved in their children's education.

Other chapters utilize qualitative approaches, focusing on the perspectives of educators, parents, and children to provide contextualized perspectives. Children's narratives of their experience of school expulsion and suspension in the United States, described in Chapter 2 by Baiyee, Polakow, and Hawkins, show the detrimental impact of a system that does not give voice to marginalized children, or respect their rights. Perspectives of young people in Québec (Canada) by Blanchet-Cohen (Chapter 3) show the impact of their political participation in fighting an announced tuition hike, and the risks of violating rights of freedom of association (Article 15), of expression (Article 12), and to education. Other chapters, including those by Emerson and Lundy (Chapter 1), Smith (Chapter 5), and Peters and Lacy (Chapter 6), foreground children's voice and also consider children's participation rights to include being research collaborators or consultants.

Throughout these chapters it appears that children's right to participate is rarely recognized in the mainstream education system, including by parents. In Chapter 9, Ndimande and Swadener report on the priority that parents place on education as provision and how Black students are still educationally excluded in both subtle and explicit ways. However, as suggested by the experience undertaken by Shier and colleagues in Guatemala (Chapter 10), involving children in the design and delivery of education can be an effective way of improving the quality of education. In countries where the state has been unable to provide for quality education because of a lack of economic or social resources, involvement of a community including young people and educators may be a way of providing more relevant education.

Community involvement is equally important in minority world countries such as the United States and Canada as a way of encouraging more socially and educationally inclusive practices. We, as editors, would advocate that states pay more attention to the innovative education programs that are emerging globally as a way of responding to the diverse needs of communities. A one-size-fits-all education model cannot serve the needs of everyone, especially children and youth from marginalized groups. We also recognize the agency, resistance, and energy of children and their allies in such struggles for inclusion and voice. Another theme expressed throughout this volume relates to the need to pay attention to the relationship between the right to culture (stated in Article 30) and to education. One is reminded that the right to education has often resulted in the promotion of singular dominant/state models of "education" and assimilation, at the cost of ethnic minority and indigenous languages and ways of knowing (Battiste, 2010). The case of Irish Travellers, as discussed by Murray (Chapter 11), or South African families concerned about indigenous language loss in their children, examined by Phatudi and Moletsane (Chapter 8), both underscore these concerns. Yet fulfillment of ethnic minoritized/indigenous children's rights as articulated in Article 30 provides for educational programs that reflect their languages, content, and cultural appropriateness (Stavenhagen, 2005). While progress has been made by states formally adopting policies that support indigenous education, chapters in this book point to the challenges in practice. In Chapter 7, Ritchie and Rau discuss the case of New Zealand, where embedding the collective and holistic indigenous concept in early education (i.e., *mana*) has not been very successful, despite formal adoption of indigenous children's education rights (i.e., *Te Tiriti o Waitangi*). Narratives with Māori educators show the need for more training, resources, and parental support. Similarly, the chapters on education in South Africa—Chapter 9 by Ndimande and Swadener, and Chapter 8 by Phatudi and Moletsane—point to parents choosing to send their children to formerly White-only schools or learn in English instead of their own African mother tongue, despite a policy that supports instruction in their primary language, and evidence that learning in the mother tongue in the early years will improve the future schooling experience.

The voices of educators and parents are a reminder that preconceived notions of what type of education will lead to "success" affect parents' decisions. Policy adoptions that support minority/indigenous education are on their own insufficient; the solution also requires undoing historical and cultural patterns of a society that are based on exclusion and discrimination. As noted by Karagianni, Mitakidou, and Tressou in Chapter 4, education cannot be examined in isolation; it reflects the social fabric of a society and, as such, must be viewed in both local and global contexts.

Organization of the Book

Children's Lives and Education in Cross-National Contexts: What Difference Could Rights Make? is organized around three broad themes: Complexities and Perspectives in Promoting Participation and Inclusion, Child-Rights Approaches in the Early Years, and Education Rights Issues in Diverse Contexts. All the authors engage with many of the questions discussed earlier in our introduction, particularly the broad question of the book: What difference could rights make and, implicitly, what does it mean to children, families, and allies when children are marginalized and educationally excluded? Collectively, the authors in this volume suggest that a commitment to children's education rights could be beneficial at multiple levels, with increased awareness of the potential of a rights framework and meaningful engagement of stakeholders in processes and decisions about education policy and classroom practice—and beyond.

Section 1 of the book, "Complexities and Perspectives in Promotion Participation and Inclusion," frames issues of children's rights and education in four nation-states, each reflecting particular issues of the geopolitical and social context, as well as children's experiences and perspectives. In Chapter 1, "Education Rights in a Society Emerging from Conflict: Curriculum and Student Participation as a Pathway to the Realization of Rights," Lesley Emerson and Laura Lundy examine the implementation of children's rights *in*, *to*, and *through* education in a society emerging from over 30 years of violent conflict. Although international human rights law has been deployed successfully to effect change within the Northern Ireland education system at a structural level, fundamental challenges remain, particularly in on-going attempts to address the effect of religious segregation in and the impact of the conflict on education. This chapter reflects on the implementation of Article 29 of the UNCRC in societies emerging from conflict and argues that children and young people are entitled to influence what they are taught in school.

Chapter 2, "Children's Rights and Educational Exclusion: The Impact of Zero-Tolerance in Schools," focuses on children's education rights in the context of U.S. public school discipline policies. Authors Martha Baiyee, Celeste Hawkins, and Valerie Polakow deal with children's experiences of corrosive consequences of zero-tolerance policies in U.S. public schools and their disproportionate impact on poor children and children of color. Each year more than 3 million children are suspended and/or expelled from kindergarten through grade 12. Zero-tolerance policies have infused educational policies and practices in the United States to the extent that punishment, rather than supportive remediation and rehabilitation, has become the norm. Vulnerable children are pushed out and/or permanently expelled from their schools, legal protections are rarely enforced, and many youth are funneled into the juvenile or adult prison system, creating a school-to-prison pipeline. Once expelled, children are actually deprived of their fundamental right to an education.

In Chapter 3, "The Protagonism of Under-18 Youth in the Québec Student Movement: The Right to Political Participation and Education," Natasha Blanchet-Cohen draws on discussions with youth leaders of the Québec student movement and frames themes from their narratives in the right to political participation and education. From young people's leadership and resilience in the events, what can we learn about political participation and education rights as identified in the CRC? Given a growing interest in how young people actively participate in the construction and implementation of their rights, this case of young people's activism provides a fresh perspective on what is often a circumscribed international narrative on children's political participation. In examining the context and impact of a youth-led grassroots movement, one can better understand the dynamic role of young people as actors, and give deeper meaning to the idea of "rights from below."

In Chapter 4, "What's Right in Children's Rights? The Subtext of Dependency," Panagiota Karagianni, Soula Mitakidou, and Evangelia Tressou draw from their extensive experience in anti-racist/inclusive education work, particularly with Roma communities in northern Greece, to unpack discourses of dependency as constructed in public policy. They address the ideology of dependency that affects institutional policies (including education programs) versus the autonomy implied in the agenda of children's right to education. The ideology of dependency, deeply rooted in the "private charity" and "welfare mother" tradition, permeates every aspect of human rights–related issues. Their chapter provides an example of ways to rethink work with marginalized communities toward a shared social vision.

Section 2 focuses on "Child-Rights Approaches in the Early Years." Chapter 5, by Kylie Smith "A Rights-Based Approach to Observing and Assessing Children in the Early Childhood Classroom," addresses a rights-based approach to assessment of children's learning and development in early childhood education. Using a case study from an Australian early childhood center, the chapter examines what happens when teachers ask children about learning and engagement from their perspective. The chapter illustrates that children's voices shine a different light on how we see, assess, and support what is happening for children, and provides new insight into the subjectivities of the teacher's gaze. Changing images of the child are offering motivation and inspiration for early childhood educators to begin to think about how young children might offer their opinions and have them taken into account in curriculum development and implementation.

In Chapter 6, "'You're Not Listening to Us': Explicating Children's School Experiences to Build Opportunity for Increased Participation Within School Communities in the United States," Lacey Peters and Lisa Lacy situate children's rights to participation and education in the context of the United States. They unpack their experiences working with children, outlining the procedures used to support collaboration and consultation with younger people. They draw from a larger study (Joanou, Holiday, & Swadener, 2012) and other work to understand children's perspectives about engaging in formal education, as well as participants commonly described as having "special needs" within classroom environments. Given that the United States has yet to ratify the UNCRC, they make a case for the need for broader support for children's rights and participation and explore possibilities that manifest when acknowledging that children's rights matter.

In Chapter 7, "Renarrativizing Indigenous Rights-Based Provision Within 'Mainstream' Early Childhood Services," Jenny Ritchie and Cheryl Rau draw on recent research to consider ways in which the early childhood education sector in Aotearoa New Zealand has responded to the challenge of recognizing indigenous children's rights to their language, and how this attention to the indigenous culture can affect all children attending early childhood services. Ritchie and Rau argue that generic attention to notions of "children's rights" may in fact have unintended exclusionary effects, and that it is important to open the dialogue about specific types of "rights" and how these can be acknowledged in early childhood education practice. Their research has demonstrated the potential for renarrativizing the application of an indigenous rights-based provision within "mainstream" early childhood services, for the potential benefit of all participants.

In Chapter 8, "Restoring Indigenous Languages and the Right to Learn in a Familiar Language: A Case of Black South African Children," Nkidi Phatudi and Mokgadi Moletsane frame children's rights in early childhood in terms of access to mother tongue/indigenous languages in South Africa. The authors critically examine the language of learning and teaching and its appropriateness in reaching learners and in creating a rich and engaging atmosphere that benefits learners. The chapter interrogates language policies from a child-rights perspective and analyzes how they are being interpreted on the ground. By engaging with questions of how schools and parents promote and sustain indigenous languages, they make recommendations for early childhood programs.

The third and final section of the book, "Education Rights Issues in Diverse Contexts," addresses cultural complexities and issues of education rights in diverse geopolitical and sociocultural contexts. In Chapter 9, "Pursuing Democracy Through Education Rights: Perspectives from South Africa," Bekisizwe Ndimande and Beth Blue Swadener draw on two related studies conducted with Black parents to discuss children's rights issues as they relate to education in post-apartheid South Africa. They analyze the extent to which children's rights have been understood and achieved, both in terms of equity in access to education and broader understandings of children's rights. Discussions with Black parents in townships revealed tensions between the Children's Act of 2007 and traditional childrearing views, particularly in terms of participatory rights. Education rights were embraced by parents in both studies, but were limited by persistent racism in desegregated, formerly white-only schools.

In Chapter 10, "Claiming the Right to Quality Education in Nicaragua," Harry Shier, Martha Lidia Padilla, Nohemí Molina Torres, Leonilda Barrera López, Moisés Molina Torres, Zorayda Castillo, and Karen Alicia Ortiz Alvarado analyze the project *Safe Quality Schools*, run by local NGO CESESMA in rural communities in the remote coffee-growing region of northern Nicaragua. This project tackled rights *in* education by recognizing children not only as "consumers" of education but as researchers, advocates, and change agents. The chapter points to the interdependence of rights *to*, *in*, and *through* education. Families make decisions on their children's schooling based on multiple factors. In addition to poverty and the pressure for children to work, also important are perceptions about the safety of the school, how children are treated, the quality of teaching, and the relevance of what is taught. If rights *in* education are not attended to, the result is that many children will not enjoy their right *to* education, nor will they go on to enjoy other rights *through* education.

Chapter 11, Colette Murray's "Getting an Education: How Travellers' Knowledge and Experience Shape Their Engagement with the System," draws on experiences and practices from an Irish early childhood diversity and equality initiative. It examines how NGOs have worked to promote the respect and recognition of Travellers within the Irish education system. The chapter shows that while key policy documents ensure Traveller participation and inclusion, implementation of these documents has been lagging. The voices of Traveller children and young people talking about their educational experience suggests that emphasis on integration by the state has resulted in reduced support to the Traveller communities, resulting in oppression and discrimination. Murray explores an alternative approach to education that would include attitudinal change and the competencies of adults involved in education.

In Chapter 12, "When Boys Are Pushed-Pulled out of School: Rights to Education in the Philippines," Leodinito Y. Cañete addresses the school dropout patterns of boys growing up in poverty as a growing area of concern in the Philippines. Using data from the 2008 Annual Poverty Indicators Survey, the chapter reveals that, despite free access to school, boys identified lack of interest as the main reason for not attending school. The chapter discusses the implications of the phenomenon of boys being outperformed by girls in school and participating less in formal education as a child rights issue with social and economic repercussions.

In the final chapter of the book, "Intersections of Education and Freedom of Religion Rights in the UNCRC and in Practice," Janette Habashi raises questions about and presents an analysis of the relationship between the achievement of the right of education and the right to express religion, as well as how these two articles of the UNCRC contribute to children's development of tolerance and world harmony. Habashi argues that these questions are important to analyze, in part because the right of education and the right to religious freedom are contradictory at times, specifically in respect to compulsory religious education. The chapter deconstructs two components of this relationship: (1) religious education models that enhance or undermine Articles 14 and 29; and (2) the current response to the interaction between religious education and its violation of children's right of education and the UNCRC.

Conclusion

One of the most cited facts about the UNCRC is that it is the most-ratified UN Treaty—a badge of honor that can be turned into a criticism in light of the fact that many of the signatories have very poor records when it comes to human rights generally and/or the treatment of children. Critics of the CRC point to its "weak" enforcement mechanisms and, in particular, its lack of a right of individual petition to a court. While the Committee on the Rights of the Child has played a role in defining and shaping education policy, keeping children's rights at the forefront of policymakers' attention and ratcheting up the pressure and degree of specificity in its comments over time (Lundy, 2012), the ultimate efficacy of the reporting process is dependent on the availability of information on the state of children's rights in the signatory nation.

The Special Rapporteur on the Right to Education has observed that "what happens in schools is seldom examined through the human rights lens, the most important reason being that the notion of rights in education is new. Evidence of abuses of education and in education is not systematically collected" (Tomasevski, 2006, p. 43). While much educational research is being done on issues that have human rights implications (e.g., equality of access, bullying, and child abuse), there is an absence of an explicit rights-based framing. This collection seeks to begin to address that gap in the existing knowledge and advocacy base. The more the educational research community goes beyond the simple collecting of relevant data and frames its research questions, analysis, discussion, and findings in terms of children's rights, the greater the pressure will be on states to comply with their obligations (Lundy & McEvoy, 2012). Likewise, the more educators, parents, child advocates, and children themselves foreground children's rights in everyday sites of learning, the more powerful their role will be in providing for an inclusive and meaningful education.

As Bill Ayers, a U.S. education professor and social justice activist, wrote in an open letter to President Barack Obama on his re-election:

Education is a fundamental human right, not a product. In a free society education is based on a common faith in the incalculable value of every human being; it's constructed on the principle that the fullest development of all is the condition for the full develop-ment of each, and, conversely, that the fullest development of each is the condition for the full development of all. Further, while schooling in every totalitarian society on earth foregrounds obedience and conformity, education in a democracy emphasizes initiative, courage, imagination, and entrepreneurship in order to encourage students to develop minds of their own. (Ayers, 2012, p. 2)

We share this commitment to the human right not only to education, but also to education that encourages equity, inclusion, transformation, and democratic principles grounded in a respect for the rights of all children.

References

Ayers, W. (2012). An open letter to President-Elect Obama. Retrieved February 2, 2013, from http://www.beaconbroadside.com/broadside/2012/11/bill-ayers-an-open-letter-to-president-obama.html

Battiste, M. (2010). Indigenous knowledge and indigenous peoples education. In S.M. Subramanian & B. Pisupati (Eds.), *Traditional knowledge in policy and practice: Approaches to development and human well-being* (pp. 31–51). Tokyo, New York, Paris: United Nations University Press.

Beiter, K.D. (2006). *The protection of the right to education by international law.* Leiden, Netherlands: Martinus Nijhoff.

Coomans, F., Grunfeld, F., & Kamminga, M.T. (2009). *Methods of human rights research.* Antwerp, Belgium: Intersentia Publishing.

Feldman, D. (2002). *Civil liberties and human rights in England and Wales.* Oxford: Oxford University Press.

Freeman, M. (2000). The future of children's rights. *Children and Society, 14,* 277–293.

Freeman, M. (2010). The human rights of children. In C. O'Cinneide (Ed.), *Current legal problems* (Vol. 63, pp. 1–44). Oxford: Oxford University Press.

Habashi, J. (2008). Palestinian children crafting national identity. *Childhood: A Journal of Global Child Research, 15*(1), 12–29.

Howe, B.R., & Covell, H. (2005). *Empowering children: Children's rights education as a pathway to citizenship.* Toronto: University of Toronto Press.

Joanou, J., Holiday, D., & Swadener, B.B. (2012). Family and community perspectives: Voices from a qualitative statewide study in the Southwest U.S. In J. Duncan & S. Te One (Eds.), *Comparative early childhood education services: International perspectives* (pp. 101–123). New York: Palgrave Macmillan.

Kilkelly, U., & Lundy, L. (2006). The Convention on the Rights of the Child: Its use as an auditing tool. *Child and Family Law Quarterly, 18*(3), 331–350.

Kirby, P. (2002). Involving young people in research. In B. Franklin (Ed.), *The new handbook of children's rights: Comparative policy and practice* (pp. 268–284). Abingdon, UK: Routledge.

Liebel, M., with Hanson, K., Saadi, I., & Vandenhole, W. (2012). *Children's rights from below: Cross-cultural perspectives.* London: Palgrave Macmillan.

Lundy, L. (2012). Children's rights and educational policy in Europe. *Oxford Review of Education, 38*(4), 293–411.

Lundy, L., & McEvoy, L. (2012). Childhood, the United Nations Convention on the Rights of the Child and research: What constitutes a "rights-based" approach? In M. Freeman (Ed.), *Law and childhood* (pp. 75–91). Oxford: Oxford University Press.

Lundy. L., McEvoy, L., & Byrne, B. (2011). Working with young children as co-researchers: An approach informed by the United Nations Convention on the Rights of the Child. *Early Education and Development, 22*(5), 714–736.

MacNaughton, G., & Smith, K. (2008). Engaging ethically with young children: Principles and practices for listening and responding with care. In G. MacNaughton, P. Hughes, & K. Smith (Eds.), *Young children as active citizens: Principles, policies and pedagogies* (pp. 31–43). London: Cambridge Scholars Publishing.

Stavenhagen, R. (2005, January 6). *Indigenous issues: Human rights and indigenous issues: Report of the Special Rapporteur on the situation of human rights and fundamental freedoms of indigenous people* (E/CN.4/2005/88). Geneva: UN Economic and Social Council.

Swadener, B.B., & Polakow, V. (2011). Introduction to special issue: Children's rights and voices in research: Cross-national perspectives. *Early Education and Development, 22*(5),1–7.

Tomaševski, K. (2001). Removing obstacles in the way of the right to education. Right to Education Primers No. 1. Retrieved April 12, 2013, from http://www.right-to-education.org/sites/r2e.gn.apc.org/files/B6e%20Primer.pdf

Tomaševski, K. (2006). *Human rights obligations in education: The 4A scheme.* Nijmegen, Netherlands: Wolf Legal Publishers.

Una Children's Rights Learning Group. (2010). *Children's rights in Una and beyond: Transnational perspectives.* Una Working Paper 7. Belfast, Northern Ireland: Una.

Una Children's Rights Learning Group. (2011). Una Working Paper 8. *Children's rights in cultural contexts.* Belfast, Northern Ireland: Una.

United Nations. (1989). *United Nations Convention on the Rights of the Child.* Geneva: United Nations.

United Nations Committee on the Rights of the Child. (2001). *General comment No. 1 on the aims of education* (CRC/GC/2001/1). Geneva: United Nations.

United Nations Committee on the Rights of the Child. (2010). *Treaty-specific guidelines regarding the form and content of periodic reports to be submitted by states parties under Article 44, paragraph 1(b) of the Convention on the Rights of the Child* (CRC/C/58). Geneva: United Nations.

Veerman, E. (2010). The ageing of the United Nations Convention on the Rights of the Child. *International Journal of Children's Rights, 18*(4), 585–618.

Verhellen, E. (1993). Children's rights and education. *School Psychology International, 14*(3), 199–208.

Complexities and Perspectives in Promoting Participation and Inclusion

CHAPTER ONE

Education Rights in a Society Emerging from Conflict

Curriculum and Student Participation as a Pathway to the Realization of Rights

Lesley Emerson & Laura Lundy

In societies emerging from conflict, the rhetorical and aspirational aspects of transition to peace are often framed in the context of the next generation, with children's rights portrayed as central to the rebirth of the society (Lundy, 2006). The focus of peace-building initiatives at times of transition is both retrospective and prospective: remedying past injustices and creating the conditions for a more stable future. Children are likely to have been disproportionately affected by the conflict (Connolly & Healy, 2004; Machel, 1996), and children's rights instruments provide a set of benchmarks for determining what is necessary to redress the social, psychological, and physical impacts of violence upon children. In terms of future planning, children's rights are thought to form the building blocks for a human rights culture and are therefore recognized increasingly as core aspects of political settlements in transitional societies (see, e.g., Sacramento & Pessoa, 1996). More pragmatically, children's rights are often perceived as politically neutral territory, making it easier to garner political and popular support for initiatives that benefit children than it is in other, more contentious spheres of engagement. Thus, not only are children's rights regarded as "a powerful tool with which to kick-start the reconstruction of society" (Sloth-Nielsen, 1996, p. 328), but they also provide a potential rallying point for consensus in the early, and therefore potentially most fragile, times in the transition process.

Within the broad sphere of children's rights, education rights are particularly significant. While recognition of children's rights is a relatively recent development, the right to education has long been regarded as a fundamental human right, first articulated in the Universal Declaration of Human Rights (UDHR) (United Nations [UN], 1948), itself an attempt to build a peaceful future in the wake of violence. Moreover, the Convention on the Rights of the Child (CRC) (UN, 1989) contains a wide range of rights that can potentially be applied to the domain of education. These rights are commonly categorized as the child's right *to*, *in*, and *through* education. In general terms, the right *to* education can be taken to denote children's right of equal access to education. The right *in* education refers to their right to be treated with dignity, respect, and equality while at school, and their right *through* education describes the content and aims of the education they are entitled to receive in order to prepare them "for responsible life in a free society." With respect to the latter, Article 29 of the CRC provides that State Parties agree that the education of the child shall be directed to:

(a) The development of the child's personality, talents and mental and physical abilities to their fullest potential;

(b) The development of respect for human rights and fundamental freedoms, and for the principles enshrined in the Charter of the United Nations;

(c) The development of respect for the child's parents, his or her own cultural identity, language and values, for the national values of the country in which the child is living, the country from which he or she may originate, and for civilizations different from his or her own;

(d) The preparation of the child for responsible life in a free society, in the spirit of understanding, peace, tolerance, equality of sexes, and friendship among all peoples, ethnic, national and religious groups and persons of indigenous origin; and

(e) The development of respect for the natural environment.

The value of securing children's rights through education is not limited to the individual child. There is a compelling public interest in guaranteeing children's right to education since the social and economic well-being of society depends upon having a well-educated citizenry and one that respects democratic values, including human rights. The national and international interests in realizing the aims of education in Article 29 are essentially the same: it is important for the stability of individual nations and the global community that children are educated to respect difference and to value peaceful means of resolving conflict (Lundy, 2005). While this is always important, it acquires enhanced significance in societies that are making the transition from violence to peace and in which new democratic processes are being established (Limber, Kask, Heidmets, Hevener-Kaufman, & Merton, 1999). Thus the Committee on the Rights of the Child has emphasized the centrality of human rights education, starting "with the reflection of human rights values in the daily life and experiences of children." This is considered to be not only relevant for children living in zones of peace, but "even more important for those living in situations of conflict or emergency" (UN, 2001, para. 16). A further key element of a rights-based approach to education is children's right to have their views given due weight in all matters affecting them (Article 12), a cornerstone of the CRC that reinforces the status of the child as an active participant in the promotion, protection, and monitoring of his or her rights (Fortin, 2003; Freeman, 2000). The right applies to all aspects of education and all levels of decision making, from government policy to school policy to classroom practice (Lundy, 2007). The UK's record in implementing this right within education has been criticized by the committee's consecutive reports (UN, Committee on the Rights of the Child, 1995, 2002, 2008). As a result, there has been a range of government initiatives to involve children in decision making in education, including new statutory obligations on public authorities to consult children on policies that affect them directly (Harris, 2009). Likewise, there has been significant academic interest in the concept of "pupil voice" and in practices that enable children to participate in, and be consulted on, their learning (Flutter & Rudduck, 2004; Noyes, 2005). In spite of this, however, evidence of the impact of Article 12 in the context of decisions about the curriculum remains rare, with children's input into school decision making often being channelled through school councils and largely limited to "minor issues" rather than the core business of schools (teaching and learning), where teacher authority and professionalism reign (see, e.g., Wyse, 2001).

This chapter aims to examine the implementation of Article 29 in Northern Ireland, a society emerging from 30 years of violent conflict. First, it provides an analysis of the Northern Irish context, including the transition to peace, the legacy of the conflict, and the ways in which the education system has sought to respond to the divided nature of this society. Second, it examines a number of aspects of the aims of education as articulated in the CRC, pertinent to societies transitioning from conflict to peace. In particular, we focus on the implementation of two separate but related aspects of Article 29. The first of these is the requirement in Article 29(1d) to develop respect for cultural identity and the promotion of tolerance. Following that, we consider how government has attempted to develop respect for human rights and fundamental freedoms in the context of the new democratic structures that accompanied the peace process. In doing so, we suggest that a rights-based approach to education in societies emerging from conflict means not only ensuring that the curricular content aligns with the aims of education in Article 29 (in terms of the promotion of cultural identity and tolerance) but also that children and young people are provided with meaningful opportunities to shape and determine the nature of the curriculum and associated education policies in accordance with their right to have their views taken seriously (Article 12).

The Northern Ireland Context: Conflict and Transition to Peace

While the roots of the most recent phase of sustained conflict in Northern Ireland (colloquially, "The Troubles") and the explanation for its protraction over 3 decades are inevitably subject to historical and political debate (see Dixon & O'Kane, 2011; McGarry & O'Leary, 1995), it is accepted that the outworking of political violence, from both state and non-state actors, had a significant impact on the small population of just over 1.6 million people (Emerson, 2012).

The impact of the conflict on young people was particularly acute. In terms of deaths during the Troubles, 26% of all fatalities were 21 years old or younger (Smyth, 1998), and many children lost parents or family members, witnessed violence, or grew up in contexts of fear and mistrust (Cairns, 1987). The direct legacy of this violence and other consequences of the conflict, such as increased community division and high levels of social deprivation, "created the societal milieu for a prolonged peace process" (Emerson, 2012, p. 280) that culminated, in 1998, in the Belfast/"Good Friday" Agreement.

The agreement committed all participants to exclusively democratic and peaceful means of resolving differences and to a future based on acceptance of diversity and on the principles of partnership, equality, and mutual respect. In particular, it committed participants to "the protection and vindication of the human rights of all." The role of human rights as key "safeguards" to the agreement was cemented further through the establishment of an independent Human Rights Commission, incorporation of the European Convention on Human Rights (ECHR) into domestic legislation, and the promise of a custom-made Bill of Rights for Northern Ireland. This central positioning of human rights within the peace process effectively shifted human rights discourse from a previously marginalized position in Northern Irish society to the mainstream of public and political debate (Mageean & O'Brien, 1999) and secured its place as the primary discourse surrounding the ongoing processes of transition (Bell, 2003).

However, the end of a conflict does not necessarily result in the cessation of violence, nor does it mean that the problems underpinning the conflict have been resolved completely. Consequently, the transitional context of Northern Ireland is often politically contentious and at times disrupted by residual violence. In particular, many young people, chiefly those living in interface areas, remain affected by sporadic sectarian violence directed toward their homes and families (Leonard, 2007; Magill, Smith, & Hamber, 2009), and some are also at risk of "punishment" shootings and assaults from dissident "paramilitary" groups (McAlister, Scraton, & Haydon, 2011). Young people are also engaging in violence such as so-called "recreational rioting" (Jarman & O'Halloran, 2001, p. 2; see also Leonard, 2010), often pre-planned and organized through social media (Reilly, 2011). Further, there are concerns in relation to some young people's desire to be involved in, and their actual recruitment into, "residual terrorist groups" (McAlister et al., 2011; Smyth & Campbell, 2005). This exposure to sectarian and community violence, according to evidence, is likely to have an impact on children and young people's psychological well-being, resulting in depression, low self-esteem, risk of suicide, and substance abuse (Forbes, Sibbett, Miller, & Emerson, 2012; Muldoon & Trew, 2000). Furthermore, children are at risk of transgenerational transmission of trauma due to the long-term psychological effects of the Troubles on the adult population (Muldoon, 2004).

In addition to the impact of the legacy of violence and continued violence within and between communities, children and young people are also dealing with the largely segregated nature of their society. This "separate living" extends to the education system, where over 94% of children receive their education in schools that are almost exclusively Catholic or exclusively Protestant in nature, and only 6% of children attend planned integrated (mixed-religion) schools. While the majority of young people would prefer to live in "mixed" communities (ARK, 2011), there is evidence to suggest that many children hold negative attitudes toward those from "the other" community and feel "unsafe" when outside their own community (Schubotz & Devine, 2008).

Thus, children and young people in Northern Ireland are growing up in a politically complex society where the peace, though relatively stable, is not altogether secure, and where the effects of violence and the factors that generated, exacerbated, and sustained the conflict are not altogether in the past. Given the impact this may have on children's lives, it is incumbent upon the state to guarantee that social policy is directed toward ensuring that children and young people growing up in this context enjoy their right to life, survival, and development (CRC, Article 6) and their right to be safe from harm (CRC, Article 19). In particular, there is a need for educational policy to align with the aims of education, as articulated in Article 29 of the CRC, specifically in relation to developing respect for human rights, respect for cultural identity, and the promotion of tolerance, if children and young people are to be assisted in understanding and functioning in their current sociopolitical context. The extent to which this is the case is discussed below.

State Response: Policy and Practice

Government policy in Northern Ireland attends in general to matters relating to the legacy of the conflict (Office of the First Minister and deputy First Minister, OFMdFM, 2005, 2010a) and in particular to its impact on children (OFMdFM, 2006). Notably, these policies tend to be situated broadly within rights discourse.

For example, the *Ten Year Strategy for Children and Young People* commits government to seek progress in relation to an outcomes framework that includes, *inter alia*, indications that children and young people are living in safety and with stability, contributing positively to the community and society, and living in a society that respects their rights (OFMdFM, 2006). The strategy recognizes that in order to deliver on these outcomes, there is a need to respond to the challenges faced in a society emerging from conflict and to recognize that "our children and young people are key to ensuring a more stable and peaceful future and a society which is inclusive and respectful of difference" (OFMdFM, 2006, p. 17). More recently, government policy has made further commitment to seeking ways of preventing young people at risk from becoming disaffected and involved in conflict and interface violence and to "empower them to engage in positive activities and programs that will have beneficial impacts and outcomes for them" (OFMdFM, 2010a, p. 24).

In this respect, policy has consistently pointed to the role that education should play in securing a future free from conflict and intolerance (see OFMdFM, 2005, 2010a). For example, government has set clear objectives in relation to "promoting civic-mindedness via citizenship education through school and life-long learning" and to "encouraging understanding of the complexity of our history" through the school curriculum (OFMdFM, 2005, p. 10). Policy states further that for this to "make a real impact it is essential that this work tackles the reality of living in a divided society" (OFMdFM, 2005, p. 25). Likewise, the Department of Education (DE) has acknowledged the need to "develop learners who will understand and respect the rights, equality and diversity of all groups in Northern Ireland and who have the skills, attitudes and behaviours to enable them to value and respect difference and engage positively with it" (DE, 2011, p. 21). In particular, it promotes the development of educational programs that aim to develop young people's "skills and the resilience needed to deal with prejudice" and to provide them with support to "recognise prejudice, to overcome it and to respond in positive ways to negative influences" (DE, 2011, p. 16).

However, evidence suggests that more progress needs to be made in achieving these objectives. It is noteworthy that a significant number of people in Northern Ireland do not believe that schools are adequately preparing young people for life in a diverse society and, in particular, are failing to encourage their understanding of the complexity of our history and the causes and consequences of the conflict (see OFMdFM, 2009, 2010b). There are several ways in which the education system can respond to this challenge. To date there has been "a tripartite approach of supporting systemic/structural change, encouraging cross-community contact schemes, and promoting curriculum initiatives" (McEvoy, 2007, p. 137). While structural changes (such as planned integrated schools or collaborative arrangements between schools) are often proposed as the best way to address the divided nature of the education system, these are often slow and contentious and, as such, the segregated nature of the education system persists. In addition, cross-community contact schemes between schools, though laudable in intention, appear to have had limited impact. For example, a review of the government-funded community relations program in schools indicated that while there were isolated examples of good practice, by and large contact schemes between schools were afforded low strategic importance, were deficient in terms of training and support for teachers, and lacked coherence in terms of the articulation of their community relations outcomes (O'Connor, Hartop, & McCully, 2002). Further, research into young people's experience of these cross-community contact schemes indicated that there was little evidence of pupils being given opportunities to genuinely mix with their peers from the other community and that young people's understanding of community relations having engaged in contact schemes remained vague. The research also suggested that schools tended to be selective in relation to the pupils they allowed to participate in the programs, meaning that only a minority of pupils could avail of the opportunity, particularly in post-primary settings (O'Connor, Hartop, & McCully, 2003).

Thus, as we have suggested elsewhere, it would appear that the curriculum holds the greatest potential for addressing these issues (McEvoy & Lundy, 2007), particularly since the statutory curriculum is an entitlement of all children and young people, irrespective of where they attend school. The degree to which young people in Northern Ireland are provided with opportunities to engage with a curriculum aligned (both in policy and practice) to those aspects of Article 29 of the CRC pertinent to societies emerging from conflict, and other associated relevant human rights standards, is discussed below. In particular, we focus on two interrelated aspects of Article 29: the requirement to promote cultural identity and tolerance and the requirement to provide education in human rights, both of which are particularly significant in divided societies and those affected by conflict.

Developing Respect for Cultural Identity and the Promotion of Tolerance

Article 29 of the CRC requires that the education of the child should be directed to, among other things, the development of respect for the child's parents, cultural identity, language, the country in which the child is living, and from where he/she originates, as well as for "civilisations different from his or her own" (UN, 1989). The Committee on the Rights of the Child has highlighted the links between this aspect of Article 29 and the struggle against racism, racial discrimination, xenophobia, and related intolerance. In particular, it notes that discrimination thrives "where there is ignorance, unfounded fears of racial, ethnic, religious, cultural and linguistic or other forms of difference, the exploitation of prejudices, or the teaching or dissemination of distorted values" (UN, 2001, para. 11). Further, it recognizes that approaches to promoting tolerance and friendship among "all peoples" (UN, 2001, para. 4) might appear to sit in tension with policies designed to develop respect for the child's own cultural identity, language, and values (UN, 1989, Article 29(1c). However, the committee argues that this provision recognizes the need for a "balanced approach to education…which succeeds in reconciling diverse values through dialogue and respect for difference." Moreover, it suggests that children are "capable of playing a unique role in bridging many of the differences that have historically separated groups of people from one another" (UN, 2001, para. 4). This is particularly significant in societies emerging from conflict, where the choice of knowledge transmitted in the curriculum can have consequences for how education is positioned as either a factor in creating or exacerbating conflict or as a transformative component of peace building (McEvoy & Lundy, 2007). It is unsurprising, therefore, that curricular reform, particularly in relation to attending to issues of diversity, is a common feature of post-conflict situations (Emerson, 2012). The nature of reform, though context specific, in general requires the revision of a number of subjects, including, for example, geography, history, languages, and religious education (Tawil & Harley, 2004). Reform also often involves the introduction of new curricular programs designed to address the needs of the particular transitional society, for example citizenship education and peace education programs (Smith, 2010). In the context of Northern Ireland, major curricular reform occurred during the conflict (Education Reform Order, 1989) and in more recent years with the introduction of a revised curriculum (Education Order, 2006). In particular, this has involved reform and revision of the history curriculum, alongside the development of programs for mutual understanding and latterly citizenship education (McEvoy, 2007), discussed below.

Mutual Understanding and Citizenship Education

In Northern Ireland, attempts were made during the conflict to introduce elements of "peace education" into the statutory curriculum. This was in the form of a cross-curricular theme: Education for Mutual Understanding (EMU) (Education Reform Order, 1989). Notwithstanding its laudable objectives and the praise it received on the international stage (see, e.g., Bush & Saltarelli, 2000), it is accepted generally in the Northern Ireland context that EMU failed, due in no small part to its refusal to engage with the political nature of the conflict, its weakness in handling issues of social justice, and its lack of reference to human rights—all compounded by teacher reluctance to address controversial issues (McEvoy, 2007). During the development of the revised Northern Ireland Curriculum, attempts were made to address the factors contributing to the lack of impact of EMU, resulting in new components of the curriculum that, in policy terms at least, arguably take a more robust approach to the development of tolerance and respect for diversity (Arlow, 2011).

The statutory curriculum, introduced in 2007, therefore includes a general provision for teaching and learning in relation to tolerance and respect through the inclusion of "mutual understanding" and "cultural understanding" as key elements of the curriculum to be addressed by *all* subjects. In addition, *specific* provision is made to address these issues within the new subjects of Personal Development and Mutual Understanding (PDMU) (primary) and Local and Global Citizenship (post-primary). For example, at primary level children are required to explore similarities and differences and to value and celebrate cultural differences and diversity. At post-primary level, in Key Stage 3 (ages 11–14), young people are required to explore "diversity and inclusion," which includes a statutory requirement to investigate "prejudice, stereotyping, sectarianism, and racism" and "ways of managing conflict and promoting community relations, reconciliation." This theme is continued into Key Stage 4 (ages 14–16) but is less specific in nature, focusing on "challenges and opportunities of diversity in NI and the wider world," which arguably addresses a core aspect of Article 29, albeit in the most general terms possible.

However, despite the focus of the statutory curriculum on diversity and tolerance and the non-statutory guidance and resources provided to support teachers in its delivery, it appears that young people are not satisfied with the extent to which issues pertaining to life in a diverse and conflicted society are being addressed. For example, research suggests that young people are keen to learn more about these issues but that teachers still lack the confidence to deal with more controversial aspects of "difference." So, while young people report increased learning in relation to issues such as "community relations," they also indicate superficial engagement with the more complex and contentious aspects of citizenship in a divided society, such as sectarianism and community conflict (University of Ulster [UU], 2010). Indeed, young people appear frustrated that the curriculum in general and the citizenship curriculum in particular are not providing them with opportunities to explore the origins and legacy of the Troubles (see Magill et al., 2009), arguably part of the remit of the history curriculum, discussed below.

History Education in a Divided Society

The potential manipulation of history curricula (Smith & Vaux, 2003) and the vulnerability of history teaching to oversimplification and partiality (Cole & Barsalou, 2006) undoubtedly have implications for the promotion of tolerance and respect for diversity in conflict-affected societies. Moreover, attempts to develop an official *single* history for inclusion in statutory curricula in deeply divided societies is self-evidently problematic, particularly when "official" histories clash with narratives and unofficial histories from home or the community (Bird, 2007; Freedman, Weinstein, Murphy, & Longman, 2008).

Prior to curricular reform in 1989, children and young people's exposure to history in schools in Northern Ireland was largely determined by the nature of the school they attended: children in Catholic schools learned predominantly Irish history, and children in state-controlled or Protestant schools learned predominantly British history. In the late 1980s, efforts were made to establish a common statutory history program. Evidence suggests, however, that schools continued to place emphasis on the history associated politically with their own community and, in addition, tended to avoid more recent aspects of history related to the antecedents of the Troubles (Barton & McCully, 2005; Kitson, 2007; McCully, 2010). The "revised" history curriculum, however, requires an exploration of the impact of history on identity and the "causes and consequences of the partition of Ireland" (Education [Minimum Content] Order, 2007). Nonetheless, there is still no statutory requirement to study the more recent phase of the conflict and the impact of its legacy.

It has been suggested, therefore, that young people for the most part have serious gaps in their knowledge and understanding of the recent conflict (Barton & McCully, 2010). Resonating with other contexts, the concern in Northern Ireland is that if young people do not learn explicitly about the conflict and its implications, "there is a danger that as [they] get older they selectively assimilate aspects of formal learning into the dominant popular narrative in their respective communities" (McCully, 2010, p. 167) and as such perpetuate associated myths and partial understandings.

While the statutory curriculum, both in policy and practice, tends to avoid explicit engagement with matters relating to the conflict and its legacy, other non-statutory educational programs in Northern Ireland are attempting to fill this lacuna. One example of this is an initiative that aims to assist young people in exploring the conflict from the point of view of those who were directly involved in the conflict. The initiative, *From Prison to Peace: Learning from the Experience of Political Ex-Prisoners* (Prison to Peace Partnership, 2011) is a 12-week program designed for use in post-primary schools within the citizenship and history curricula. This was developed as part of a wider program administered by the Community Foundation for Northern Ireland, which combines the political ex-prisoners support groups from loyalist and republican former combatant constituencies. Based on the narratives of 15 political ex-prisoners, the program invites young people to explore the reasons why people became involved in the conflict, the impact of prison, and the contribution former prisoners are now making to the community. During the program, young people are also provided with opportunities to engage directly in dialogue with former combatants in order to further explore their personal stories. In doing so, the program allows young people to explore the reality of conflict, including its complexities and the intricacies of transition from conflict to peace. In particular, it seeks to challenge sectarian attitudes and behaviors and engender within young people a confidence in their own identity along with respect for the rights of others to hold alternative political views. (For a fuller analysis of the program, see Emerson, 2012.)

As noted at the outset of this chapter, respect for human rights is a key aspect of the aims of education pertinent to societies emerging from conflict. The extent to which children and young people in Northern Ireland are provided with access to human rights education is discussed below, again in the context of relevant human rights standards and commitments made by the international community.

Development of Respect for Human Rights and Fundamental Freedoms

Since the UDHR enshrined human rights education (HRE) as a universal entitlement, the "right to human rights education" has been established further through explicit references to it in numerous human rights instruments as a state obligation, and implicit references to its intrinsic value (McEvoy & Lundy, 2007), culminating in its endorsement by the international community in the General Assembly's adoption of the Declaration on Human Rights Education and Training (UN, 2011). While the target audience for HRE in international law is wide ranging, the CRC is more specific in its focus. Article 29(1b) requires that education be directed to "the development of respect for human rights and fundamental freedoms, and for the principles enshrined in the Charter of the United Nations." Moreover, Article 42 of the CRC identifies education as a key mechanism for effective implementation of children's rights. This is endorsed further by the Committee on the Rights of the Child, which maintains that "states should develop a comprehensive strategy for disseminating knowledge of the Convention throughout society" (UN, 2003, para. 67) and place special emphasis on children acquiring knowledge of their rights through "incorporating learning about the Convention and human rights in general into the school curriculum at all stages" (UN, 2003, para. 68). In particular, the committee has stipulated that HRE should provide information on the content of human rights treaties and that children should learn about human rights by seeing human rights standards implemented in practice, whether at home, in school, or within the community (UN, 2001, 2003). More recently, the UN has articulated further its vision of effective HRE in primary and secondary schools through the World Programme for HRE, which encourages states, *inter alia*, to specifically include HRE in the curriculum in general and citizenship and history curricula in particular; to provide opportunities for young people to put human rights learning into practice; to relate human rights to issues in young people's daily lives; to base HRE programs on international human rights standards; and to develop a comprehensive training policy on human rights education for educational personnel, including a focus on "knowledge about human rights, their universality, indivisibility and interdependence and about protection mechanisms" (UN, 2006, 2010).

In addition to the fact that international law dictates that children have a *right* to human rights education in general and children's rights education in particular, academic debate endorses HRE in terms of its potential contribution to social transformation (McEvoy & Lundy, 2007). For example, it has been suggested that HRE can contribute to the reduction of human rights violations; the perpetuation of stable, peaceful, and tolerant societies (Reardon, 1997; Salomon & Nevo, 2002); conflict resolution and peace building (Andreopoulos & Claude, 1997); and the maintenance of democracy (Osler & Starkey, 2005). Such issues are self-evidently pertinent to a society emerging from conflict, underscoring further the rationale for the inclusion of HRE in the statutory curricula of transitional societies. Moreover, since human rights provide a language around which conflict can be framed and addressed (Ignatieff, 2001), HRE in conflict-affected societies should seek not only to provide children and young people with a knowledge of their rights but also aim to ensure that they are initiated into this discourse in order to facilitate their participation in the reconstruction of their societies (McEvoy & Lundy, 2007).

In the light of this compelling rationale for HRE and the central role afforded to human rights in the Northern Ireland peace process discussed above, it would be reasonable to expect human rights to be put at the forefront of the statutory curriculum. However, specific mention of human rights as part of the statutory NI Primary Curriculum appears only at Key Stage 2 (that is, for children ages 8–11), where reference is made to "developing knowledge, understanding and skills in human rights and social responsibility" as part of the Personal Development and Mutual Understanding (PDMU) learning area (Education [Minimum Content] Order, 2007). Non-statutory guidance in elaborating on this, however, makes no reference to human rights, children's rights, or any international human rights standards. In reference to the values underpinning PDMU, the non-statutory guidance suggests that schools may wish to use the UDHR or CRC as vehicles through which children can explore their own values. No reference is made to human rights in any other aspect of the primary curriculum.

As noted above, the NI Post-Primary Curriculum contains specific provision for citizenship education, which at Key Stage 3 (for children ages 11–14) contains the core theme "Human Rights and Social Responsibility." The content of this theme makes reference to upholding human rights standards, investigating human rights principles, balancing and limiting rights, and investigating examples of infringements of rights. Core human rights instruments, however, are not statutory—the UDHR and CRC are offered only as examples that might be included (Education [Minimum Content] Order, 2007). In practice, however, non-statutory supporting resources build this aspect of the curriculum around the UDHR and CRC, which should have the effect of encouraging teachers to engage with international standards. Arguably, other components of the statutory curriculum provide the opportunity to explore human rights (although the terms are not explicitly used). The English curriculum requires young people to "use literature and drama, poetry or moving image to explore other's needs and rights," and the curriculum for drama makes reference to "balancing rights," though this is not statutory. The history curriculum refers to "women's rights" and "workers' rights," though again as examples of issues to explore only, not as statutory content (Education [Minimum Content] Order, 2007). Beyond this, no specific reference to human rights is made in any other aspect of the statutory Post-Primary Curriculum. At Key Stage 4 (for young people ages 14–16), the statutory curriculum for citizenship education makes no specific reference to *human* rights, instead referring more broadly to "exercising rights and social responsibilities." However, the non-statutory guidelines again urge schools to interpret this to mean "human rights" and to develop curricula around international and regional human rights instruments.

Research suggests that young people's learning in relation to human rights in general has increased, especially since the introduction of citizenship education and PDMU into the statutory curriculum (UU, 2010). In particular, children and young people's awareness of the CRC has increased. For example, prior to the introduction of the revised NI Curriculum, a Commonwealth study indicated that only 4% of children and young people surveyed in Northern Ireland had heard of the CRC (Bourne et al., 1998). More recent surveys (the *Kids' Life and Times* and *Young Life and Times* surveys, administered annually to children age 11 and young people age 16, respectively) have shown that this percentage has increased to 28% for children at the end of their primary education (Ark, 2012) and 39% for young people at the end of their compulsory post-primary education (Ark, 2010). While only a small percentage of children are aware of the CRC, they are nonetheless able to identify some of their convention rights. For example, the latest *Kids' Life and Times* survey asked 11-year-olds to identify the rights that they possessed and found that 67% of children knew they had the "right to have a safe place to play," 53% could identify the "right to education" as a child's right, and 59% knew that they had a "right to have our ideas listened to and taken seriously" (Ark, 2012).

While this increase in awareness of the convention and the rights within it is promising, the survey findings suggest that more needs to be done to ensure that *all* children and young people are made aware of the existence of the CRC in addition to familiarity with their particular rights within it. Moreover, research indicates that there is a need to ground the knowledge of human rights in the lived reality of children and young people, as young people are reporting limited opportunities to put their learning into practice (UU, 2010), suggesting that the curriculum provides for only a superficial engagement with the nature of both human rights and children's rights.

This is to an extent unsurprising, since little support has been given to teachers to develop their own understanding of human rights (McEvoy, 2007), and as a result they by and large lack confidence in relation to engaging with HRE (see UU, 2010). Despite expressed governmental commitment to human rights and the requirement that schools attend to these issues, no comprehensive strategy has been established in relation to teacher education for HRE. Investment in in-service teacher training for the implementation of citizenship education in general was significant. However, the training focused primarily on active and participatory pedagogical approaches to learning (of course necessary for effective HRE), arguably to the detriment of a sound conceptual understanding of the concepts underpinning the curriculum, in particular human rights (McEvoy, 2007). Further, the professional competence framework (which guides teacher education from initial teacher training through continued professional development) makes no reference to human rights or children's rights. While recent Department of Education guidelines include an amended form of some of the relevant competencies, which refer to a need for teachers to develop an understanding of contemporary debates in relation to human rights (DE, 2011, p. 46), these are non-statutory.

It is worth noting that non-governmental organizations (NGOs) are providing teachers with the support and resources required to deliver effective HRE in their classrooms. For example, at the primary level, many schools have incorporated Amnesty International's *Lift Off* program into their PDMU curriculum. This program, which introduces primary school children to the language of rights in a child-friendly and age-appropriate manner, has been acknowledged by the UN as an effective way of engaging young children in understanding the nature of human rights and children's rights. Moreover, it has undoubtedly provided children in the primary sector with opportunities to enjoy their right to human rights education, despite the lack of reference to it in the statutory primary curriculum and lack of state-funded support and training for teachers. Amnesty International has also produced resources to augment the curriculum and support teachers in the delivery of effective HRE in the post-primary sector. The resource "Making Human Rights Real," aimed at young people ages 14–16, focuses on the historical development of human rights discourse, core human rights concepts, international, regional, and national human rights instruments, and the application of these to the context of Northern Ireland. In doing so it seeks to support teachers and young people in developing a sound understanding of the nature of human rights and the processes through which rights become realized. Hence, while the statutory curriculum is, to an extent, providing some opportunities for children and young people to "develop respect for human rights and fundamental freedoms," NGOs are at the forefront of ensuring the delivery of effective HRE.

In sum, it is acknowledged that attempts have been made in the statutory NI curriculum to attend to matters relevant to the nature and legacy of the conflict. This has, however, been driven largely by policy commitment to improving community relations and promoting social cohesion rather than a core commitment to human rights standards and their implementation in education (McEvoy, McEvoy, & McConnachie, 2006). Thus, while current policy aligns to some degree with the aims of education as articulated in Article 29 of the CRC, it does so more coincidentally than by design. While research suggests that curriculum policy and practice need to attend more deeply to the complexity of issues relating to the promotion of tolerance and respect for human rights, teacher engagement with grassroots initiatives developed by NGOs (such as those presented above) suggests at least a "ripeness" within the educational community for teaching the more controversial aspects of the history and citizenship curricula. Further, as noted above, research evidence indicates that young people are keen to engage with these issues and want to understand the transitional context in which they are growing up.

Conclusion

The content of what children and young people are taught at school is clearly a "matter which affects them" and is, therefore, in accordance with Article 12 of the CRC, a matter about which they are entitled to have their views sought, listened to, and taken seriously. This is especially important in the context of transitional societies, where knowledge relating to the causes and consequences of conflict is essential to the realization of a range of their other rights. In practice, however, it is adults involved in the processes of curriculum development who decide what children need to know. This is then mediated further by teachers who "approximate" the curriculum policy to suit their own classroom context (McEvoy, 2007, p. 143). Teachers have considerable discretion in relation to curriculum implementation and are then able to exercise this with caution when faced with issues of controversy, conflict, and rights. In relation to the latter, reasons for teacher avoidance of controversial issues are well rehearsed within the literature and include teacher unease in relation to classroom management implications, anxiety about parental response, fear of being accused of or being complicit in indoctrination, or genuine concern that dealing with such issues may make the world seem even more chaotic for children who are perhaps struggling to cope with their own personal circumstances (see, e.g., Chikoko, Gilmour, Harber, & Serf, 2011; Hess, 2002). In addition, effective engagement with controversial issues poses challenges to teachers' pedagogical practice, requiring them to possess a "tolerance for ambiguity" in educational contexts that tends to stress certainty and fact (Howe & Covell, 2005, p. 167).

In addition to the tendency to steer clear of controversy in the classroom, there is also a reluctance among adults to engage children in school decision making, particularly in relation to decisions regarding the curriculum, where teacher professionalism and authority usually hold sway (Flutter & Rudduck, 2004). Thus, not only does curricular content and its implementation in Northern Ireland fall somewhat short of the aims of Article 29, but the processes through which the curriculum is designed and developed also fail to engage meaningfully with children and young people, as required by Article 12—a situation that may resonate with other societies emerging from conflict. When aversion to dealing with conflict and controversy *in* the curriculum is combined with reluctance to consult young people *on* the curriculum, the combined effect amounts to a denial of their rights to, in, and through education. As always, responsibility for ensuring the implementation of the CRC in this context lies with the state, which has the duty to take the lead in relation to ensuring that law, policy, and practice are compliant with the international standards to which it has committed. Educational policy needs to attend to this and support teachers in exploring the issues young people want to address, even when these are sensitive and contentious in the context in which they live.

If, as Article 29 states, a key aim of education is to prepare children and young people for responsible life in a free society, then curricula developed and enacted need to provide young people with the necessary knowledge and skills for the life they lead now and the life they may have in their community. A rights-based approach requires that their best interests are a primary consideration in all matters affecting them (Article 3). Moreover, there is an indubitable sufficiency of interest (at the foundation of all rights) in their knowing and understanding the context in which they find themselves. In doing so, this enables fulfilment of a range of rights beyond Article 29, including the right to life, survival, and development (Article 6), the right to seek, receive, and impart information (Article 13), the right to be safe from harm (Article 19), and the right to guidance and direction from the adults in their lives (Article 5).

In societies emerging from conflict, this means explicitly addressing the origins, nature, and legacy of the conflict in order that children and young people can make sense of, contribute to, and live securely in their own transitional context. In particular, this requires space to be created in the curriculum that will allow young people to explore and understand the issues that are confronting them. A rights-based approach obliges those charged with developing and implementing such a curriculum to engage with children and young people in order to ascertain from *their* perspective the issues they are dealing with and how best the curriculum can address their needs. As we have suggested elsewhere, "in order to know what will work *for* children there is no option but to work *with* children to secure the realisation of their rights" (McEvoy & Lundy, 2007). In short, children and young people are entitled to have input into shaping the curriculum to ensure that it is relevant to the transitional context in which they live.

References

Andreopoulos, G.J., & Claude, R.P. (Eds.). (1997). *Human rights education for the twenty-first century*. Philadelphia, PA: University of Pennsylvania Press.

ARK. (2010). *Young Life and Times Survey 2010*. Retrieved from http://www.ark.ac.uk/ylt

ARK. (2011). *Young Life and Times Survey 2011*. Retrieved from http://www.ark.ac.uk/ylt

ARK. (2012). *Kids' Life and Times Survey 2012*. Retrieved from http://www.ark.ac.uk/klt

Arlow, M. (2011). Diversity, mutual understanding and citizenship. In N. Richardson & T. Gallagher (Eds.), *Education for diversity and mutual understanding* (pp. 311–330). Oxford, UK: Peter Lang.

Barton, K.C., & McCully, A.W. (2005). History, identity, and the school curriculum in Northern Ireland: An empirical study of secondary students' ideas and perspectives. *Journal of Curriculum Studies, 37*(1), 85–116.

Barton, K.C., & McCully, A.W. (2010). "You can form your own point of view": Internally persuasive discourse in Northern Ireland students' encounters with history. *Teachers College Record, 112*(1), 142–181.

Bell, C. (2003). *Peace agreements and human rights*. Oxford: Oxford University Press.

Bird, L. (2007). Learning about war and peace in the Great Lakes region of Africa. *Research in Comparative and International Education, 2*(3), 176–190.

Bourne, R., Gundara, J., Dev, A., Ratsoma, N., Rukanda, M., Smith, A., & Birthistle, U. (1998). *School-based understanding of human rights in four countries: A Commonwealth study*. London: Department for International Development.

Bush, K., & Saltarelli, D. (Eds.). (2000). *The two faces of education in ethnic conflict*. Florence, Italy: UNICEF Innocenti Research Centre.

Cairns, E. (1987). *Caught in crossfire: Children and the Northern Ireland conflict*. Belfast, Northern Ireland: Appletree.

Chikoko, V., Gilmour, J., Harber, C., & Serf, J. (2011). Teaching controversial issues and teacher education in England and South Africa. *Journal of Education for Teaching: International Research and Pedagogy, 37*(1), 5–19.

Cole, E., & Barsalou, J. (2006). *Unite or divide? The challenges of teaching history in societies emerging from violent conflict*. Washington, DC: US Institute of Peace.

Connolly, P., & Healy, J. (2004). *Children and the conflict in Northern Ireland: The experiences and perspectives of 3–11 year olds*. Belfast, Northern Ireland: OFMdFM.

Department of Education Northern Ireland. (2011). *Community relations, equality and diversity in education*. Bangor, Northern Ireland: Department of Education.

Dixon, P., & O'Kane, E. (2011). *Northern Ireland since 1969*. London: Pearson.

Duffy, A. (2010). A truth commission for Northern Ireland? *The International Journal of Transitional Justice, 4*, 26–46.

Education (Minimum Content) (NI) Order. (2007). Belfast, Northern Ireland: HMSO.

Education (NI) Order. (2006). Belfast: HMSO.

Education Reform (NI) Order. (1989). Belfast: HMSO.

Emerson, L. (2012). Conflict, transition and education for "political generosity": Learning from the experience of ex-combatants in Northern Ireland. *Journal of Peace Education, 9*(3), 277–295.

Flutter, J., & Rudduck, J. (2004). *Consulting pupils: What's in it for schools?* London: RoutledgeFalmer.

Forbes, T., Sibbett, C., Miller, S., & Emerson, L. (2012). *Exploring the community response to multiple deaths of young people by suicide.* Belfast, Northern Ireland: Centre for Effective Education, Queen's University Belfast.

Fortin, J. (2003). *Children's rights and the developing law.* Cambridge: Cambridge University Press.

Freedman, S.W., Weinstein, H.M., Murphy, K., & Longman, T. (2008). Teaching history after identity-based conflicts: The Rwanda experience. In E. Cole (Ed.), *Teaching the violent past: History education and reconciliation* (pp. 123–155). Lanham, MD: Rowman & Littlefield.

Freeman, M. (2000). The future of children's rights. *Children and Society, 14*(4), 277–293.

Hansson, U. (2005). *Troubled youth? Young people, violence and disorder in Northern Ireland.* Belfast, Northern Ireland: Institute for Conflict Research.

Harris, N. (2009). Catch-up in the schoolyard? Children and young people's "voice" and education rights in the UK. *International Journal of Law, Policy and the Family, 3*, 331–366.

Hess, D. (2002). Teaching controversial public issues discussions: Learning from skilled teachers. *Theory and Research in Social Education, 30*(1), 10–41.

Howe, R.B., & Covell, K. (2005). *Empowering children: Children's rights education as a pathway to citizenship.* Toronto: University of Toronto Press.

Ignatieff, M. (2001). *Human rights as politics and idolatry.* Princeton, NJ: Princeton University Press.

Jarman, N., & O'Halloran, C. (2001). Recreational rioting: Young people, interface areas and violence. *Child Care in Practice, 7*, 2–16.

Kitson, A. (2007). History education and reconciliation in Northern Ireland. In E. Cole (Ed.), *Teaching the violent past: History education and reconciliation* (pp. 123–155). Lanham, MD: Rowman & Littlefield.

Leonard, M. (2007). Trapped in space? Children's accounts of risky environments. *Children and Society, 21*, 432–445.

Leonard, M. (2010). What's recreational about recreational rioting? Children on the streets in Belfast. *Children and Society, 24*, 38–49.

Limber, S., Kask, V., Heidmets, M., Hevener-Kaufman, N., & Merton, G. (1999). Estonian children's perceptions of rights: Implication for societies in transition. *International Journal of Children's Rights, 7*, 365–383.

Lundy, L. (2005). Family values in the classroom: Balancing parents' wishes with children's rights in state schools. *International Journal of Law, Policy and the Family, 19*(3), 1–27.

Lundy, L. (2006). Mainstreaming children's rights in, to and through education in a society emerging from conflict. *International Journal of Children's Rights, 14*(4), 339–362.

Lundy, L. (2007). Voice is not enough: Conceptualising Article 12 of the United Nations Convention on the Rights of the Child. *British Education Research Journal, 33*(6), 927–942.

Lundy, L., & McEvoy, L. (2009). Developing outcomes for education services: A children's rights–based approach. *Effective Education, 1*(1), 43–60.

Machel, G. (1996). *The impact of armed conflict on children.* Geneva: United Nations.

Mageean, P., & O'Brien, M. (1999). From the margins to the mainstream: Human rights and the Good Friday Agreement. *Fordham International Law Journal, 22*, 1499–1539.

Magill, C., Smith, A., & Hamber, B. (2009). *The role of education in reconciliation: The perspectives of young people in Bosnia and Herzegovina and Northern Ireland.* Coleraine, Northern Ireland: UNESCO Centre, University of Ulster.

McAlister, S., Scraton, P., & Haydon, D. (2011). *Childhood in transition: Experiencing marginalisation and conflict in Northern Ireland—Executive summary and key findings.* Belfast, Northern Ireland: Childhood, Transition and Social Justice Initiative.

McCully, A.W. (2010). History teaching, "truth recovery," and reconciliation. In C. Mitchell, T. Strong-Wilson, K. Pithouse, & S. Allnutt (Eds.), *Memory and pedagogy.* London: Routledge.

McEvoy, L. (2007). Beneath the rhetoric: Policy approximation and citizenship education in Northern Ireland. *Education, Citizenship and Social Justice, 2*(2), 135–158.

McEvoy, L., & Lundy, L. (2007). "In the small places": Human rights culture, education and conflict-affected societies. In G. Anthony, K. McEvoy, & J. Morison (Eds.), *Judges, transition and human rights culture.* Oxford: Oxford University Press.

McEvoy, L., McEvoy, K., & McConnachie, K. (2006). Reconciliation as a dirty word: Conflict, community relations and education in Northern Ireland. *Journal of International Affairs, 60*(1), 81–106.

McGarry, J., & O'Leary, B. (1995). *Explaining Northern Ireland.* Oxford: Blackwell.

Muldoon, O. (2004). Children of the troubles: The impact of political violence in Northern Ireland. *Journal of Social Issues, 60*(3), 453–468.

Muldoon, O., & Trew, K. (2000). Children's experiences and adjustment to political conflict in Northern Ireland. *Peace and Conflict: Journal of Peace Psychology, 6*(2), 157–176.

Noyes, A. (2005). Pupil voice: Purpose, power and the possibilities for democratic schooling. *British Educational Research Journal, 31*(4), 533–540.

O'Connor, U., Hartop, B., & McCully, A. (2002). *The Schools Community Relations Programme: A review.* Bangor, Northern Ireland: DENI.

O'Connor, U., Hartop, B., & McCully, A. (2003). *A research study of pupil perceptions of the Schools Community Relations Programme.* Bangor, Northern Ireland: DENI.

OFMdFM. (2005). *A shared future—Policy and strategic framework for good relations.* Belfast, Northern Ireland: OFMdFM.

OFMdFM. (2006). *Our children and young people—Our pledge: A ten year strategy for children and young people in Northern Ireland 2006–2016.* Belfast, Northern Ireland: OFMdFM.

OFMdFM. (2009). *Good relations indicators—2009 update.* Retrieved from http://www.ofmdfmni.gov.uk/good_relations_indicators_-_2009_update.pdf

OFMdFM. (2010a). *Programme for cohesion, sharing and integration consultation document.* Belfast, Northern Ireland: OFMdFM.

OFMdFM. (2010b). *Good relation indicators—2010 update.* Retrieved from http://www.ofmdfmni.gov.uk/gr-pubs

Osler, A., & Starkey, H. (2005). *Changing citizenship: Democracy and inclusion in education.* London: McGraw-Hill.

Prison to Peace Partnership. (2011). *From prison to peace: Learning from the experience of political ex-prisoners.* Belfast, Northern Ireland: Prison to Peace Partnership.

Reardon, B. (1997). Human rights as education for peace. In G. Andreopoulos & R. Claude (Eds.), *Human rights education for the twenty first century* (pp. 21–34). Philadelphia, PA: University of Pennsylvania Press.

Reilly, P. (2011). Anti-social networking in Northern Ireland: Policy responses to young people's use of social media for organizing anti-social behavior. *Policy & Internet, 3*(1), article 7.

Sacramento, L., & Pessoa, A.M. (1996). Implementation of the rights of the child in the Mozambican context. In M. Freeman (Ed.), *Children's rights: A comparative perspective* (pp. 145–164). Aldershot, UK: Dartmouth Publishing.

Salomon, G., & Nevo, B. (Eds.). (2002). *Peace education: The concept, principles, and practices around the world.* Mahwah, NJ: Lawrence Erlbaum Associates.

Schubotz, D., & Devine, P. (Eds.). (2008). *Young people in post-conflict Northern Ireland: The past cannot be changed but the future can be developed.* Dorset, UK: Russell House Publishing.

Sloth-Nielsen, J. (1996). The contribution of children's rights to the reconstruction of society: Some implications of the constitutionalisation of children's rights in South Africa. *International Journal of Children's Rights, 4*(4), 323–344.

Smith, A. (2010). *The influence of education on conflict and peace building: Background paper prepared for the Education for All Global Monitoring Report*. Paris: UNESCO.

Smith, S., & Vaux, T. (2003). *Education, conflict and international development*. London: DFID.

Smyth, M. (1998). *Half the battle: Understanding the impact of the troubles on children and young people*. Derry, Northern Ireland: INCORE.

Smyth, M., & Campbell, P. (2005). *Young people and armed violence in Northern Ireland*. São Paulo, Brazil: COAV: Children in Organised Armed Violence.

Tawil, S., & Harley, A. (2004). *Education, conflict and social cohesion*. Geneva: International Bureau of Education, Department of International Development (DFID).

United Nations. (1948). *Universal declaration of human rights*. Geneva: United Nations.

United Nations. (1989). *United Nations Convention on the Rights of the Child*. Geneva: United Nations.

United Nations. (2001). *Committee on the Rights of the Child. General comment no. 1 (2001): The aims of education* (UN/CRC/GC/2001/1). Geneva: United Nations.

United Nations. (2003). *Committee on the Rights of the Child. General comment no. 5 (2003): Implementation* (UN/CRC/GC/2003/1). Geneva: United Nations.

United Nations. (2006). *Plan of action: World Programme for Human Rights Education first phase*. Geneva: United Nations.

United Nations. (2010). *Plan of action: World Programme for Human Rights Education second phase*. Geneva: United Nations.

United Nations. (2011). *United Nations declaration on human rights education and training* (A/RES/66/137) Geneva: United Nations.

United Nations, Committee on the Rights of the Child. (1995). *Concluding observations: United Kingdom of Great Britain and Northern Ireland*. Geneva: United Nations.

United Nations, Committee on the Rights of the Child. (2002). *Concluding observations: United Kingdom of Great Britain and Northern Ireland*. Geneva: United Nations.

United Nations, Committee on the Rights of the Child. (2008). *Concluding observations: United Kingdom of Great Britain and Northern Ireland (para 67)*. Geneva: United Nations.

University of Ulster. (2010). *Evaluation of local and global citizenship: Final report*. Coleraine, Northern Ireland: University of Ulster.

Wyse, D. (2001). Felt tip pens and school councils: Children's participation rights in four English schools. *Children & Society, 15*(4), 209–218.

CHAPTER TWO

Children's Rights and Educational Exclusion

The Impact of Zero Tolerance in Schools

Martha Baiyee, Celeste Hawkins, & Valerie Polakow

Everyone has the right to education.... Education shall be directed to the full development of the human personality and to the strengthening of respect for human rights and
fundamental freedoms....
—Universal Declaration of Human Rights, 1948

This chapter addresses children's rights in the United States and the crisis of
educational exclusion caused by zero-tolerance policies in public schools and
their disproportionate impact on poor children, children of color, and children
with disabilities. Zero tolerance for student misconduct is now embedded in the
symbolic universe of schooling and the punitive discourse of consequences. The
social spaces for error and youthful indiscretions have constricted as young people
increasingly inhabit institutions of surveillance where their rights to privacy, participation, and voice are checked at the schoolhouse door, where metal detectors
frame them as potential threats. Harsh punishment, rather than remediation and
rehabilitation, has become the disciplinary norm as young children and youth
constructed as "trouble" are pushed out and/or are permanently barred from
school; legal protections are rarely enforced, and many children are funneled into
the juvenile justice system, creating a school-to-prison pipeline.

What does it mean to experience a disrupted education and the attendant
marginalization that results when students are exiled from school? For a developing child or adolescent, there is not only a violation of fundamental educational
rights, but also an experience of exclusion and shaming and, frequently, a threat

to the family's stability and economic self-sufficiency, particularly if the student is young and in need of alternative care arrangements. Children's voices are rarely heard or attended to by the adults who control and restrict their educational access. What do children and youth think about zero-tolerance policies? How do they perceive the critical incidents that result in exclusion from their schools? How might educators learn from students who experience suspensions and expulsions? In this chapter, the voices of suspended and expelled students are presented in order to illuminate the impact of zero-tolerance policies on their lives and analyze the consequences in terms of their rights and future life trajectories.

The Wide Reach of Zero Tolerance

The federal Gun Free Schools Act (GFSA) of 1994 marked a radical shift in educational policies in the United States. Mandatory expulsion for weapons and drug violations became the norm across the country and ushered in an era of unprecedented educational exclusion from schools for millions of American children over the next 2 decades. Denied access to educational services, suspended and expelled for minor infractions such as fighting, bringing Midol (for menstrual cramps) to school, demonstrating grandfather's Swiss army knife at "show and tell" in kindergarten—children have been criminalized, dragged out of schools crying in handcuffs, and forbidden re-entry after long periods of exile. Such is the story of zero tolerance, a dramatic unfolding of how two generations of discarded children and youth have lost part of their childhoods.

Dohrn (2000) points out how the shift toward the criminalization of children has resulted in the widespread detention and incarceration of youth, and that the general policing of schools, with consequent school-based arrests, rapidly turns misconduct into criminal acts. In addition, the increasing surveillance and arrest of young people for status offenses such as truancy, loitering, or curfew violations, and the transfer of children to adult criminal courts raises fundamental questions about our civic responsibility and accountability. Robbins (2008) argues forcefully that current zero-tolerance policies, embedded in increasingly militarized schools and abetted by surveillance technologies, erode students' rights, their educational opportunities, and, ultimately, their life chances as the school-to-prison pipeline weaves an inexorable downward trajectory. His analysis of the policies of exclusion points to the radical transformation of public education that has taken place as a consequence of zero tolerance: the shrinking of the public space, disproportionate racial exclusions, and the perpetuation of further inequality—all intricately tied to the erosion of democratic ideals of schooling.

Students of color, poor students, and those with special needs are disproportionately impacted by zero-tolerance policies and are two to three times more likely to be disciplined than White students for the same or similar school offenses. Over 3 million children were suspended in 2006, and 102,080 more were expelled; yet the majority of offenses were non-violent and included violating school rules such as dress code infractions, tardiness, and insubordination (American Civil Liberties Union [ACLU], 2008; Losen & Gillespie, 2012; U.S. Department of Education, 2012). The overrepresentation of African American students (15%) in comparison to White students (5%) raises fundamental concerns about civil rights, racial bias, and the impact on youth whose school lives are frequently derailed by punitive disciplinary policies, with many school districts now pursuing long-term suspensions (LaMarche, 2011).

Several disturbing trends have emerged nationwide that point to the lack of available, accessible, and alternative education options while students serve "time" during suspensions and expulsions. The Georgetown Law Human Rights Institute (2012) documents how children face barriers when attempting to re-enroll and in many instances are steered away from school altogether, thus contributing to repeated suspensions, expulsions, and overrepresentation in the juvenile justice system. For students who are impoverished and confronting multiple risk factors, it is clear that "denying access to education can produce life altering results...and for these vulnerable youth the effects are often especially dire" (p. 7).

Education and Children's Rights

In the United States, education is not a constitutional right, and it falls to state constitutions to ensure a free public education for all children. While the importance of education has been affirmed by numerous Supreme Court cases such as *Brown v. Board of Education* (1954), there is no federal framework to ensure that students have a right to a quality education. In 1982, *Phyer v. Dyer* established the vital importance of education "in maintaining the fabric of our society" (quoted in Georgetown Law Human Rights Institute, 2012, p. 76), yet the proliferation of school exclusion policies now tears apart that prized "fabric of our society," as educational opportunities are denied to growing numbers of youth and extend downward to the youngest of our children, who may experience such exclusion before they even enter elementary school.

From a rights-based perspective, children and youth who are excluded from school experience fundamental violations of their human rights—rights juxtaposed against the backdrop of the struggle for educational equity and social justice in the United States. The International Convention on the Rights of the Child (CRC) was adopted in 1989 and has been ratified by 191 countries, yet the United States remains an outlier in failing to ratify the CRC. The CRC incorporates civil, cultural, economic, social, and political rights and recognizes children as "rights bearers" and as active agents of their own lives (Kilbourne, 1999). The four key principles of the CRC incorporate respect for the child's human dignity and address the best interests of the child, non-discrimination, the right to healthy development, and the right of the child to express his/her own views. Article

12(1) specifically refers to "the right to express those views freely in all matters affecting the child." Article 28(2) addresses the right to education, emphasizing that state parties (governments) are obligated under the CRC to both establish educational systems and to ensure access to them, and that the administration of "school discipline (be implemented)…in a manner consistent with the child's human dignity." Article 29(1) addresses education as a developmental process promoting "the child's personality, talents, and mental and physical abilities to their fullest potential" as well as the "preparation of the child for responsible life in a free society." The *General Comments* of the CRC (United Nations, 2001) that elaborate on "The Aims of Education" point to Article 29 as articulating a specific quality of education that is "child-centered, child-friendly, and empowering."

Yet these fundamental rights, articulated by the CRC and other international conventions such as the International Covenant on Economic, Social and Cultural Rights (ICESCR), are violated by zero-tolerance policies and educational practices in the United States, pointing to the vast distance between U.S. domestic policy and internationally accepted rights. In the United States, educational reform efforts have largely focused on increasing students' educational achievement, teacher quality and accountability, and comprehensive and "smarter" testing, while the dominant discourse of punishment and sanctions for non-compliant behavior ignores students' voices and the question of rights, and maintains a silence about the toxic impact of educational exclusion.

Educational Exclusion, Poverty, and Race

In contrast to wealthy industrialized countries with commitments to eradicating child poverty and ensuring children's rights in alignment with the CRC, the United States ranks highest in child inequality among 24 wealthy, industrialized nations (UNICEF, 2010), with over 15.5 million children living in poverty (Addy & Wight, 2012). For school-age children, life in impoverished communities may mean enduring the daily dangers of street and community violence, under-resourced and inferior schools, and isolation from networks of support, creating further conditions of social toxicity (Garbarino, 1995). The American Psychological Association (APA) points to the relationship between poverty and school dropout rates: poor students are five times more likely than their affluent peers to drop out of school. In addition, so-called "dropout factories" (schools that graduate less than 60% of their students) produce half of the dropouts nationwide, two-thirds of whom are ethnic minority students (APA, 2012). Given the high rates of exclusion from school, dropout rates might be better characterized as push-out rates (ACLU, 2008), as long-term suspensions and expulsions cast hundreds of thousands of youth into the streets, and in many school districts there are few viable alternative education programs. The trajectory from exclusion to the streets to incarceration is glaring testimony to the erosion of educational rights.

A recent report by Rich (2012) on an analysis of federal data by the Center for Civil Rights Remedies (CCRR) at UCLA indicates that students with disabilities are twice as likely to be suspended than non-disabled students and that in 10 states, 25% of African American students with disabilities were suspended in the 2009–2010 school year. CCRR (2012) documents that in some states the disproportionality is startling. In Henrico County in Virginia, for example, 92% of African American males with disabilities were suspended, in comparison with 44% of White male students with disabilities. CCRR also points to the general overrepresentation of African American students who undergo suspensions and expulsions in contrast to other ethnic groups. In Escambia County, Florida, African American students made up 36% of the school population, yet 65% received out-of-school suspensions, leading the Southern Poverty Law Center to file complaints against that school district and four other counties for civil rights violations. Some of the reported violations included cell phone usage or dress code violations!

The analysis of federal data by CCRR documents school practices of rampant exclusion with pernicious outcomes for children and their communities, leading Orfield to comment:

> Students who are barely maintaining a connection with their school often are pushed out, as if suspension were a treatment.... Every dropout costs society hundreds of thousands of dollars over the student's lifetime in lost income, and removing a large number of students from school undermines a community's future. (2012, p. 4)

When these deplorable outcomes are viewed as inextricably linked to poverty and race and placed in an international context, it is clear that zero-tolerance policies erode not only children's rights, but also their human capabilities. As Amartya Sen (2001) points out in writing about global poverty and freedom, material poverty certainly restricts freedom and life opportunities, but it is *capability deprivation* that leads to long-lasting social exclusion. Martha Nussbaum (2011) similarly argues that the fundamental question to ask when examining life conditions is: "What is each person able to do and to be?" (p. 18). When we translate such questions into the U.S. educational context, it becomes apparent that the lost educational opportunities and eviscerated life chances for discarded youth mean they can neither "do" nor "be"—and such inequality of life chances must be critically juxtaposed against the promise of democratic schooling for all.

In order to understand students' perceptions and experiences of exclusion, we interviewed middle and high school students during a 3-month period in 2012. In the following sections, we briefly describe our qualitative research approach followed by thematic narratives that capture the voices of suspended and expelled students.

Narratives of Exclusion

> I came to understand better than ever before the power of one's story, the value of one's personal narrative in making sense of experience. (Garbarino, 2000, p. xi)

This qualitative study is shaped by the work of interpretive ethnography, which focuses on "thick" description and local knowledge (Geertz, 1973, 1983), documenting and witnessing "truths that shame...us" (Behar, 1996, p. 33), and exploring the meanings and lifeworlds of young people from an emic perspective (Guajardo & Guajardo, 2008; Polakow, 1993; Soto & Swadener, 2005). Influenced by Articles 12 and 13 of the CRC, with its emphasis on child and youth participation, an international, interdisciplinary field of childhood studies has developed, committed to constructing theory and methods that favor child agency, by listening to children's voices and soliciting their views about their own learning and schooling experiences (Christensen, 2004; Mauthner, 1997). Viewing children as agents of their own lives raises critical questions about issues of power, social agency, voice, and the representation of children's perspectives in research (Brady, 2007; Christensen, 2004; Tisdall & Davis, 2004).

Interviews with a small sample of African American and White students in southeast Michigan between August and October 2012 focus on their experiences and perceptions of suspension and expulsion. Open-ended and semi-structured interviews were conducted with individual students outside their school settings, and they were asked to describe their experiences and to reflect on their own perspectives about fairness and school discipline policies. The interviews were audiotaped, and narratives were analyzed in order to understand students' experiences of suspension and/or expulsion. The sample consisted of five female and four male middle and high school students, all of whom experienced a suspension or expulsion during the past 3 years. The students (ages 12–19 years) were recruited from personal and professional contacts, community networks, and advocacy agencies outside of their original school settings, and pseudonyms have been used to protect their confidentiality.

The Students

Nineteen-year-old Charmaine is one of four children in a two-parent family; both parents have college degrees and work full-time. Charmaine was suspended several times in high school for tardiness and insubordination. Simone, a 19-year-old, grew up in a single-mother household; her mother works full-time. She was expelled from school for fighting during her junior year. Bridgette, a high school freshman raised by her mother and grandmother in a household where the primary source of income is from state disability benefits, received several suspensions in middle and high school for inappropriate conduct and disruptive behavior; she attends an alternative education program. Melanie, an 18-year-old senior in high school, lives with her single mother, who supports the family on a fixed income consisting of Social Security benefits. Melanie was suspended for disruptive behavior. Jason is a sophomore who currently attends an alternative education program. He is being raised by his single mother and his grandmother, who receive state disability benefits as their sole income. Jason has served multiple suspensions in middle and high school for tardiness. Nick, a junior suspended for inappropriate conduct, attends a school with a diverse population of students and is being raised by a single mother who receives disability benefits. Andre is an 18-year-old male who attended a private Christian school. He was suspended on multiple occasions and was expelled a few months before graduation for fathering a child. Andre lives with his single mother, who receives state disability benefits. Fourteen-year-old Jenny lives in a low-income household with her grandmother, who has cared for her since she was a young child. Her grandmother also takes care of Jenny's great-grandmother. Jenny has just completed serving a one-year expulsion for being in the presence of students who were smoking marijuana on school grounds. Sean, the youngest participant in the study, was a sixth grader when he received a 5-day suspension for fighting on the school bus. He lives in a two-parent professional family and has just begun the seventh grade. All the students, except Andre, attended public schools, and with the exception of Jenny, who is White, all are African American. Seven of the nine students live in poor or low-income households.[1]

Lack of Care
Several of the students expressed feelings of disappointment and disillusionment because adults in the school environment appeared indifferent to the challenges they were confronting. Teachers were perceived as uncaring and distant, compounding students' sense of isolation and disengagement. Charmaine faced many social and emotional challenges in high school, yet she did not receive emotional support nor was she given the space to share those feelings.

> Most of the time I needed to talk to someone, I went through a period where I was depressed and angry and didn't know what to do…the teachers missed that, they didn't care what was going on in your life…it didn't click for them.

Charmaine also compares her high school experience unfavorably as she recalls a different, more caring atmosphere in her elementary school.

> The thing I realized is as you get older, people start not to care…. I remember elementary school teachers spend a lot of time with you…in middle school, it's like "hmmm you'll get it"…then in high school they don't give a dang. I remember I had a teacher who would actually say, "I'm getting paid anyway."… I disengaged and didn't wanna be there…. I'm not getting an education if you're not teaching!

Jason seems to echo these sentiments, stating, "Teachers should talk to kids more; most kids just need someone to talk to…sit them down and talk to them or give them a warning before just jumping to suspending them." Simone recounts her attempts to resolve escalating problems with another student, with no support from her teachers. She felt that she was not heard. In telling her story about the fight that led to the expulsion, she states:

> She kept messing with me, so I busted her in her face…they don't care, they have these rules and they want us to follow them, the rules just say don't fight! What is the rule if someone is bothering you and you tell the staff and they don't do anything about it?

When Simone was expelled from school, her principal and teachers did not give her any specific information about how long she would be out of school, nor did they provide her with any alternative educational options. "They told me…since I would miss so much school I may as well not come back till next year, they just didn't care…it was my eleventh grade year, like what was I supposed to do?" Melanie sums up the lack of care and sense of rejection she feels, stating, "I think the real problem is the teachers and principals 'cause they really don't want you to learn from what you did, they want to make an example of you to the other kids."

Consistently Inconsistent: Lack of Fairness

Students were uniformly critical of what they perceived as inconsistent and unfair discipline meted out to them and to others. They saw themselves frequently targeted for collective punishment and guilt by association. These were common disciplinary practices in cases where students happened to be "in the wrong place at the wrong time," where just witnessing a situation could result in being disciplined just as severely as the person who was guilty of breaking the rule.

Consequences did not match the offense, and discipline policies were viewed as excessively harsh and did not "make sense." Melanie states:

> I mean, no matter what, the teacher or adult is always right and we wrong. I mean some kids are bad and they deserve what they get, you know…fightin' and stuff over dumb boys or whatever. But little stuff like talking or wearing certain clothes isn't something you should get in trouble for.

Nick, too, is critical of school discipline that he views as unfair, saying, "If you get in a fight and you didn't start it, you both get 10 days. I think the person who defended themselves should get less days than the person who started the fight!" Charmaine corroborates Nick's criticism, saying:

> Someone got suspended for being around a situation, they got suspended for the same amount of time as the person who was directly involved…if there was a fight…they would bring everyone into the room, they would tell the person "Well, you were there

and you didn't tell anybody so you are getting suspended too," and it happened quite frequently…you just had to be in the wrong place at the wrong time.

Jason comments on the lack of fairness and inconsistency at his former middle school:

> The policy at my old middle school was not fair, like if someone fought they would suspend you and not the other person, if you started the fight you would get suspended but if the other person fought you back they would not get suspended…. I think they both should get the same consequence for fighting.

Sean, who was suspended because another student assaulted him and he defended himself, comments on the arbitrary penalties that are meted out to students, even when they are unwitting victims.

> Because I was just talking to somebody and someone comes up and just punches you and you are just sitting there while he jumps on you. That's not really doing anything and getting in trouble for that doesn't really make sense.

As Jenny looks back at suspensions she received in middle school, she feels she was inconsistently and unfairly treated.

> I believe that some people are treated more harshly than others. I remember a few times last year Mr. D he gave me 5 days suspension because I walked down to the high school… and then they had another girl in there and she only got one day and she was doing the same thing. Either she didn't get in as much trouble as me or he [Mr. D] just doesn't like me or he like[s] her a lot better, thinks she has more potential or something….

Andre, too, feels aggrieved that he received unfair treatment as he comments on his expulsion from his former school: "There have been plenty of children who had babies and they got to stay in school, walk with their class and graduate, like I can name a few who didn't get any punishment at all." Bridgette recounts a racial incident where she was treated unjustly, stating: "A kid spit on me and he was White and I threw a ball at him and I got suspended, but he didn't, it was like only our kind who would get in trouble…she sent me to the principal's office, the kid who spit on me did not get in trouble!"

Silenced Voices

Students also experienced a complete disregard for their views, resulting in a silencing of their voices. Charmaine's anger is palpable as she states: "I felt like I was being done wrong, you were suspending me because you wanted another student out of your class…you're telling me when I grow up no one is going to listen to me!" A prevailing sense of not being heard—and worse, an atmosphere of intimidation—actively discouraged students from speaking out, as Charmaine recounts: "They don't want to hear any feedback, if they (students) give somebody lip they will get suspended for longer...students know this and don't feel comfortable speaking out." Sean, who feels he was unfairly penalized when he was suspended, despite the fact that he was not the aggressor, echoes Charmaine's criticism.

> The school doesn't always take all of the situation into consideration. And they don't really like think about what you're trying to say sometimes, like once they've heard what they need to, or what they want, that's when they make the decision. Not with or after you tell them more of the details....

Jenny, who was expelled for a full academic year as a consequence of being in the wrong place at the wrong time when friends were smoking marijuana, also feels that no one listened to her.

> It was really hard 'cause they don't care what we have to say. They think that they already know the situation so they don't care. Like, it's kind of sad that they can't hear from all of us.... I think I was treated unfairly by the school board...and they already had their mind made up that they were going to expel all of us....

Andre describes his feelings when he was told he would be expelled, and how he felt he was given no voice, saying, "At first I was hurt and then I didn't care and then I felt like it was unfair. I had a lot of mixed emotions about it...they never gave me a chance to explain...."

It was clear that students who shared their stories found discipline policies to be inconsistent and unfair. There was a pattern of injustice that permeated their stories, where harsh discipline policies targeted them in arbitrary ways and just did not "make sense." Their views were not taken into consideration, their accounts of incidents were disregarded, and their voices were silenced.

Disrupted Education

It is ironic that schools emphasize individual responsibility and individual accountability, yet in disciplinary situations they resort to collective punishment, and the disruption of student learning does not seem to be a priority concern. If one considers all the budgetary costs and the sanctions directed at students who are truant in Michigan and other states, as well as the fines and possible jail time meted out to their "delinquent" and often impoverished parents, it is again paradoxical that coerced and involuntary truancy under zero-tolerance policies does not seem to elicit the same educational concerns about disrupted schooling. Students, however, are very aware of the losses they incur and consistently articulate the importance of not disrupting their learning. As Charmaine states, "I'm not getting an education if you're not teaching." Sean, an academically successful student, worries about lost time, saying, "Being suspended felt weird, because you weren't at school and you were missing a lot of things." Nick, too, expresses concern about missed classroom assignments: "Ten days is way too much...if you miss 10 days they are setting you up for failure, because like when the teachers go over something there is no way you can make up all that work." Jenny expresses her anxiety about her future after having been suspended for 3 weeks and then expelled.

When I first heard I was expelled, my heart just dropped and I was like, "Oh my God!" Then I thought about it and I was like "Oh, I'll go to a different school and start fresh." Then we tried to get into…another school for expelled kids, and they could not let me in. I'd have to be special needs to go there. So we waited 6 months to get an IEP, and through that whole time I was depressed not being around anybody, being alone, not getting an education. Just what am I going to do? Now I'm expelled and it's going to be on my record forever. Now I'm not going to get into a good college and I just hated it!

According to the ACLU, Michigan's zero-tolerance policies are described as some of the harshest in the nation, placing students at higher risk for suspension and expulsion. Students in Michigan have no inherent "right" to an education; rather, Article 8 of Michigan's constitution requires only that the state "maintain and support" a system of free schools in a "non-discriminatory manner" (ACLU of Michigan, 2009, p. 11). Michigan is also one of 11 states that do not provide suspended or expelled students with a right to some form of alternative education. Violations of educational rights often include lack of due process and lengthy periods out of school, with no accommodation made to providing access to an equal education. Children who become victims of punitive disciplinary policies are left with few options to cope with their push-out punishments. If their parents are well educated, have access to power and influence, and possess the confidence, social capital, and system knowledge to challenge unfair disciplinary policies, their children are likely to emerge as privileged survivors and will experience the suspension or expulsion as a temporary setback. But for poor children, children of color, and disabled children, the educational exclusion may be far more traumatic and disruptive. Excluding children from school in an impoverished neighborhood has potentially dire consequences, and when we consider the racial and economic disparities in suspension and expulsion data, it is clear that millions of vulnerable children and youth are viewed as discards. Their lives are deemed to be of little value, as denied educational access leads to an irreversible downward trajectory that feeds the school-to-prison pipeline.

The downward trend of zero-tolerance policies has also severely impacted young children's educational futures, as more and more expulsions take place before children even enter public schools. Preschool expulsion is emerging as a new crisis of access in early childhood education. For vulnerable young children who already experience multiple stressors—poverty, unstable housing, inadequate nutrition, lack of access to health care, and dangerous neighborhoods—an expulsion may be the tipping point in terms of family viability. Once expelled, a young child risks exclusion from other settings, and developmental risks compound. For single-parent families in particular, an expulsion may induce a downward spiral of events that threatens to destabilize the entire family: lack of child care leads to loss of a job, which in turn leads to eviction, homelessness, and destitution (see Polakow, 2007). Gilliam's (2005) study of almost 4,000 pre-K classrooms across 40 states indicates that the pre-K expulsion rate is 3.2 times higher than for K–12 students. In a subsequent study in Massachusetts, Gilliam and Shahar (2006) document that during a 1-year period, 39% of teachers expelled one or more pre-K children and that the expulsion rate was more than 34 times the K–12 expulsion rate in Massachusetts! The increasing trend toward "Get Out," with its accompanying denial of access, begins early and creates multiple circuits of damage.

As the student narratives in this study indicate, educational exclusion has the potential to violate students' educational futures. Their voices are silenced, due process provisions are not in place, and many spend lengthy periods out of school, with minimal or no accommodation made to providing access to alternative education.

Student Recommendations

Keep Students in School

The learning spaces in our education systems could and should empower and create voices for all students, especially those who are vulnerable and disenfranchised. Those who feel powerless often have fewer options and access to opportunities, and thus their social capital is greatly diminished. Fostering agency among youth increases their power and voice, thereby increasing their ability to advocate for themselves and become more actively engaged in their education. All too often, policy and school decisions affecting youth are created for and about them—but not with them. It is critical that educators value, respect, and listen to students' voices.

The students in this research study provided examples of what they believe would be fairer and more consistent disciplinary policies. They repeatedly denounced policies that kept students out of school. Sean displays an awareness and sensitivity to the impact of suspension on different socioeconomic households and argues for "proper evidence" before making decisions, stating:

> Suspension does not help a student really. It depends on what type of household the child is living in. Like if the parents are the type that make them do work at home, then suspension wouldn't be that much of a problem. But then in some households the parents just let their kids do whatever and they are just staying home watching TV, playing their video games.... I think it would be better if instead of taking the student out of school, you could keep them in school.... Also, you could keep them separated in school and monitor their behavior.... Again, use proper evidence to make the right choice.

Jenny, who suffered grievously from a year's expulsion, recommends only in-school suspensions.

> I don't think people need to get expelled 'cause that just doesn't help anybody. And not like a long-term suspension either, just do detentions or in-school suspensions…where you sit in a room by yourself and work on stuff like schoolwork but you're just by yourself. Or detentions, like if you got in trouble you'd just have a whole bunch of detentions and maybe it would sink in to your mind that "Oh, I shouldn't do this then." 'Cause [that way] you get an education and the school gives you work….

Nick, too, supports in-school suspensions and detentions, pointing to the wasted educational time when kids are out of school.

> Instead of suspension, I would have them get a lunch detention; when kids are at home all they do is get on Facebook, Twitter, their phones, go to the mall…at lunch time you are only missing social time, when you are out of school you are missing all of your work… they don't learn anything from being at home…they should give students inside school suspension.

Bridgette expresses similar concerns, remarking, "Being out of school doesn't teach anything, you are missing school and they wonder why our grades are down!"

Listen to Us

Throughout the students' interviews, a clear and consistent pattern of not being heard was noted. Students expressed how important it is to listen to their voices and to take their views seriously. Charmaine's recommendation emphasizes the need to listen.

> Hire some staff who would sit down and listen. I understand you cannot listen to everyone, but…if a teacher sees a pattern they could pull that child aside to see what is going on in their lives…. Teachers should talk to kids more. Most kids just need someone to talk to….

Bridgette echoes Charmaine's emphasis on listening and suggests some form of conflict resolution.

> I would have everyone sit down and talk…. The people's stories are going to have to match up and somebody is going to have the finger pointed at them, it still leads up to the one person who did it…they could be doing other things besides missing school…they should have better methods other than suspension this and suspension that, it doesn't solve anything.

As Simone reflects on her own situation and wonders about different outcomes, she, too, feels things could have been different if she had a voice. "The only thing that could've been different is if they would have listened to me when I told them I was having problems, if they did it would have helped me deal with it differently...." Andre, who attended a Christian school, felt there was an ethical obligation on the part of his school to help him.

> Well with my situation, the pregnancy one, I think they should change that 'cause one, you're a Christian school, and you should uplift students and not put them down, and I felt like I was put down in my situation, so I say they should change it, modify it and help others.

The Damaging Impact of Zero-Tolerance Policies: The School-to-Prison Pipeline

During the 18 years since zero-tolerance policies were enacted, there have been numerous reports and scholarly publications documenting the overrepresentation of poor and minority students in suspension/expulsion rates, special education, and referrals to juvenile court. These practices have led to educational exclusion and violations of student rights, and are inextricably linked to issues of race and class (ACLU, 2008; ACLU of Michigan, 2009; Advancement Project, 2000; APA, 2012; Bell, 2000; Dohrn, 2000; Robbins, 2008; Skiba & Noam, 2002). Historically, the racial and social class status of children and youth in public education correlates closely with the level of investment in their education and subsequent school achievement (Anyon, 2005). The interrelationships of poverty, race, and educational inequality form a critical backdrop for the analysis of educational marginalization—the dropouts and push-outs who comprise the underserved and ill-served of America's K–12 public education system.

The diminished social and cultural capital of poor children and children of color (Maeroff, 1998; Noguera, 2003) and the impact of racism in the classroom result in a poverty discourse that "invidiously highlights the social construction of difference" and otherness (Katz, 1989, p. 5) and leads to an educational discourse that stigmatizes children and youth who do not "fit" as deficient, at-risk, and impaired (Swadener, 1995). A structural and systemic critique is frequently absent, since the source of educational failure is problematized as an individual, family, or cultural pathology.

Noguera (2003) points specifically to the experiences of African American males who are stigmatized, excluded, and made "other" in school systems. They experience more severe punishments than other students and are less likely to be placed in academically rigorous classes or to benefit from supportive educational services and opportunities so that "rather than serving as a source of hope and opportunity, schools are sites where Black males are marginalized and stigmatized" (p. 3). In Michelle Fine's *Framing Dropouts* (1991), the majority of African American students during the mid-1980s attended predominantly segregated schools, were overrepresented in special education, and experienced disproportionate suspensions and expulsions. Yet over 2 decades later, those same patterns are still pervasive across the nation. For example, in Pontiac, Michigan, 67.5% of

African American students were suspended during the 2009–2010 school year, and in Heidelberg, Mississippi, 63.5% of African American students were suspended (Rich, 2012).

In their analysis and critique of Michigan's zero-tolerance policies, Zweifler and DeBeers (2002) argue that due process protections are not in place, that many families have no access to legal advice and are unaware of how to challenge violations of their children's rights, and that most students' families (predominantly from poor and minority households) cannot afford to sue school boards. Furthermore, students who are permanently expelled from their schools for weapons violations are denied access to other public schools in Michigan, and students who experience expulsion for non-weapons violations are also denied access in other school districts. Private school options are not readily accessible to the majority of students, and poverty and transportation barriers frequently create further obstacles that result in large numbers of youth being excluded—not only from school, but from their adolescent social worlds as well. In addition, students with disabilities receive minimal or no special education services, which severely impacts their learning and leads to school push-outs and entry into the school-to-prison pipeline.

The shift from rehabilitation to punishment, with the mantra of "adult time for adult crime," has occurred amid an increase in prison budgets and a concomitant decrease in education and mental health spending as hundreds of thousands of youth—ethnic minority, disabled, poor, and predominantly male—are inducted into the incarceration industry. Concerns about discarded, disabled youth have received national attention, leading *The New York Times* to comment that "many of America's juvenile jails would be empty if schools obeyed federal law and provided disabled children with the special instruction that they need" ("Writing Off Disabled Children," 2008). When children are referred to juvenile justice, the stigma associated with being on probation upon their release often creates additional barriers, making it difficult for them to re-enroll in mainstream schooling, with schools often turning children away by steering them toward alternative education services. Schools also face enormous pressure to meet accountability standards and performance benchmarks, and because they view these "problem" students as having a negative impact on overall school performance, they are often reluctant to readmit them (Georgetown Law Human Rights Institute, 2012).

Large numbers of adolescents now spend their formative years in juvenile lock-up facilities or, even worse, in adult prisons. Human rights abuses of juveniles have been reported by organizations such as Amnesty International (1998) and Human Rights Watch, documenting appalling conditions of confinement and abuse. The outsourcing of youthful offenders to private, for-profit prison facilities has resulted in several high-profile U.S. Department of Justice investigations into allegations of violence and sexual abuse of juvenile offenders. In

Mississippi a federal judge commenting on the charges against the GEO Group, the nation's second-largest private, for-profit prison system operator, described the treatment of juveniles as "a cesspool of unconstitutional and inhuman acts" ("Private Prison," 2012).

The socially toxic environments (Garbarino, 1995) that so many vulnerable youth are condemned to—impoverishment and destitution, domestic violence and abuse, street violence, drug trafficking, educational exclusion, and disrupted schooling—all presage diminished futures as healthy developmental pathways are cut off. Woodhouse (2008), who has written extensively about children's rights in the United States, calls for recognition of the responsibility to ensure that children's human dignity and well-being are recognized as fundamental factors in formulating public policies and legal decisions. The current "demonization of children" ignores their developmental needs and the socially toxic worlds they inhabit. Woodhouse claims that during the 1990s, the criminal justice system became "a yawning pit swallowing large numbers of children," and she cites the bitter conclusions of a civil rights attorney: "There is only one thing we promise our children. We don't promise them good schools, or food, or a roof over their heads. But we do promise them a jail cell" (2008, p. 286).

The path from expulsion to the juvenile justice system and to adult prison is a recurring threat for adolescents nationwide. Over 50% of young African American men who have not completed high school have prison records (Western, Shiraldi, & Ziedenberg, 2003). The Pew Center (2008) has documented that 2.3 million adults (1 in 100) are incarcerated, and for African American men ages 20–34, the figure jumps to 1 in 9. The female incarceration rate has also risen, particularly for young African American women, and 80% of the women behind bars are mothers. In the 2 decades between 1980 and 2000, prison spending (state and local) rose by 104%, in stark contrast to the 21% drop in higher education spending. Overall state expenditures for corrections are 2.5 times higher than for education, which includes K–12, vocation, and higher education (Western et al., 2003).

As prison increasingly replaces education as the social space of adolescence, vulnerable children and youth in need of education and mental health services lose their rights to childhood and adolescence as a period for development and self-formation. Instead, their "felon" identities are fixed, and they are framed as ex-children, written off, discarded, and consigned to lives on the margins. William Schulz, executive director of Amnesty International, accuses the courts of functioning as indifferent agents, destroying any future life chances for the young, describing them as "assembly lines that mass produce mandatory life without parole sentences for children" (Human Rights Watch and Amnesty International, 2005, p. vl). Legislation in 42 states now permits youth to receive life-without-parole sentences.

What is to be done? There are multiple areas for redress that cover due process, pedagogy and educational interventions, alternative education, and student activism. In the following section we briefly describe possible points of intervention and change.

Due Process

Very few due process protections are in place for suspended and expelled students—and only long-term suspensions and permanent expulsions require "formal procedures" that derive from the *Goss v. Lopez* Supreme Court decision of 1975. Zweifler and DeBeers (2002) argue that this "leads to casual and capricious decisions to expel…. There is no requirement for vigorous scrutiny of evidence before making the life-affecting decision to expel a student" (p. 212). The GFSA of 1994 and the subsequent state legislation do not mandate due process procedures, and while there is some discretion on the part of school superintendents in terms of modification of an expulsion, that discretion is not often in play. Insley (2001) points out that *Goss v. Lopez* established minimal due process procedures only when there is deprivation of an individual's property interest, such as the right to public education, resulting from a suspension or expulsion. However, in reviewing court decisions, Insley notes that most procedural and substantive due process challenges are not successful unless there are blatant violations of procedures or policies.

In order to curb the rampant violation of students' constitutional right to due process as they are suspended or expelled from school, civil rights advocates have proposed that school officials be given training on how to hold due process hearings (Southern Poverty Law Center, 2012). There is increasing evidence that schools circumvent due process protections for students who are suspended and/or expelled. In addition, critics of high-stakes testing argue that this has created greater incentives to exclude low-performing students, contributing to the push-out crisis, which has targeted students with disabilities despite existing special education protections (ACLU, 2008).

Culturally Responsive Pedagogy and Reflective Teaching

Educators advocate addressing the disproportionate representation in special education and discipline rates among poor and minority students through Culturally Responsive Pedagogy (CRP) (Ladson-Billings, 2009), which empowers students by building on their strengths and by incorporating their histories, traditions, and identities into classroom teaching. Many African American students use African American Vernacular English (AAVE) or Ebonics when communicating, yet AAVE is viewed as a stigmatized dialect. Student disengagement and marginalization in the classroom and the mismatch of language and culture have also been linked to disproportionate suspensions, exclusions, and referrals to special education.

Several studies focus on the qualities of teachers that adolescent African American males consider effective. Students consistently voice their preference for teachers who are strict and caring—teachers who have high expectations and challenge their academic prowess, yet are responsive and supportive (Foster & Peele, 1999). Noguera (2008) proposes specific characteristics of effective schools for African American boys. These include a commitment to inclusive and intentional teaching, an academically demanding curriculum, high expectations, an organized and safe school climate, respect for and validation of students' parents and families, and a "problem-solving" rather than a punitive orientation to student misconduct.

Critical reflection is central to the development of teachers in order to unpack assumptions and biases and to understand students' diverse ways of knowing. Teachers who are skilled and critically reflective about their pedagogy and practice effectively engage students and promote student-centered learning in the classroom, respecting the "power of their ideas" and creating safe and inclusive spaces that embrace diversity (Meier, 2002; Thompson, 2013). To this end, it is important to develop approaches that help educators understand, embrace, and incorporate cultural and linguistic diversity in their pedagogy, where differences among students are seen as an opportunity to self-examine personal assumptions and beliefs (Ladson-Billings, 2009). In addition, it is important to recruit and retain effective teachers who are reflective and who critically examine their practices, in order to impact change among youth facing barriers of poverty, marginalization, and institutionalized racism.

Alternative Education

There is limited data available on the actual number of accessible alternative education service options for vulnerable children. Alternative education definitions vary from state to state, as do the services they provide. Some states have comprehensive alternative education plans, but others have minimal policies and practices in place (Lehr, Lanners, & Lange, 2003). In Michigan, where there is no comprehensive plan in place, a Catch-22 frequently obstructs students from re-enrolling in school. Zweifler and DeBeers (2002) charge that Michigan expulsion laws place the burden of alternative education on parents, since students can be denied readmission to their home schools if they have been out of school for a protracted period of time and have been unable to access alternative programs because of cost or transportation difficulties. The wide disparities in alternative education services further compound the crisis of push-outs. There are only six states—California, Idaho, Iowa, Minnesota, Oregon, and Wisconsin—that have adopted comprehensive alternative education policies. These states also maintain separate statutes that explicitly outline a process that specifies how vulnerable children will be identified, supported, and engaged in alternative education programs to promote successful futures and academic outcomes (Martin & Brand, 2006).

Other programs and practices that have met with some success include Restorative Justice programs, the use of evidence-based positive behavior management strategies, in-school suspensions, and the provision of mental health services for students experiencing post-traumatic stress disorder (PTSD), abuse, and other mental health challenges. Another promising program is Response to Intervention (RTI), which exemplifies a positive behavior support model. RTI is a three-tiered, data-based, non-special education intervention approach that blends assessment, instruction, and intervention to minimize challenging behaviors deemed to put students at risk for school failure (Bayat, Mindes, & Covitt, 2010).

Student Activism and Building Social Networks

Well-resourced schools with supportive interventions that provide access to rich extracurricular offerings in low-income school districts contribute to building social capital among youth. Engaging our youth and creating spaces for students to play a major role in the decision-making processes that govern their schools is another critical component that can help to reduce the overrepresentation in disciplinary referrals, suspensions, and expulsions among marginalized youth. Strengthening school-community partnerships and actively engaging students in community building and community activism also serve to connect young people with civic and political power that advance their own best interests. One such example of youth activism in Oakland, California, involved high school students protesting, marching, and testifying before the County Board of Supervisors to stop the "super jail for kids," a 540-bed juvenile facility. Students organized action campaigns against the local county authorities who had approved plans to build an expanded juvenile facility (see Tilton, 2009). With slogans like "Books not Bars" and "Schools not Jails," the youth argued in public forums for more investment in their schools and prevention programs for youth. One of the young women who led the "Books not Bars" campaign was quoted as challenging adults to take public responsibility for youth, saying, "Where's the leadership.... Kids don't need to be incarcerated. They don't need funding for their schools and recreation centers and health care and social services to be spent on prisons" (Tilton, 2009, p. 120).

It is clear that there is a fundamental difference between viewing children as problems in need of discipline and seeing them as active agents of their own lives whose voices and views must be respected. School environments that value students' perspectives and treat children and youth as developing human beings whose dignity must be affirmed are far more likely to create engaged and inclusive learning environments. In such child- and youth-centered settings, challenging situations are viewed as opportunities for teaching and learning about self and others, so that developmental goals include not only educational success but also sustained outcomes such as self-regulation and the building of resilience.

Exclusion and the Right to Education

The students whose voices are presented in this chapter provide an on-the-ground perspective of suspension and expulsion in their harsh and unforgiving school worlds. Their anger and frustration, their sense of being unfairly treated, their anxiety about missed and disrupted school time, all speak to a profound disrespect of their young lives and the silencing of their voices. And the nine students' narratives profiled here do not tell the worst of stories—there is no evidence of police brutality, of being dragged out of school in handcuffs, of being sent to juvenile prison, of assaults, of sexual abuse by guards and other offenders. That, too, happens, all too frequently in the morass of snowballing repercussions that ensue once zero-tolerance policies are put into play. Yet even for these nine students, damage was done; youthful lives were put on hold, derailed, disrupted, and, in some cases, futures were threatened.

When coerced educational exclusion is juxtaposed against the international conventions that confer rights of dignity, agency, and self-expression on children, it becomes disturbingly clear how far the United States has strayed from the original commitments of the Universal Declaration of Human Rights in 1948. All four key principles of the CRC that articulate the best interests of the child, respect for human dignity, the right to healthy development, and the right to express one's views, are violated by zero-tolerance policies. None of our nine students was given the right to freely articulate his or her views (Article 12), and school discipline was certainly not implemented "in a manner consistent with the child's dignity" (Article 28). Pushing the students out of school did not demonstrate the principle of viewing education as a developmental process that promotes the child's "mental and physical abilities to their fullest potential," nor do such exclusionary actions prepare them "for responsible life in a free society" (Article 29).

The UN Special Rapporteur who investigated racism, racial discrimination and xenophobia in the United States has singled out zero-tolerance policies as an area of strong concern, citing the "failure of the school system to educate pupils adequately, serving rather as a conduit to juvenile and criminal justice" (UN Human Rights Council, 2009). Among the chief targets of criticism were severe punishments for minor offenses, the criminalization of school misconduct, excessive use of force by police officers in schools, and the clear racial disparities indicated by the disproportionate out-of-school suspensions and expulsions of African American students.

Other international conventions also point to the violation of children's human rights when they are deprived of the right to an education. The International Covenant on Economic, Social and Cultural Rights (ICESCR) affirms "the right of everyone to an education" and states that "education shall be directed to the full development of the human personality and the sense of its dignity" (Article 13). However, the students in this study and millions of their fellow students are denied that right arbitrarily, and the students who are marginalized by such policies and practices are accorded neither dignity nor support for self-development and an identity as an engaged learner.

Much more remains unsaid about the violation of the educational rights of children in the United States, particularly for students of color, students with disabilities, and young children banished from preschool before they ever begin formal education—all forms of exclusion that speak to disrupted education, damaged childhoods, and the unmaking of young lives. Changing the discourse about "at-risk" youth destined for the school-to-prison pipeline to one that holds schools responsible for affirming children's rights and educational futures is critical to changing public sensibilities. Educational exclusion inexorably erodes the possibility of democratic schooling. Ensuring educational access and opportunities for *all* our nation's children and youth must be at the forefront of our national policy agenda.

Note

1. A three-person family with household income below $19,090 was classified as living below the federal poverty level (FPL) in 2012 (U.S. Department of Health and Human Services, 2012). A three-person family with a household income that is 200% of the FPL is classified as low income (See Addy & Wight, 2012).

References

Addy, S., & Wight, V.R. (2012, February). *Basic facts about low-income children, 2010: Children under age 18.* New York: National Center for Children in Poverty. Retrieved from http://www.nccp.org/publications/pub_1049.html

Advancement Project and Harvard Civil Rights Project. (2000). *Opportunities suspended: The devastating consequences of zero tolerance and school discipline policies.* Retrieved from http://civilrightsproject.ucla.edu/research/k-12-education/school-discipline/opportunities-suspended-the-devastating-consequences-of-zero tolerance-and-school-discipline-policies

American Civil Liberties Union. (2008, June 6). *What is the school to prison pipeline?* Retrieved from http://www.aclu.org/racial-justice/what-school-prison-pipeline

American Civil Liberties Union of Michigan. (2009). *Reclaiming Michigan's throwaway kids: Students trapped in the school to prison pipeline.* Retrieved from http://www.aclumich.org/sites/default/files/file/ACLUSTPP.pdf

American Civil Liberties Union of Northern California. (2008). *Schools for all campaign: The school bias and pushout problem.* Retrieved from https://www.aclunc.org/s4a/full_report.pdf

American Psychological Association. (2012). *Facing the school dropout dilemma.* Retrieved from http://www.apa.org/pi/families/resources/school-dropout-prevention.aspx

Amnesty International. (1998, November). *Betraying the young: Children in the US justice system.* Retrieved from http://www.amnesty.org/en/library/info/AMR51/060/1998

Anyon, J. (2005). *Radical possibilities: Public policy, urban education, and a new social movement.* New York: Routledge.

Bayat, M., Mindes, G., & Covitt, S. (2010). What does RTI (Response to Intervention) look like in preschool? *Early Childhood Education Journal, 37,* 493–500.

Behar, R. (1996). *The vulnerable observer: Anthropology that breaks your heart.* Boston, MA: Beacon Press.

Bell, J. (2000). Throwaway children: Conditions of confinement and incarceration. In V. Polakow (Ed.), *The public assault on America's children: Poverty, violence, and juvenile injustice* (pp. 188–210). New York: Teachers College Press.

Brady, B. (2007). Developing children's participation: Lessons from a participatory IT project. *Children & Society, 21,* 31–41.

Center for Civil Rights Remedies. (2012). Retrieved from http://civilrightsproject.ucla.edu/resources/projects/center-for-civil-rights-remedies/front-matter

Christensen, P.H. (2004). Children's participation in ethnographic research: Issues of power and representation. *Children & Society, 18,* 165–176.

Convention on the Rights of the Child (CRC). (1989, November 20). Retrieved from http://www2.ohchr.org/english/law/crc.htm

Dohrn, B. (2000). Look out kid, it's something you did: The criminalization of children. In V. Polakow (Ed.), *The public assault on America's children: Poverty, violence, and juvenile injustice* (pp. 157–187). New York: Teachers College Press.

Fine, M. (1991). *Framing dropouts: Notes on the politics of an urban public high school.* Albany: State University of New York Press.

Foster, M., & Peele, T.B. (1999). Teaching black males: Lessons from the expert. In V.C. Polite & J.E. Davis (Eds.), *African American males in schools and society: Practices and policies for effective education* (pp. 8–19). New York: Teachers College Press.

Garbarino, J. (1995). *Raising children in a socially toxic environment.* San Francisco, CA: Jossey-Bass.

Garbarino, J. (2000). *Lost boys: Why our sons turn violent and how we can save them.* New York: Anchor Books.

Geertz, C. (1973). *The interpretation of cultures.* New York: Basic Books.

Geertz, C. (1983). *Local knowledge.* New York: Basic Books.

Georgetown Law Human Rights Institute. (2012). *Kept out: Barriers to meaningful education in the school-to prison pipeline.* Retrieved from http://www.law.georgetown.edu/academics/centers-institutes/human-rights-institute/fact-finding/upload/KeptOut.pdf

Gilliam, W. (2005, May 4). *Prekindergarteners left behind: Expulsion rates in state prekindergarten systems.* Retrieved from http://www.plan4preschool.org/documents/pk-expulsion.pdf

Gilliam, W., & Shahar, G. (2006). Preschool and child care expulsion and suspension: Rates and predictors in one state. *Infants & Young Children, 19*(3), 228–245.

Guajardo, M., & Guajardo, F. (2008). Transformative education: Chronicling a pedagogy for social change. *Anthropology and Education Quarterly, 39*(1), 3–21.

Human Rights Watch and Amnesty International. (2005, October 12). *United States: Thousands of children sentenced to life without parole.* Retrieved from http://www.hrw.org/news/2005/10/11/united-states-thousands-children-sentenced-life- without-parole

Insley, A.C. (2001). Suspending and expelling children from educational opportunity: Time to reevaluate zero tolerance policies. *American University Law Review, 50,* 1039–1074.

International Covenant on Economic, Social and Cultural Rights (ICESCR). (1976, January 3). Retrieved from http://www2.ohchr.org/english/law/cescr.htm

Katz, M.B. (1989). *The undeserving poor: From the war on poverty to the war on welfare*. New York: Pantheon.

Kilbourne, S. (1999, Spring). Placing the convention on the rights of the child in an American context. *Human Rights, 28*(2), 27.

Ladson-Billings, G. (2009). *The dreamkeepers: Successful teachers of African-American children*. San Francisco, CA: Jossey-Bass.

LaMarche, G. (2011, April 11). The time is right to end "zero tolerance" in schools. *The Huffington Post*. Retrieved from http://www.huffingtonpost.com/gara-lamarche/the-time-is-right-to-end_b_847622.html

Lehr, C.A., Lanners, E.J., & Lange, C.M. (2003). *Alternative schools: Policy and legislation*. Alternative School Research Project, Institute on Community Integration, University of Minnesota.

Losen, D.J., & Gillespie, J. (2012, August 7). *Opportunities suspended: The disparate impact of disciplinary exclusion from school*. The Civil Rights Project, Los Angeles, CA. Retrieved from http://civilrightsproject.ucla.edu/resources/projects/center-for-civil-rights-remedies/school-to-prison-folder/federal-reports/upcoming-ccrr-research

Maeroff, G. (1998). *Altered destinies: Making life better for school children in need*. New York: St. Martin's Press.

Martin, N., & Brand, B. (2006). Federal, state, and local roles supporting alternative education. Washington, DC: American Youth Policy Forum. Retrieved from http://www.doleta.gov/youth_services/pdf/ae_current_policy_and_funding_environment.pdf

Mauthner, M. (1997). Methodological aspects of collecting data from children: Lessons from three research projects. *Children and Society, 2*, 16–28.

Meier, D. (2002). *The power of their ideas: Lessons for America from a small school in Harlem*. Boston, MA: Beacon Press.

Noguera, P.A. (2003). *City schools and the American dream: Reclaiming the promise of public education*. New York: Teachers College Press.

Noguera, P.A. (2008). *The trouble with Black boys: And other reflections on race equity, and the future of public education*. San Francisco, CA: Jossey-Bass.

Nussbaum, M. (2011). *Creating capabilities: The human development approach*. Cambridge, MA: Harvard University Press.

Orfield, G. (2012). Foreword. In D.J. Losen & J. Gillespie (Eds.), *Opportunities suspended: The disparate impact of disciplinary exclusion from school*. Retrieved from http://civilrightsproject.ucla.edu/resources/projects/center-for-civil-rights-remedies/school-to-prison-folder/federal-reports/upcoming-ccrr-research

Pew Center on the States. (2008, February 28). *One in 100: Behind bars in America 2008*. Retrieved from http://www.pewstates.org/uploadedFiles/PCS_Assets/2008/one%20in%20100.pdf

Polakow, V. (1993). *Lives on the edge: Single mothers and their children in the other America*. Chicago: University of Chicago Press.

Polakow, V. (Ed.). (2000). *The public assault on America's children: Poverty, violence, and juvenile injustice*. New York: Teachers College Press.

Polakow, V. (2007). *Who cares for our children? The child care crisis in the other America*. New York: Teachers College Press.

Private prison for juveniles in Mississippi plagued by violence, despite federal settlement. (2012, June 14). *The Huffington Post*. Retrieved from http://www.huffingtonpost.com/2012/06/14/private-prison-mississippi_n_1598293.html

Rich, M. (2012, August 7). Suspensions are higher for disabled students, federal data indicate. *The New York Times*, p. A10.

Robbins, C. (2008). *Expelling hope: The assault on youth and the militarization of schooling.* Albany: State University of New York Press.

Sen, A.K. (2001). *Development as freedom.* New York: Oxford University Press.

Skiba, R., & Noam, G.G. (Eds.). (2002). *Zero tolerance: Can suspensions and expulsions keep schools safe?* San Francisco, CA: Jossey-Bass.

Soto, L.D., & Swadener, B.B. (2005). *Power and voice in research with children.* New York: Peter Lang.

Southern Poverty Law Center. (2012, August 15). *Alabama's Mobile County public schools continue to violate student rights.* Retrieved from http://www.splcenter.org/get-informed/news/alabama-s-mobile-county-public-schools-continue-to-violate-student-rights

Swadener, B.B. (1995). Children and families "at promise": Deconstructing the discourse of risk. In B.B. Swadener & S. Lubeck (Eds.), *Children and families "at promise": Deconstructing the discourse of risk* (pp. 17–49). Albany: State University of New York Press.

Thompson, P. (2013). Learner-centered education and "cultural translation." *International Journal of Educational Development, 33*(1), 48–58.

Tilton, J. (2009). Stop the super jail for kids: Youth activism to reclaim childhood in the juvenile justice system. In L. Nybell, J. Shook, & J. Finn (Eds.), *Childhood, youth and social work in transformation* (pp. 113–124). New York: Columbia University Press.

Tisdall, E.K., & Davis, J. (2004). Making a difference? Bringing children's and young people's views into policy-making. *Children & Society, 18*, 131–141.

UNICEF Innocenti Research Centre. (2010, November). *The children left behind: A league table of inequality in child well-being in the world's rich countries* (Report Card 9). Retrieved from http://www.unicef-irc.org/files/documents/d-3796-The-Children-Left-Behind-.pdf

United Nations CRC. (2001, April 17). *The aims of education.* Retrieved from http://www.unhchr.ch/tbs/doc.nsf/%28symbol%29/CRC.GC.2001.1.En?OpenDocument

United Nations Human Rights Council. (2009, April 28). *Report of the Special Rapporteur on contemporary forms of racism, racial discrimination, xenophobia and related intolerance.* Retrieved from http://www.ushrnetwork.org/sites/default/files/u.n._special_rapporteur_on_contemporary_forms_of_racism_2009_u.s._report_0.pdf

United States Department of Education, Office for Civil Rights. (2012). *Civil rights data collection.* Retrieved from http://www2.ed.gov/about/offices/list/ocr/docs/crdc-2012-data-summary.pdf

United States Department of Health and Human Services. (2012). *2012 HHS poverty guidelines.* Retrieved from http://aspe.hhs.gov/poverty/12poverty.shtml

Universal Declaration of Human Rights. (1948). Retrieved from http://www.un.org/en/documents/udhr/index.shtml

Western, B., Shiraldi, V., & Ziedenberg, J. (2003, August 28). *Education and incarceration.* Retrieved from http://www.justicepolicy.org/images/upload/03-08_REP_EducationIncarceration_ACBB.pdf

Woodhouse, B. (2008). *Hidden in plain sight: The tragedy of children's rights from Ben Franklin to Lionel Tate.* Princeton, NJ: Princeton University Press.

Writing off disabled children. [Editorial]. (2008, August 8). *The New York Times*, p. A19.

Zweifler, R., & DeBeers, J. (2002, Fall). How zero tolerance impacts our most vulnerable youth. *Michigan Journal of Race and Law, 8*(1), 191–220.

CHAPTER THREE

The Protagonism of Under-18 Youth in the Québec Student Movement

The Right to Political Participation and Education

Natasha Blanchet-Cohen

The tuition increase is a giant step toward the wall in front of us. Humanity needs to take a collective breath of air in order not to suffocate. In order to continue moving forward. Our demonstration is legitimate, fair and the beginning of a new era.

My name is Adèle Surprenant, I'm 14, and on Friday, April 27, I became a victim of your putrid blindness.[1]

The 2012 Québec student movement, coined the Maple Spring, is challenging the stereotype that young people are individualistic, apathetic, and politically disengaged. Sparked by the Québec government's announcement that it would increase university tuition fees by 82% over 5 years, the movement is responsible for the longest and largest student strike in North American history (Hallward, 2012). Following the government's attempt to end student protests by enacting legislation limiting freedoms of speech, association, and assembly, citizens also mobilized with pot-clanging marches held throughout the province and beyond its borders (Montgomery, 2012). Heated conversations centered on young people's right to protest and pressure government by disturbing the state of order.

What can we learn from young people's leadership and resilience in these events about political participation and education rights as identified in the United Nations Convention on the Rights of the Child (CRC)? Given a growing interest in how young people actively participate in the construction and implementation of their rights, this case of young people's activism provides a fresh perspective on what is otherwise an often-circumscribed international narrative on children's political participation (Liebel, 2012). In examining the context and impact of a youth-led grassroots movement, one can better understand the dynamic role of young people as actors and give deeper meaning to the idea of "rights from below."

This chapter focuses on the perspectives of youth under 18 years of age who actively participated in the movement, even though higher tuition fees do not have an immediate impact on them. First, I present *why* these youth participated in the movement, then *how* they participated. Finally, I discuss young people's perspectives on duty-bearers' respect of specific rights that relate to participation and on the participants' concept of "citizenship."

Education and Participation Rights: Policy and Practice

While United Nations narratives may be critiqued for being idealistic or Western, they set global principles and serve as a benchmark for assessing progress (Moore & Mitchell, 2008). Framing this chapter is the CRC's holistic conceptualization of education and participation (David, 2003). The two articles that deal directly with education convey an all-encompassing view of learning as foundational to fundamental human rights (Hart, 2001; United Nations [UN], 2001). Article 28 covers the right to access education, while Article 29 focuses on the goals of education, including the development of the child to his or her "fullest potential" and "the preparation of the child for responsible life in a free society" (UN, 1989).

Along with the right to education, the CRC, in Article 12, establishes children's right to participate in making decisions in all matters affecting him or her. Furthermore, Article 13 specifies the right to freedom of expression, Article 14 the right to freedom of beliefs, Article 15 the right to freedom of association, and, finally, Article 17 the freedom to access appropriate information, both imparting and receiving information through media of their choice. The CRC mentions higher education in Article 28(c) and *General Comment No. 12*, which interprets the participation article, identifies children's right to participation in educational policy at the local and national levels, in independent student organizations, and in decisions about the transition to the next level of schooling (UN, 2009).

In general, the significance of young people's political participation has been debated. In considering that political participation and citizenship are interrelated, various perspectives prevail on the meaning of human rights education and citizenship education. On the one hand, the focus has been on citizenship as a right to education, and on the other of education as a way of acquiring more effective citizenship (McCowan, 2009). In the context of Canada, my focus is on education as "enabling" citizenship, which raises the question of where citizenship education takes place and who defines it. School curriculum on citizenship education has dealt with teaching skills, knowledge, and attitudes related to citizenship as "apprenticeship" (Liebel, 2012, p. 177) rather than actually practicing citizenship as children (Howe & Covell, 2005). Emphasis has been placed on preparing children for political life in the future in terms of voting, with no real effect on the wider polity. This narrow focus ignores the fact that children in different cultural contexts actively participate in political processes related to their own everyday life and that the CRC encompasses a broader understanding of political participation where citizenship is enacted in both formal and non-formal settings (Smith, 2009).

Biesta, Lawy, and Kelly (2009) point to the significance of citizenship learning beginning early, in both formal and informal contexts. Participation in the construction, maintenance, and transformation of social and political life are key aspects of democracy, as contended by educational philosopher John Dewey. James and James (2004) further argue that children as agents actively respond to their environments and incrementally contribute to redefining childhood and establishing social policies toward young people. Their analysis of social policy in education in the UK shows that young people's engagement in policies involved "sometimes responding obediently to the controls which are placed upon their actions, while at other times refusing to do what they have been told" (p. 9). Young people can influence both small "p" politics, referring to the implicit conventions and customs of ordering, as well as capital "P" politics, relating to national laws. Their influence depends on their interactions with the structures that affect their lives.

Considering that political participation involves both expressing viewpoints as well as making changes in the present, young people's political participation can be contested in various ways. Christens and Kirschner (2011) refer to the "reactionary delegitimizing attempts" (p. 38) in which the authorities question the capabilities of young leaders or, without justification, seek to punish them for organizing activities. Indeed, youth and society often experience a paradoxical relationship (Wyn & White, 2000). At times, youth's agency is profiled, while in other instances it is their vulnerability. In questioning adults and possibly disobeying rules, young people may be trespassing adults' notion of "good citizenship behaviour."

Thus, adult views may impact the interpretation of restrictions that accompany the participation-related article. Article 13, for instance, states that restrictions are necessary "for the protection of national security or of public order (*ordre public*), or of public health or morals" (UN, 1989). Article 15, on the right to gather with others and to join or form associations, may be limited, given concerns for the safety, health, and rights of others. Indeed, application of these articles is influenced by whose social order is given priority.

Inherent in the CRC's provision for protection and participation rights is the understanding that although children are vulnerable, they are also able to participate. The duality calls for a careful balancing act, particularly for middle to late adolescents (Lansdown, 2005) who, though still considered children under the CRC, are actively forming their self-identity and are developmentally competent enough to make decisions.

This chapter considers how young people can promote and advocate for wider collective rights, an involvement referred to by Cussiánovich (2001) as "protagonist participation." In this sense, political participation involves extending beyond the individual and reaching out to the collective interests. Liebel (2012) defines children's social movements as "organized protagonism" when "they are directed by children themselves and the structures and norms [allow] children's participation…[and when] young people can influence the social and political decisions that affect them" (p. 207). Children's social movements can defend collective rights, as in the case of promoting social justice.

The first question for this study concerns why young people participated in this political movement. The literature on citizenship shows that motivating factors for a young person's political involvement include a sense of collective efficacy and a feeling of contributing to a set of shared values (Sherrod, Flanagan, & Youniss, 2002). In this context, I examine the reasons for young people's protagonist participation. The second question deals with how these young people participated politically. As persons under the age of 18, restrained by their status as minors and unable to vote, what means did young people use to pressure government?

The third question focuses on young people's perspectives on how the state as the primary duty-bearer responsible for implementation of the CRC fulfilled (or not) its responsibility in relation to specific participation rights. This is followed by a discussion about the impact on participating children's views of citizenship. Underlying these questions is the recognition that youth's position and role in politics depend on the dynamic between youth and society. Context determines the extent to which young people are able to influence regulatory frameworks.

The Context of Education in Québec

As background, it is important to recognize that the CRC is not part of Canadian domestic law (Senate of Canada, 2007). However, as a signatory to the convention, the country reports on the progress of children's rights to the Committee on the Rights of the Child, an independent body of experts responsible for monitoring. Domestic and international pressure groups have also used feedback from the committee to make progress toward fulfilling CRC obligations, including integrating children's rights into formal school curricula (Canadian Coalition on the Rights of the Child, 2003). Under provincial jurisdiction, however, variations exist in the delivery of and ethos surrounding education, particularly when comparing Québec to the rest of Canada. Predominantly French speaking, the province has retained a distinct identity and status in Canadian society and law.

The student movement, therefore, cannot be dissociated from the history of education in Québec, particularly the Quiet Revolution in which the provincial government took over responsibility for education from the Roman Catholic Church (Rocher, 2004). As a result of the "Rapport Parent," education became mandatory until 16 years of age, primary and secondary school education were reformed, college (called CÉGEP) was created as a 2-year transition before university (for those who would be between 17 and 19 years of age), and post-secondary education was made more accessible. The democratization and taking control over education were integral to the Quiet Revolution's cultural and political transformation, including the struggle for self-determination and sovereignty from English-speaking Canada.

Québec's post-secondary education fees have historically remained the lowest in the country, and attempts to increase them have met with resistance. In 2005, the government tried to convert student bursaries to loans, but the proposal was abandoned because of student demonstrations. Six years later, the government announced its intention to increase fees by $1,625 over a 5-year period, representing an 82% hike. It is noteworthy that the government making the announcement was accused at the time of corruption after 9 years in power and criticized for forging ahead with a highly contested development plan in the north of the province.

Student protests began in November 2011, with 30,000 marching in the streets of Montreal. By March the numbers grew to 200,000, with an unprecedented number of marches held thereafter (Curran, 2012). People started pinning small red squares of fabric to their clothing and backpacks as symbols of support for the movement. (Green squares, seen less frequently, indicated a desire to resume classes.) To garner media attention, students also organized several disruptive events, including blocking bridges and traffic in the city centre and disrupting the Montreal Grand Prix auto race, which the students saw as a symbol of capitalism. Apart from scattered incidents, protests were non-violent (Blatchford, 2012).

To pressure the government, students also stopped attending classes. At the peak of protests in March, over half of the CÉGEPs across the province (25 of 48) were on strike, representing 79% of students (Breton, 2012). Two months later, 43% of the province's students remained on strike, disrupting the education year for CÉGEP and university students. CÉGEP students were represented by two province-wide associations: the CLASSE ("Coalition large de l'association pour une solidarité syndicale étudiante"), a militant coalition of university and CÉGEP students, and the Québec Federation of CÉGEP Students (FECQ) (Gervais, 2012). Secondary students also participated in 3-day strikes, though their involvement was less covered by mainstream media, given that they were not represented by a single organization. This chapter addresses that gap by examining their participation.

Government attempts to negotiate with student leaders were unsuccessful, reportedly frustrating for both sides, and resulted eventually in the education minister's resignation. In response to the perseverance of the student movement and the failed negotiations, the government passed Bill 78 (later renamed Law 12), which restricted freedom of association and assembly and included fines for individuals and student organizations. The law was strongly criticized for infringing on the rights guaranteed in Québec's Charter of Human Rights and Freedoms and eventually resulted in demonstrations across the province and beyond its borders in solidarity with the students and also against a perceived attack on democracy (Bherer & Dufour, 2012). The police responded with force, arresting more than 500 people on the night of May 23rd (Shaw Media Inc., 2012). An article reported that more than 50 minors had been arrested in the protests and that delays in informing parents had caused anxiety (Duchaine, 2012). Data for this chapter were gathered during the summer of 2012, after the Québec government called for a provincial election on September 4th. It is widely believed that the student demonstrations contributed to the calling of the election, and some people attribute the election results in part to the student movement (Seymour, 2012).

Method

Qualitative methods informed this chapter, as they are particularly conducive to exploring and illuminating the meaning attributed to certain events or social phenomena (Maxwell, 1996). The research has a phenomenological quality to it: young people's lived experiences of the student movement served as a point of departure, and I used a deliberative, selective sample and both participant observation and interviews to seek meaning (Van Manen, 1990). As a Québec resident working in the post-secondary education system, I participated in key protests, read English and French media coverage, discussed the issues with neighbours and students, and keenly observed responses in my milieu. In the context of Spradley's (1980) typology of participation, my involvement was limited but provided background on the context, defining my research inquiry.

Interviews and focus groups provided rich material. Nine 14- to 19-year-olds (four boys and five girls) recounted their lived experience of the movement, five of them as secondary school students and the others as CÉGEP students. The two 19-year-olds in the group shared their perspectives as recent graduates. Participants self-identified as supporting the student movement, with a range of involvement: one was a spokesperson for the FECQ, while others were involved at the level of their schools. Interviewees were identified either through an invitation letter sent through Facebook or by word of mouth. The five individual interviews lasted an average of 50 minutes, and the focus groups took 2.5 hours. Open-ended questions focused on the three theme areas, with an emphasis on how individuals personally experienced the movement. Conducted in public spaces (i.e., parks or cafés) agreeable to both participant and researcher, interviews and focus groups were carried out in French, providing for an appropriate fluidity of language and comfort level (Kvale, 2008). Because the study was carried out 4 to 5 months after the movement had taken shape, participants were close to the experience, a lack of distance commented on in the discussion.

In selecting to transcribe and thematically code the material based on the study's research questions, I depart from phenomenology. The use of an *a priori* theoretical standpoint served to define the focus and answer my research questions (Jackson & Mazzei, 2012).

Perspectives of People Under 18 Years of Age on Political Participation

Three dominant themes are discussed in this chapter: reasons for participating, means of participating, and young people's perspectives on duty-bearers' fulfillment of participation rights and the concept of citizenship. Combined, these three elements have important implications for understanding young people's role in political participation and education rights.

Reasons for Participating

While the increase in student tuition fees propelled the movement, the reasons for participating went deeper. Study participants explained that their involvement originated in feelings that their right to education was threatened, and that they were defending a vision of society.

Right to education threatened. Beyond the fact that the increase in tuition fees would be coming into full effect when attending university, which was generally after age 19 in Québec because of the 2-year CÉGEP, young people participated because they felt their view of education was under siege. The fee increase represented a shift in society's priorities. "The increase as such is not necessarily the end of the world as we know it, but it is the end of something that said education was important for us," explained Joseph, age 17. Students considered higher education to be a right, although an unusual usage of the term.

With education becoming less accessible, greater priority would be placed on the pursuit of education for economic goals instead of learning for knowledge and social development. Emma, age 14, condemned this commercialization of education: "It changes our right to education because education becomes a commodity.... Education is transformed, and that prevents and perverts the right to education." Joseph, age 17, explained that the decision would compromise the freedom of students' to choose their own educational path: "Education is about deciding to do a BA in philosophy and perhaps not finding work or making money with that degree." The movement made young people aware of the role of schools in molding future citizens: "We ended up discovering that school is political. I didn't used to see it as having anything to do with the kind of society we want to build. I saw it as being a personal investment," explained Colette, age 18. There was a realization that school and state were connected, with schools often transmitting dominant norms and values.

Vision of society. Young people explained that their involvement in the movement also came from a broader concern for society. Emma, age 14, evocatively expressed her concern: "The real issue with the increase is far bigger than a bank account or our so-called selfishness. The real issue of this increase is the people who are drowning in terrible swamps of student loans and underhanded policies." Underlying the movement was a concern for social justice and collective well-being. Participants spoke about "defending their vision of the community" and "we're doing this for the good of everyone." Colette, age 18, evoked her concern: "I find it completely unfair."

Students felt they were defending a way of life. George, age 19, explained that his involvement came from wanting a more socialist society: "I didn't want us to end up here in 10 or 20 years, making the same choices the United States has made, for example." Students recognized that their collective views could clash with individualism: "People who are, like, I'm 40, I've got my car, my family, my house. Of course they're going to think that the student who is blocking the Jacques Cartier Bridge is a first-class asshole." On the other hand, young people recognized the advantages of their position:

Old people might not have the courage to do it, because they have "experience," in quotation marks, because they say it won't work, but for people our age, that might be it, that we don't have experience. We have hope. So we have the courage to stand up and say that we refuse.

Young people interviewed considered that adults' experiences might prevent them from speaking up and taking risks to defend collective interests.

In summary, young people experienced the movement as an opportunity to defend a collective and more egalitarian society. Their engagement came out of a concern for the collective, rather than an individual interest, an expression of protagonist participation. Participants each clarified that they would not be prevented from attending university by the increase because of financial support from parents or their own part-time jobs. Providing for the process and momentum for young people's activism was the multiple means of participation. The section below examines what nourished young people's engagement.

Means of Participating

Being younger than 18 years of age raised the question of how to politically participate. Young people were limited in their options to participate. They have no right to vote, and those in secondary are also legally required to attend school. If they wanted to attend a demonstration, they also had no secondary student organization to represent them. Their engagement was often critiqued, reflecting society's discomfort with young people expressing political beliefs that challenge the status quo. Despite constraints, young people felt they had been effective with the movement and that their political weight had counted. Below, we describe the four main political actions undertaken by these young people and the risks associated with each: (1) being informed and participating in discussions, (2) creating general assemblies, (3) wearing red squares, (4) street demonstrating and going on strike.

Being informed and participating in discussions. Youth spoke expansively about the importance of being well informed, as well as of taking part in discussions. Julia, age 17, pointed out the importance, as a minor, of "being well informed, knowing what is going on, not giving in to generalizations, or letting yourself be influenced by just anything." Creating spaces for discussions was a means to "bring arguments from both sides, to help understand a little," explained Joseph, age 17. Discussions had the potential to be transformative. Colette, 18, said: "Having discussions with people, exchanging ideas, listening to ideas, adopting new ones, it completely changed my vision of what I want to be in society."

Among families, peers, and, more broadly, in society, an unprecedented number of conversations centered on the movement. A focus group participant evoked the interest and enthusiasm for politics among her friends: "This is the first time in our lives when we can talk only about politics for an entire night and no one gets sick of it." At times the movement was divisive. Emma, age 14, commented: "I also lost friends because I was a little too involved and not them. It is hard to remain friends when the person is 'green.'" In families, the topic could also be contentious, and some spoke of avoiding it at family gatherings. Half of the parents in the study supported the movement from its inception, whereas the other half became supportive as a result of their children's engagement. Young people spoke about having lively conversations with their parents and discovering new aspects of their parents' personalities and opinions.

The preferred means of communication were social media such as Facebook, certain blogs, and YouTube, because they provided a wide array of viewpoints and information unavailable in mainstream media. Eagerness for current information meant that social media were perfect for remaining informed and participating. Felix, age 19 and a student organizer in the CÉGEP, commented on the context: "The social media are not a good tool for mobilizing people in normal circumstances…but in this case, since people wanted to demonstrate, since they were hungry for it…it really became an easy, effective way to reach people." Social media offered proximity to the events and real-time updates that complemented mainstream media.

General assemblies. General assemblies in schools and CÉGEPs were the main means for young people to express themselves collectively. They provided a forum to come together, discuss the issues, and vote on striking. Emma, age 14, described their function in this way: "The point is to open the debate. People really get into it, sometimes too much, but the point is to hear people's point of view. It's a great example of democracy, because the people who came were really interested." General assemblies assisted young people in making informed decisions. Julia, 17, described how hearing the different viewpoints helped her take sides.

> I think that's what really convinced me. When you hear the arguments of the "greens," they're really egocentric. They're like, "My decision, I want to go to university next year" and the Reds defend the ideas of society. I think that's when I understood that, yeah, I was going on strike.

Interviewees valued the process of deciding on a position. Many were critical of young people who wore the red square or protested without first knowing the reasons for their involvement.

Voting to go on strike also took place in general assemblies. Of significance is that unlike CÉGEPs, secondary schools did not have organizational structures such as general assemblies to make decisions at the level of the school to strike, so they had to be created independently by each school. Two of the interviewees, Emma and Marie, attended secondary schools that each created a general assembly where a vote for a 3-day strike was made. In Emma's school, 88% voted for the 3-day strike, with 93% of students participating. Prior to voting, they had held two meetings to discuss different viewpoints. Students valued the process in making well-informed decisions.

Red square. Wearing a red fabric square became a symbol that peacefully but publicly showed support for the student movement. "It is a way of continually protesting," noted an interviewee. Colette and Julia referred to their knowledge of the history of the red square, which gave it additional meaning: "Before wearing it, I became very interested in the history of the red square. So, I went to search the why, the what…. I was rich with power knowing its history." The red square had been used in the 2005 student demonstrations and also in campaigns against poverty. Becoming knowledgeable about one's actions was empowering.

Young people spoke about the sense of community created among those who wore the red square. Sarah, 17, observed: "In public transit there are lots of people wearing it…it creates a sense of belonging. Like we're connected with everyone who's wearing it." Given the controversy around the student movement, wearing the red square could place young people in difficult situations. Marie, 14, described how she was forced to remove her red square after a threat of suspension from school. She explained: "That's when I decided to take off my red square. I wasn't going to let myself get booted out of school in mid-March.... I think that was really the kicker.... There was such a sense of revolt then." When the government passed Bill 78, there was also a fear of being arrested for wearing the red square, breaching the right to freedom of self-expression.

Street demonstrating and taking action to strike. To pressure government, young people used street protests and strikes. A focus group participant reasoned, "I can't vote, so according to some people, I have no political power.... But with these demonstrations, now I can make my political weight count." Félix, age 19, remarked on the durability of the protests: "It is a completely surreal atmosphere. And I think that in the history of students, anyway, there have never been such frequent, regular demonstrations in Montreal and all across Québec." The possibility of making history fed young people's enthusiasm.

Participating in protests was also risky. Marie and Colette described being "kettled" by the police, a technique in which police block off escape routes in large crowds, allowing them to arrest everyone drawn in the "kettle." Colette, 18, referred to her involvement as "stressful." Emma, 14, who was arrested, recalled her fear vividly: "It's scary to be chased by police, the SQ, horses, to have rifles with rubber bullets pointed at you, to be pepper sprayed in the eyes." The seemingly unjustified violence by police was considered an attack on their right to associate, as discussed below.

Along with protesting in the streets, students stopped attending classes in high schools and colleges. As described by Emma, 14, secondary students going on strike had a particular impact.

> When people saw us with our posters blocking the school, it made the CÉGEP realize something. We're young, but in high school they're really young, and kids who are 12 or 13 can have a conscience that adults don't have. And they can discuss political topics. That makes them [adults] think.

Young people gained confidence in expressing themselves. With this new self-assurance, under-18 youth defended their capacity to politically participate despite their age. Marie, 14, said:

> They say "Oh, it's just children, they don't need opinions, they don't need to take an interest in anything, they're still young. They'll do it when they get to CÉGEP." But at 15, 16, 17 is when you start having opinions and wanting to defend them.

There was pride in taking on their newfound power. "You know, before, it was often young people in a basement. Now, it's young people out in the streets making their opinions heard. And I think that's great," commented Pierre, age 15. He was evoking a break from the stereotype of youth being in the basement doing nothing. Now one of the youth was outside.

Perspectives on Fulfilling Participation Rights

This last section deals with young people's perspectives on how duty-bearers facilitated participation rights, and their own evolving concept of citizenship. Emerging from the study are the young people's feeling that duty-bearers were ambivalent about their participation; for young people the combination of mixed responses and their own actions contributed to a deeper reflection on the meaning of citizenship.

Duty-bearers' interpretation of specific participation rights. While young people asserted rights normally upheld in a democracy—including the CRC's right to expression (Article 13), freedom of association (Article 15), and access to information (Article 17)—these rights were not willingly granted to the youth. Emma, 14, explained how the right to expression had to be defended.

> Yes, we were able to express ourselves, to go on the streets, to wear the red square but we did not have the right to do so. With Bill 78, it was illegal to have an opinion different from the government's. We gave ourselves the right to speak, it was not offered to us.

Young people criticized the harshness of the state, particularly given their status and limited options as minors. Annie, age 17, said:

> We should have the right to express ourselves without being afraid of being beaten or cut down because other people don't share our opinions. It's about the only method we have because we're not corporations. We have no money to lobby the government.

Young people felt unsupported in voicing opinions, given their limited ability to pressure government.

The freedom of association was most directly attacked under Bill 78, which regulated the terms of association, including restricting protests. Young people expressed deep concern. One said, "This law is a violation of two fundamental rights." Another called the bill "a putrid law." Still another categorized it as "incomprehensible." Marie, 14, pointedly stated: "On the night Bill 78 was passed, I really cried because it was like my world was ending, and I realized that really terrible things were happening." Seeing the bill as unfair, young people justified civil disobedience.

The state's interpretation of its role as protector was considered confusing. An interviewee's repeated use of the verb "suppose" reflected the gap. Julia, 17, said: "You're supposed to be able to go demonstrate because it is your right and you're supposed to be able to do it safely...it's not supposed to be the police who take over." The use of force by police was distressing. According to Marie, age 14, "When the police are beating you and beating the people around you, establishing that kind of fear, you just don't know what to do. You're completely on your own. It's really really disconcerting." Young people commented on the police's paradoxical behaviour: "He picks up his mic and he's like, 'Hello everyone, it's time to go home.' He was practically telling us to go brush our teeth and put on our pyjamas," commented Sarah, age 17. There was wavering between harshly reprimanding young people and a concern for them as children needing protection.

With respect to freedom of information, young people observed the inconsistent and selective coverage by mainstream media. There was anger in realizing the gap between reality and the media's portrayal of events. Julia, 17, explained:

> It makes you angry when you listen to the news and you see 200 people were arrested yesterday for no reason. I was there, I know nothing was being broken. If you have never been you think all the demonstrators are violent but you know it is all peaceful.

While critiquing the reporting, young people also recognized that the public had a responsibility: "It is also the fault of citizens who decide to watch TVA [a television channel] and satisfy themselves with what they hear. Because it is so much easier that way."

In general, young people felt that duty-bearers, primarily the state, condemned young people's right to participate because they were voicing disapproval of the state's actions. "It's okay for people to get involved as long as it doesn't bother anyone…. But the day it starts to bother them, then it's not okay anymore," explained Felix, age 19. Thus, young people's political involvement was considered unnecessary, given their stage in life. "The message he [government in power] is sending to the youth is, you know, shut up, go about your business, study and one day, when you start paying taxes, then you'll have the right to complain." For the government, the right to participate was being associated with income.

Young people felt pleased, however, when witnessing their power. "It might be the youth's realization of their power in society, but also society's realization of the importance of the youth. I don't think people have ever talked with the youth so much or talked so much about education," commented Leo, age 19. Another participant in a focus group stated: "It gives hope that we are able to make change whoever we are." In that sense, the student movement was already a success, even though at the time of the interviews no one knew that the student movement would contribute to actually changing the political landscape. Seeing young people's success, the state indulged in an almost intentional belittling of them: "I think that the youth have been infantilized in this debate." Joseph, 17, felt categorized and did not like the distinction adults drew between themselves and youth. "It's a new way of talking. You know, 'them' for the youth and 'us.' I find that sad because we are not just the future." Young people felt they were changing the broader public's perception of young people, who expressed surprise at their competence and saw them as people "who argued well, who were able to defend their point of view...against the sitting government, with articles and all sorts of things. They're clearly not idiots." The unfolding of responses shows how youth actively shaped the perceptions of adults and society, and how the state opposed youth's voice by attempting to diminish their capacity and arguing that the safety of the state was in jeopardy.

Evolving concept of citizenship. An unfolding of events marked by resistance, coupled with the ambiguity of duty-bearers, impacted young people's views on their citizenship. It was a revelation for many under-18 people to witness for the first time their ability to shake the system. One said, "Before I did not care, it was beyond me a bit...but now I'm really excited. We even got a minister to resign." They became aware of their influence and how that shaped the public agenda.

As a result of the movement, young people became aware of the importance of politics and their own role in political life, even at an age younger than 18. An interviewee with an immigrant background reflected on how the change had affected her home life: "Especially for children of immigrants, like at my home, [before] we rarely talked about politics." Another explained how young people realized the implications of voting. "This has allowed many young people to realize the importance of being involved...they realize what it means concretely not to vote." As a result, there was a record-high voter turnout by the public in general (increasing from 57.4% in the 2008 election to 72%). It is claimed that the prime minister lost because there was a huge concentration of students in his riding.

Discussions also focused on the deeper significance of being a citizen. Young people identified the importance of asserting a political presence that goes beyond voting and merely being a taxpayer. "I am aware that I live in an economy, but I do not want to be reduced to a taxpayer. I want to be considered a human being first," explained Sarah, age 17. In extending the concept of citizenship, participants in the study identified that citizenship education needed to begin in elementary school. As one stated, "It is important to be citizens at your developmental level from primary school." Realizing perhaps for the first time the risks of manipulation, young people emphasized the need to view different sources of information in order to develop critical thinking. Joseph, 17, argued that he wanted to "encourage the people around me to...read newspapers, several different newspapers to compare the information because in a big conflict like this, you can see the difference in how events are reported on." Being a citizen also involved actively contributing to bringing about change: "We speak a lot about having a consciousness but one has to be involved in actions for the change to become a reality. It does not just happen like that." Young people saw themselves as actors.

To develop young people's critical capacity, students spoke about the value of having political science courses starting in secondary 1 (ages 12 to 13): "In secondary, they should teach us to have opinions that are not based on what we see on T.V., but really based on the facts or on values.... You have to inform yourself, to debate." Young people criticized the lack of relevant and current content in the formal school curricula designed to make them realize the impact of politics on their daily lives. Pierre, 15, explained how removed young people often felt from politics: "Especially as young people, they do not see the link that it has with them." Young people were also aware that the education system needed to support them in developing their own views and avoid imposing any specific point of view. The challenge was encapsulated by one focus group participant this way: "How do we create citizens who will take an interest in the common good without telling them what the common good is? Because otherwise you're not creating citizens, you're creating robots." Young people recognized that citizenship needed to be nurtured without reducing the freedom to form one's own views.

Discussion

The involvement of youth under age 18 in the Québec student movement points to how young people can assume their rights despite primary duty-bearers' disapproval. When state and young people's views clashed following the announcement of an increase in post-secondary education fees, the state removed the youth's right to participate, even though Canada has signed the CRC and provinces are expected to fulfill its obligations. The state placed priority on re-establishing public order, despite the fact that such an act had the consequence of repressing young people's rights, whether they were minors or not.

Considering the movement to be legitimate and fair, young people justified their disobedience of the law, as Adèle pointed out in the opening epigraph of this chapter. Young people's protagonism contributed to a reconfiguration of Québec's political landscape, illustrating the powerful influence of bringing together young people—both those without the right to vote as well as those older than 18, who are also considered to be relatively powerless because of their lack of economic clout (James & James, 2004). A couple of months after the study was carried out, a provincial election was held in which the premier lost his electoral seat and resigned as leader of his party, and the new government announced that tuition fees would remain unchanged (Seymour, 2012). The former president of the FECQ at the height of the movement also became the youngest elected member of the National Assembly in the province's history (Curtis, 2012).

The political competence of youth under the age of 18 underscores the arbitrariness of having established 18 as the legal age for political enfranchisement (Blais, Massicotte, & Yoshinaka, 2001), as well as the myriad ways this age group can build awareness and create pressure on government and the broader public.

By discussing different viewpoints with peers and families, and with classmates in school assemblies, emphasis was placed on the process of forming opinions. Social media became a critical way to share information and also exchange perspectives to formulate a position. Youth visually expressed themselves by wearing the red square, and in order to pressure government and raise awareness, they boycotted classes and marched in the streets. As minors, young people were limited in the actions they could undertake to register their protest. However, they creatively conceived of and then implemented a range of techniques while recognizing the importance of being politically informed themselves, and of creating awareness among others.

This study illustrates the potential of locating young people's political participation in an array of private and public arenas that draws upon the richness of young people's non-formal modes of social participation. One is reminded of Hart (2009), who argues that strengthening young people's role in civil society requires broadening the opportunities for all young people to become active at the various levels of their community. The many forms of participation used by young people also represent Young's (2000) ideal of extending the understanding of democratic citizenship to include deliberation and protests.

Indeed, the resilience of the Québec student movement cannot be dissociated from the province's distinct history of education and the specific political context. The defense of rights from the "bottom up" by children identified by Liebel (2012) came from being tuned into the collective climate and feeling able to respond, given a combination of unique contextual factors. In expanding the concept of citizenship from obedience to a more critical appraisal of one's rights and responsibilities—considered a critical area of study by Sherrod and colleagues (2002)—young people's participation was in this case met with resistance. Political awakening meant opposing adults, taking risks, and being disappointed in the confusing responses of duty-bearers to their engagement. The case study shows some of the real costs associated with achieving young people's political participation, often simplified and glorified in the international discourse.

Further longitudinal studies are warranted on the impact of political participation on the future citizenship of youth under 18, and how some of the potency of the movement can be sustained beyond specific events and the education issue itself. It would also be interesting to understand the significance of the lived experience with more distance from the actual events, an aspect considered important in phenomenology (Van Manen, 1990).

Nonetheless, one of the implications of this study is reflecting on how youth participation can broaden and deepen citizenship education, providing for a more holistic and critical approach (Biesta, Lawy, & Kelly, 2009; McCowan, 2009). Young people's exercise of citizenship involved questioning the education system itself, suggesting that the understanding of political participation of youth ages 18 to 30 in Québec can no longer be confined to voting statistics (Gauthier, 2003) or relayed to the formal institution of learning. Somewhat paradoxically, it was through the movement itself that young people became aware of the interconnectedness between education and participation rights and the potential risks of the state violating both these rights. Learning about and practicing citizenship involves children realizing the direct impact of politics on their daily lives, as well as their role in giving meaning to citizenship. Our study serves as a stark reminder that even in a country like Canada, where the right to education as such is provided, the responsibility for citizenship education cannot be relegated to the state.

While young people demonstrated their capacity to innovate during the movement, sustaining their involvement in both small "p" and capital "P" politics requires that social places and spaces be provided for them to express their protagonism (Liebel, 2012). Thus, schools are a critical place for this to happen. We need to provide organizational structures that allow young people to collectively voice themselves to avoid having to improvise, like during the movement, with young people creating structures on a school-by-school basis depending on the leadership of individuals. This type of change is part of moving toward "the new era" referred to by Adèle, where under-18 youth are supported and recognized for their active and current role in shaping society.

Note

1. An unpublished excerpt from a study participant's submission to a local newspaper.

References

Bherer, L., & Dufour, P. (2012, May 23). Our not-so-friendly northern neighbor. *The New York Times*. Retrieved from http://www.nytimes.com

Biesta, G., Lawy, L., & Kelly, N. (2009). Understanding young people's citizenship learning in everyday life: The role of contexts, relationships and dispositions. *Education, Citizenship & Social Justice, 4*(1), 5–24.

Blais, A., Massicotte, L., & Yoshinaka, A. (2001). Deciding who has the right to vote: A comparative analysis of election laws. *Electoral Studies, 20*(1), 41–62.

Blatchford, A. (2012, May 28). Quebec unrest generates 3,000 news reports in 77 countries: Analysis. *Globe and Mail*. Retrieved from http://www.theglobeandmail.com

Breton, P. (2012, May 16). Grève dans les CEGEPs: Un conflit Montréalais. *La Presse*. Retrieved from http://www.lapresse.ca

Canadian Coalition on the Rights of the Child. (2003). *Monitoring children's rights: A toolkit for community-based organizations*. Retrieved from http://rightsofchildren.ca/

Canadian Press. (2012, September 6). *Marois to cautiously push agenda*. Retrieved from http://oncampus.macleans.ca/education

CBC News/Canada. (2012, May 29). *How a student uprising is reshaping Quebec*. Retrieved from http://www.cbc.ca

Christens, B.D., & Kirshner, B. (2011). Taking stock of youth organizing: An interdisciplinary perspective. In C.A. Flanagan & B.D. Christens (Eds.), *Youth civic development: Work at the cutting edge* (pp. 27–41). New Directions for Child and Adolescent Development, 134. San Fransisco: Jossey-Bass.

Curran, P. (2012, May 22). Anatomy of a conflict after 100 days of student protests. *The Gazette*. Retrieved from http://www.montrealgazette.com

Cussiánovich, A. (2001). What does protagonism mean? In M. Liebel et al. (Eds.), *Working children's protagonism: Social movements and empowerment in Latin America, Africa and Asia* (pp. 157–170). Frankfurt and London: IKO.

David, P. (2003). *A holistic vision of the rights to education*. Retrieved from http://www.cifedhop.org/Fr/Publications/Thematique/thematique11/David.pdf

Duchaine, G. (2012, June 12). Des mineurs arretés, des parents angoissés. *La Presse*. Retrieved from http://www.lapresse.ca

Gauthier, M. (2003). The inadequacy of concepts: The rise of youth interest in civic participation in Quebec [1]. *Journal of Youth Studies*, 6(3), 265–276.

Gervais, L.M. (2012, September 7). Pauline Marois promet d'annuler la hausse des droits de scolarité. *Le Devoir*. Retrieved from http://www.ledevoir.com

Hallward, P. (2012, June 1). Quebec's student protesters give UK activists a lesson. *The Guardian*. Retrieved from http://www.guardian.co.uk

Hart, R. (2009). Charting change in the participatory settings of childhood: A very modest beginning. In N. Thomas (Ed.), *Children, politics and communication: participation at the margins. Decision-making and child participation* (pp. 7–30). Bristol, UK: Policy Press.

Hart, S.N. (2001). *Children's rights in education*. London: Jessica Kingsley.

Howe, R.B., & Covell, K. (2005). *Empowering children: Children's rights education as a pathway to citizenship*. Toronto: University of Toronto Press.

Jackson, A.Y., & Mazzei, L.A. (2012). *Thinking with theory in qualitative research: Viewing data across multiple perspectives*. London: Routledge.

James, A., & James, A. (2004). *Constructing childhood: Theory, policy and social practice*. New York: Palgrave Macmillan.

Kvale, S. (2008). *InterViews. Learning the craft of qualitative research* (2nd ed.). London: Sage.

Lansdown, G. (2005). *Evolving capacities of the child*. Florence, Italy: UNICEF Innocenti Research Centre.

Liebel, M. (2012). *Children's rights from below: Cross-cultural perspectives*. New York: Palgrave Macmillan.

Maxwell, J. (1996). *Qualitative research: An interactive approach*. Thousand Oaks, CA: Sage.

McCowan, T. (2009). *Rethinking citizenship education: A curriculum for participatory education*. London: Continuum.

Montgomery, S. (2012, May 26). Students, unions join forces in bid to get rid of Bill 78. *The Gazette*. Retrieved from http://www.montrealgazette.com

Moore, S., & Mitchell, R. (2008). Introduction: Power, pedagogy and praxis—towards common ground. In S.A. Moore & R.C. Mitchell (Eds.), *Power, pedagogy and praxis: Social justice in the globalized classroom* (pp. 1–19). Rotterdam: Sense Publishers.

Rocher, G. (2004, Winter). Un bilan du Rapport Parent: Vers la démocratisation. *Bulletin d'histoire politique*, 12(2), 2–17.

Senate of Canada. (2007). *Children: The silenced citizens*. Ottawa, Canada.

Seymour, R. (2012, September 7). Quebec's students provide a lesson in protest politics. Retrieved from http://www.guardian.co.uk

Shaw Media Inc. (2012, June 7). Timeline: Events in Quebec student strike. *Global News*. Retrieved from http://www.globalnews.ca

Sherrod, L.R., Flanagan, C., & Youniss, J. (2002). Dimensions of citizenship and opportunities for youth development: The what, why, when, where and who of citizenship development. *Applied Developmental Science, 6*(4), 264–272.

Smith, A. (2009). The children of Loxicha: Participation beyond the UNCRC rhetoric. In N. Thomas (Ed.), *Children, politics and communication: Participation at the margins. Decision-making and child participation* (pp. 49–68). Bristol, UK: Policy Press.

Spradley, J.P. (1980). *Participant observation.* New York: Holt, Rinehart and Winston.

United Nations. (1989). *Convention on the Rights of the Child.* New York: General Assembly of the United Nations.

United Nations. (2001). *General comment no. 1: The aims of education.*

United Nations. (2009). *General comment no. 12. The right of the child to be heard.*

Van Manen, M. (1990). *Researching lived experience: Human science for an action sensitive pedagogy.* Albany: State University of New York Press.

Wyn, J., & White, R. (2000). Negotiating social change: The paradox of youth. *Youth & Society, 32,* 165–183. DOI: 10.1177/0044118X00032002002.

Young, I.M. (2000). *Inclusion and democracy.* New York: Oxford University Press.

CHAPTER FOUR

What's Right in Children's Rights?

The Subtext of Dependency

Panagiota Karagianni, Soula Mitakidou,
& Evangelia Tressou

The notion of dependency and its impact on the continuing exclusion of Roma from the Greek public and social domains is the focus of this chapter. The ideology of dependency affects institutional policies, including educational programs, and thus affects the autonomy implied in the broader agenda of children's right to education. Drawing from our work in a program for the education of Roma in northern Greece,[1] we unpack the issue of dependency as it is constructed in public imagery for Roma children and their families. A critical analysis of the welfare dependency pathology that informs public discourse and policy will reveal its harmful impact on the process of children's inclusion in the educational system, a right that has been traditionally undermined and violated so far.

The chapter unfolds in two parts. The first part examines the construction of a skewed public image as a result of the dependency on benefits of marginalized groups. The second part draws from our research data relating to issues of dependency in order to show how they affect Roma families' rights in general, and their children's rights in particular.

Education of Roma Children
Through the Dependency Lens

The educational scene is just a reflection of the larger picture of marginalization and exclusion that characterises Roma life in Greece, as well as in other European countries. Recent data (Papadimitriou, Mamarelis, & Niarchos, 2011) affirm that what Swadener, Tressou, and Mitakidou claimed in 2001 still holds true:

> Pervasive attitudes of people in public services, including health and education, either reflect conscious racism or are characterized by reluctance to accept and support the necessary changes in practice that might encourage greater ROM participation. (p. 191)

In this context, Roma children's right to education remains an unfulfilled goal: educational records in Greece document low attendance rates and performance scores for Roma children (Hatzisavvidis, 2007; Mitsis, 2008). Roma children still face marginalization by peers and teachers in schools. Education, apart from being a basic human right, can bridge the gap between Roma people and mainstream Greek society, given that it is both an empowering and liberating force. We chose to unpack the ideology of dependency because we recognize that it affects institutional policies and their implementation; therefore, it can undermine the struggle of the poor for freedom and human dignity recognized in the United Nations' *Universal Declaration of Human Rights* (Article 26).[2]

As Fraser (1989) suggests, needs claims cannot be "divorced from rights claims" (p. 312). Moreover, she continues,

> [t]o analyze the political imaginary of social welfare is simultaneously to shed light on the construction of social identities. It is to examine the terms in which people formulate their sense of who they are, what they deserve, and what they hope for. These in turn are bound up with assumptions about identity and difference: Who is like me and who is not? Who is my ally and who is my enemy? (Fraser, 1993, p. 9)

From the beginning of our involvement with the coordination of the above-mentioned European Union program focused on the education of Roma children, that is, their inclusion in the Greek school, their uninterrupted attendance, and the successful completion of their schooling, we have often stumbled on the dominant and persistent representation of the Roma as "inept," "sly," and "undeserving" benefit claimants. The notion of dependency informs the rhetoric and practice of dominant stakeholders—sometimes even avowed allies of the Roma population—thus marring their good intentions and energy for action. It may happen that at critical points, when decisions need to be made to support or block the implementation of practices that will lead to firm advocacy of the children's rights to education, this negative filter "sometimes prevents people from putting more energy into much needed institutional and pedagogical transformations" (Skliar & Dussel, 2011, p. 199).

Our vision for education is informed by critical pedagogy that locates the educational process in its sociopolitical context and sees it as a liberating power and a form of cultural politics (Freire & Macedo, 1987), a process that strives to turn individuals into social actors able to claim their futures (Aronowitz, 1981).

The nature of the program inevitably and directly links it to critical issues of poverty, inequality, social exclusion and human rights, at both local and national levels. In administering an educational program, there is a delicate line between being informed by past experiences and practices and being trapped by well-established and intricately interwoven economic, political, and social forces. This awareness has alerted us to the need to examine these issues through critical lenses. In this sense, we sought to examine the real ties to welfare benefits that Roma people have so that we could (a) confirm our hypothesis that they are not as dependent on benefits as the public rhetoric implies, (b) inform them of their rights and facilitate their access to them, and, based on this evidence, (c) try to restore their negative public image.

Theoretical Scene

"They make black money." "They receive welfare benefits at a time of crisis, when we all suffer income cuts." "They receive the school assistance benefit but do not send their children to school." "They are lazy, they don't want to work, and they are spoiled by being given all these benefits." "Teenage mothers have children to be entitled to welfare." These are some of the common expressions that permeate the mainstream social representations for the Roma dependency on welfare assistance. In fact, they construct the largest part of the public representation of the group, the other part being that of the defiant, independent figure that does not fit into mainstream conventions. This is an oxymoron and a puzzle that we have been striving to understand and to solve from the beginning of our involvement with the group, long before we were connected to the program.

The concept of dependency features quite prominently in the literature, mostly with negative connotations (Fraser, 1989, 1993; Harvey & Lind, 2005). In the English-language literature, the prevalent term is *welfare dependency*, and it has been amply analyzed by scientists in the fields of political philosophy (Fraser & Gordon, 1994), sociology (Levitas, 1996, 2004; Townsend, 1987; Townsend & Gordon, 2002), disability studies (Oliver, 1990, 1996; Rowlands, 2010), feminist studies (Naples, 2009), and in the area of social policy and empowerment programs for African communities (Harvey & Lind, 2005; Lind, 2005)

In the United States, discussion of dependency received great attention and a publishing boom from the 1990s through the early years of this century.[3] Correspondingly, in Europe, Levitas (1996), Townsend and Gordon (2002) in England and Honneth (2003) in Germany identified the use of the term and noted that its analysis prevailed in the discussions for social policy issues and was closely associated with the term *underclass*.

In the post-industrial era, any sense of "good" dependency disappeared, and the term's negative connotations prevailed. It is interesting to note the reversal of the terms *dependency* and *independence* over time: in the pre-industrial era, dependency was associated with subjection and labor, while independence implied privilege and freedom.

Social, economic, and political changes of the times signaled major shifts in the meaning of the term *dependency*, which definitely acquired a derogatory meaning. The word further shifted to concern the individual, whose immaturity, erratic behavior, and unstable trajectory were to blame for his/her precarious position. New, bleaker connotations of welfare dependency were nourished by discourses outside the field of welfare such as medicine and psychology, which associated dependency with pathology, obliterating its social aspect and placing all blame on the dependent. For instance, in 1980, the American Psychiatric Association made "Dependent Personality Disorder" an official psychopathology term, turning dependency into a behavioral syndrome.

> The essential feature of this disorder is a pervasive pattern of dependent and submissive behavior beginning by early childhood. People with this disorder are unable to make everyday decisions without an excessive amount of advice and reassurance from others, and will even allow others to make most of their important decisions. (American Psychiatric Association, 1987; cited in Fraser & Gordon, 1994, p. 326)

The framing of dependency within the New Deal and the Third Way diom emphasized the victim-blaming connotations of the term. Giddens (1994, 1998), an enthusiastic supporter of the New Deal, proclaimed that new policies had to be understood as "planning of positive welfare state," which was oriented toward reconstructing a self-sufficient and self-existent self. Giddens's perspective was that the new reflective subject, liberated from traditional commitments and "capable of translating potential threats into satisfactory challenges," could face danger "as an active challenge, which generated self-fulfillment" (Giddens, 1994, p. 192).

> Social democrats have to shift the relationship between *risk* and *security* involved in the welfare state, to develop a society of responsible "risk takers" in the spheres of government, business enterprise and labour markets. (Giddens, 1998, p. 100)

In Giddens's terms, redistribution of wealth does not necessarily guarantee security and happiness, and social provision stigmatizes morally and becomes the source of social exclusion of groups. Townshend (2009) claims accurately that Giddens attributes to the welfare state a spiritual rather than economic character.

Today, the term *dependency* is closely associated with the individual and carries negative connotations based on conservative morality. It is a term embraced by the ideological context of conservative and liberal politics, both of which blame social problems on people, thus defining them not only economically but also morally and psychologically.

As Fraser and Gordon (1994) argue, terms not only describe social life but also shape it. Loaded with "historical emotive and visual associations and a powerful pejorative charge," dependency carries assumptions concerning human nature, the roots of poverty, social roles, citizenship, rights, work, and everything else considered a contribution to society (p. 311).

The uncritical consumption and implementation of the dependency rhetoric by social policy planners and administrators can deepen social inequalities and further distort and stigmatize the social representation of vulnerable groups. The assumptions and attitudes of social actors often tend to neglect the structural causes of poverty and view needy individuals as "social parasites" who are responsible for their fates. Thus interactions between social workers and welfare beneficiaries further reinforce the latter's poor self-image and fail to promote their empowerment through the social provision process. At the same time, the negative implications of dependency affect individuals' self-esteem and self-image, disempowering them and annulling their motivation to pursue and absorb societal resources to improve their lives.

In the same vein, it is not a coincidence that most policy stakeholders seem to share the view that welfare policy complicates recipients' lives, since it fosters lack of motivation for self-help and employment and also stigmatizes benefit recipients morally, psychologically, and economically, stressing their condition as members of the "underclass" (Solomon, 1987).[4] As Levitas (2004) argues,

> The focus on school dropout and exclusion, in particular, when they are flatly related with potential and real criminality in combination with the theme of adolescent pregnancy recall traditional demons of the "dangerous social class"—idle young men who are criminals and young women, sexually and reproductionally violators. (p. 233; translated from Greek)

This distorted image of the undeserving benefit recipient, who is inevitably associated with transgression and delinquency, is a heavy burden on any beneficiary. Further, it leads to isolation and exclusion, with harmful consequences to his or her ability to be liberated from poverty and exclusion, to benefit from basic rights, and to achieve social mobility. Disempowered and deprived adults cannot secure basic rights and resources for their children.

In other words, instead of reaching independence through dependency, welfare beneficiaries are often trapped in a vicious circle of dependency, which, as our data below will show, is more imaginary than real. At every point in this circle, there are children who are directly affected by family poverty and destitution and have little hope of ever gaining control of their personal, societal, and political environment.

Roma, Those "Mischievous Fiends"

In the Greek social policy literature, there is no specific reference to the term *dependency*; however, it is embedded and implied in the keywords that refer to socially excluded groups—the Roma, for example (e.g., unskilled, unemployed, needy, pauper, etc.) and the measures for their social inclusion. "Keywords typically carry unspoken assumptions and connotations that can powerfully influence the discourses they permeate—in part by constituting a body of *doxa*, or taken-for-granted commonsense belief that escapes critical scrutiny" (Fraser & Gordon 1994, p. 310).

The overtones and negative connotations of the term are perceptible in the discourse of social service agents, including educators, who act as intermediaries between welfare programs and their beneficiaries. The prevalent view among administrators and staff of welfare programs is that welfare benefits lead recipients to idleness and apathy. Roma recipients, for example, are often pictured as idle and pathetic people who, despite the welfare assistance, still live in settlements and whose children, whom they do not send to school, often slip into delinquency. Culturally, they are glued to traits such as premature marriages/pregnancies that confine them to exclusionary trajectories.

Drawing from our research data, we analyze whether and how dependency on welfare benefits is affecting family welfare and rights, including education, by attempting a more detailed analysis of the Roma population and their relationship to welfare benefits.

About the Study

In the following sections, an effort will be made to draw parallels between the theoretical issues discussed above and our research findings about the Roma, framed in the larger context of human (including children's) rights. Our interview protocol included seven main themes (education, health, economic situation, employment, living conditions, participation in public life, and disability issues) and aimed at sketching the socio-demographic profile of Roma families. As Alderson (2008) suggests:

> there are strong links between poverty and lower standards of economic wellbeing, health, enjoyment…education, transport and road safety, family life and care, racism and violence, housing and children's participation…. All these areas need to be addressed together if children's rights to an adequate standard of living are to be respected. (p. 35)

For the purposes of our analysis here, we focused on four questions relevant to human and children's rights, particularly the right to wellbeing and social resources that encompasses the right to education and cannot be isolated from other basic needs. The first question related to the provision of benefits, the second to the level of education of family members, the third to material deprivation, and the fourth to adult occupation. All of these questions are related to poverty and deprivation, conditions that definitely disempower individuals obstructing them from the absorption of basic social and material resources, such as education.

Our research was conducted from March 2011 to March 2012 by going door to door among 1,666 Roma families located in 39 different areas within 9 prefectures of northern Greece, an area with the most serious economic issues and highest unemployment rate in the country. Our data showed that Roma participants lived in makeshift or more permanent settlements or in mixed neighborhoods, usually at the outskirts of cities or towns. A large percentage of the families (40.4%) lived in the prefecture of Thessaloniki, while a smaller but substantial segment of the sample (21.6%) lived in the prefecture of Imathia. The rest of the sample was scattered over the remaining seven prefectures of northern Greece. Women respondents far outnumbered men—1,321 women to 311 men (82.8% vs. 17.2%).

Findings

Allocation of benefits. The benefits that interviewees asserted they received were for families with many children (three and above), for unprotected child(ren), unmarried mother, disability, widowhood, poverty welfare, unemployment, and the school assistance benefit. At the top of the list was the benefit for families with many children, which was received by 63.9% of the sample. This was followed by the benefits for disability, unprotected child, and school assistance, received by a significantly smaller percentage, 6.5%, 5.6%, and 2.9% of the sample respectively. The percentages dropped even lower for the rest of the benefits, that is, unmarried mother, 2.0%, poverty welfare, 1.3%, unemployment, 0.3%, and widowhood, at just 0.1%.

Table 4.1 Allocation of benefits

Benefits	FREQUENCY	PERCENTAGE %
Families with many children	900	63.9
Disability	92	6.5
Unprotected child	80	5.6
School assistance	41	2.9
Unmarried mother	28	2.0
Poverty welfare	19	1.3
Unemployment	4	0.3
Widowhood	1	0.1

The only benefit received by a substantial percentage of the Roma population was the benefit for families with many children—in other words, the overwhelming majority of Roma families. The benefit received by such families at the time of the research was €215 for 2 months.[5] The rest of the benefits were received by an insignificant number of families.

The breadth of benefits is not only limited but also conditional, so that dependency on them is insignificant, if not non-existent. For instance, poor families with fewer than three children are not entitled to benefits. Disability benefits depend on the nature of the disability. Housing benefits are given on the condition of employment insurance of the recipient, and in our area of activity we did not identify a single recipient.

In other words, the common belief that the Roma live on benefits, a situation that encourages idleness and social immobility and leads to parasitism, exists in the sphere of the imaginary alone. Moreover, these myths about benefits and their influence on the character of poor people have the power not only to create misleading stereotypes of them but also to undermine their relations with other citizens, whom they may see as adversaries, each threatening and placing obstacles in the other's path.

Looking at the larger picture, the amount of benefits in Greece is the lowest in Europe. Benefits play a marginal role in what is actually a precarious, punctured safety net; they are proof of the fragmented and insufficient coverage of needs in day-to-day reality (Matsaganis, Ferrera, Capucha, & Moreno, 2004). The fragmented and insufficient needs provision becomes evident if we consider that the unemployment benefit is provided for a limited time—that is, 1 year—and only on the condition that the beneficiary has sufficient employment insurance history. Thus, only 44% of the unemployed population is entitled to it (Matsaganis et al., 2004; Papatheodorou & Petmetzidou, 2004).

The insufficient protection that provisions offer beneficiaries in Greece is further evidenced by recent data selected by the Greek Observatory in January 2012[6] showing a further decline of benefit provision to 2.4% at the same time that the extent of poverty in Greece is growing (22% of Greek households are below the poverty line) and the array of social benefits is shrinking. Indeed, in today's climate of severe economic crisis, and because of what is believed to be benefit embezzlement (for example, pensions still paid to deceased beneficiaries and disability benefits to healthy individuals), all benefits are being reassessed, and most of them are being severely cut. On the basis of these data, the scarcity of benefits hardly qualifies them as relief measures or "safety-net" policies, let alone as evidence of a redistributive tendency.

Family level of education. In our research, special emphasis was placed on family members' ability to read and write and their level of education. Our sample totaled 8,137 people and consisted of the actual interviewees and their families. Out of that number, 44% knew how to read and write, 23% had completed elementary school, 4% had completed junior high school, and only 1.7% had completed senior secondary education.

The educational level of family heads is generally associated with poverty risk for children in a family. With or without social provisions, lower education levels are related to high poverty risk (Papatheodorou & Dafermos, 2010). Poverty compromises children's educational prospects, which in turn shuts off one pathway to the avoidance of poverty. According to Townsend and Gordon (2002):

> the definition of absolute poverty implies that a child is poor if she suffers from severe educational deprivation.... There might be a number of reasons why a child does not receive primary education and low family income is often a very important factor. (p. 67)

Low educational levels, therefore, mean limited professional options and, consequently, impaired economic and social relations.

People who live in families in which the main provider has completed only primary education are also at risk for poverty (Papatheodorou & Petmetzidou, 2004), and this was the case with the majority of our sample. Low income for adults in a household translates into children directly affected by poverty and limited in their ability to attend or finish school, as they are obliged to contribute to the family income.

Material deprivation. In recent years, EUROSTAT[7] has formulated an additional index of relative poverty in which indices of material deprivation are recorded based on households ability to cover nine basic needs: (1) meal with fish or meat every second day, (2) a 1-week vacation every year, (3) facing extra expenses, (4) sufficient heating, (5) payment of rent and other bills without difficulty, (6) washing machine at home, (7) color TV at home, (8) home telephone line, and (9) car property. People or families are now considered to be experiencing material deprivation when they cannot satisfy at least three of these needs.

Our data showed that, for our sample, only three needs (TV, car, telephone) of those nine were satisfied (90%, 70%, and 84% correspondingly). Moreover, in response to the question about family nutritional habits, a disturbing 70% of our research participants claimed that in the past month they were not able to cover their family's nutritional needs. In fact, an important finding in our study was that dietary deprivation was closely associated with living conditions. Insufficient food supply was recorded by a very high percentage of Roma who lived in settlements (90.3%). That figure was only slightly lower for the Roma who lived in mixed neighborhoods (88.5%) but much lower for the Roma who lived in conventional neighborhoods (56%).

Adult occupation and children's welfare. The occupational map of our adult population predicts a further deterioration of the children's welfare and future prospects. Only 45.7% of our sample had steady jobs (most of them were self-employed) that lasted for the whole year. A quite significant percentage (13.9%) reported their employment was limited to only a few days a month; 9.4% had seasonal jobs, and 4.2% worked "rarely." A quite high percentage (22.8%) did not work at all, and 31.5% were employed seasonally or in part-time jobs. The fact that family heads cannot provide sufficient income means that Roma children experience extreme poverty and live in destitute conditions.

The poverty and social exclusion of parents usually leaves children with limited prospects of success at school. It is a vicious circle. The poor absorption of basic public resources—for example, educational resources—leads to an inability to partake equally in political decision making, which in turn weakens the decisive struggle against those negative conditions that generate exclusion and the limited absorption of public resources. Thus the circle is completed and perpetuated (Tsiakalos, 2002). This is a characteristic example of violation of children's rights.

Benefit Rights: A Case for Children's Rights

Analysis of the research data presented above reveals important points: Roma live in conditions of utter poverty, and they are uneducated and limited to pursuing poorly paid and unstable jobs. Contrary to common public belief, Roma utilize a very limited amount of welfare funds. This contradicts the dominant myth of their exploiting the system by receiving unjustified benefits. However, the power of negative social representations of the Roma, coupled with the group's own limited ability to claim their rights to those benefits, results in their utter poverty and gives their children little hope of escaping the vicious circle that plagues them. Moreover, negative encounters with social systems such as school, the police, the welfare service, the hospital, and so forth, often lead members of vulnerable groups to internalize negative societal evaluations and avoid any contact with services for fear of failure (Solomon, 1987). Implementation of policies by prejudiced state agents, including educators, may widen the gap between the Roma and the state, pushing them toward further exploitation, igniting racism, and cultivating the conditions for social exclusion. Furthermore, the negative connotations of dependency deflect policies from the ideal of universality of social provision, stigmatizing dependency with the deficiency label even when the conditions of poverty are real.

The research we engaged in was not conducted for academic reasons alone, but also served as the basis of the program's action plan. We felt that our target of securing the children's access to education could be achieved through the amelioration of their living conditions. According to Article 25 of the *Universal Declaration of Human Rights*,[8]

everyone has the right to a standard of living adequate for the health and well-being of himself and of his family, including food, clothing, housing and medical care and necessary social services, and the right to security in the event of unemployment, sickness, disability, widowhood, old age or other lack of livelihood and circumstances beyond his control.

Since welfare benefits may contribute to better living conditions, one of our basic goals was to help the population to claim the rights to social benefits they were entitled to. In our effort to accomplish this, we did the following:

- educated our associates to scaffold the Roma population, empower them, and assist them in claiming their rights;

- tried to disrupt the crooked social image of the Roma by sensitizing educational professionals to their actual living conditions and life predicament by sharing and critically discussing our research data with them;

- covered children's basic needs (vaccinations, clothing, food subsidies, toys) through the motivation and mobilization of mainstream individual stakeholders and social agents;

- worked to formulate suggestions to inform social strategies and policies.

Final Remarks

Educational programs cannot be seen in strict educational terms, as they evolve at the center of the social fabric and are directly related to the social values and relations developed within the society. Roma children live in households that lack basic necessities, so at times it seems almost offensive to make a case for the importance of education in opening up opportunities for a better future—not because you do not believe in the strength of education to empower, liberate, and elevate, but because your sense of justice and dignity is violated. In times of economic and societal crisis, such as the current one in Greece, education, stripped of the cloak of direct reciprocity for employment and/or better living conditions, does not make a very convincing case. Thus, our interest lies in dependency as one of the factors that undermines and obstructs children's rights to welfare and education: a steady and reliable benefit system could secure a viable living standard for Roma children. By revealing the true living conditions of these children and their limited dependency on benefits, we aspire to deconstruct the negative public image of the Roma as major benefit beneficiaries and to reveal society's responsibility for their exclusion from social and educational resources.

Notes

1. It is an ESF program called "Education of Roma Children in the Regions of Central Macedonia, Western Macedonia, Eastern Macedonia and Thrace," with Evangelia Tressou acting as scientist responsible for the program. The three authors comprise the coordinating team of the program.

2. (1) Everyone has the right to education. Education shall be free, at least in the elementary and fundamental stages. Elementary education shall be compulsory. Technical and professional education shall be made generally available and higher education shall be equally accessible to all on the basis of merit.

(2) Education shall be directed to the full development of the human personality and to the strengthening of respect for human rights and fundamental freedoms. It shall promote understanding, tolerance and friendship among all nations, racial or religious groups, and shall further the activities of the United Nations for the maintenance of peace.

(3) Parents have a prior right to choose the kind of education that shall be given to their children. (United Nations, 1948)

3. A description of the historical shifts in the meaning of the term from its first appearance in the pre-industrial era to the present would exceed the limitations of our research, so this essay is based on its present usage. For a detailed genealogy of the term, see Fraser and Gordon (1994).

4. This is similar to the argument of the right-wing declarations in Greece (June 2012) in support of lawful householders who work to pay their taxes and take care of their families, as opposed to those who belong to the underclass of immigrants, organized crime, and milder forms of criminality of various groups who live like parasites (http://www.tovima.gr/afieromata/elections2012/article/?aid=461878).

5. This benefit was recently reassessed and severely cut.

6. http://www.ineobservatory.gr/analyseis-kai-stoicheia/parsousiash-kai-analysh-statistikon-stoixeiwn/ti-prepei-na-gnwrizete

7. http://epp.eurostat.ec.europa.eu/portal/page/portal/pgp_ess/news/ess_news_detail?id=12499 2264&pg_id=2737&cc=EL_GREECE

8. http://www.un.org/en/documents/udhr/index.shtml

References

Greek

Levitas, R. (2004). Τι είναι κοινωνικός αποκλεισμός. Στο Μ. Πετμεζίδου & Χ. Παπαθεοδώρου (επιμ.), *Φτώχεια και Κκοινωνικός Ααποκλεισμός* (pp. 202–225). Αθήνα: Εξάντας.
[Levitas, R. (2004). What is social exclusion? In M. Petmetzidou & Ch. Papatheodorou (Eds.), *Poverty and social exclusion* (pp. 202–225). Athens: Exandas.]

Ματσαγγάνης, Μ., Ferrera, M., Capucha L., & Moreno, L. (2004). Πολιτικές κατά της φτώχειας στη Νότια Ευρώπη. Στο Μ. Πετμεζίδου & Χ. Παπαθεοδώρου (επιμ.), *Φτώχεια και κοινωνικός αποκλεισμός* (pp. 483–512). Αθήνα: Εξάντας.
[Matsagganis, M., Ferrera, M., Capucha, L., & Moreno, L. (2004). Policies against poverty in South Europe. In M. Petmetzidou & Ch. Papatheodorou (Eds.), *Poverty and social exclusion* (pp. 483–512). Athens: Exandas.]

Παπαθεοδώρου, Χ., & Πετμεζίδου, Μ. (2004). Ανισότητα, φτώχεια και αναδιανομή μέσω των κοινωνικών μεταβιβάσεων: Η Ελλάδα σε συγκριτική προοπτική." Στο Μ. Πετμεζίδου και Χ. Παπαθεοδώρου (επιμ.), *Φτώχεια και κοινωνικός αποκλεισμός* (pp. 307–367). Αθήνα: Εξάντας.
[Papatheodorou, Ch., & Petmetzidou, M. (2004). Inequality, poverty and redistribution through social transfers: Greece in comparative perspective. In M. Petmetzidou & Ch. Papatheodorou (Eds.), *Poverty and social exclusion* (pp. 307–367). Athens: Exandas.]

Παπαθεοδώρου, Χ., & Δαφέρμος, Γ. (2010). *Δομή και τάσεις της οικονομικής ανισότητας και της φτώχειας στην Ελλάδα και την Ε.Ε, 1995–2008.* Επιστημονική Έκθεση 2. Παρατηρητήριο Οικονομικών και Κοινωνικών Εξελίξεων, Ινστιτούτο Εργασίας ΓΣΕΕ.
[Papatheodorou, Ch., & Dafermos, G. (2010). *Structure and trends of economic inequality and poverty in Greece and EU, 1995–2008.* Scientific Report 1, Observatory of Economical and Social Developments, Institute of Labor, GSEE.]

Μήτσης, Ν. (2008). *Αξιολόγηση του έργου "Ένταξη τσιγγανοπαίδων στο σχολείο."* Αθήνα: Omas Synergon Ltd.

[Mitsis, N. . (2008). *Assessment of the project "Inclusion of Gypsy children in school."* Athens: Omas Synergon Ltd. .]

Townsend, P. (2004). Για μια αναθεώρηση της διεθνούς κοινωνικής πολιτικής ενάντια στη φτώχεια. Στο Μ. Πετμεζίδου και Χ. Παπαθεοδώρου (επιμ.), *Φτώχεια και κοινωνικός αποκλεισμός* (pp. 115–159). Αθήνα: Εξάντας.

[Townsend, P. (2004). Reconsidering the international social policy against poverty. In M. Petmetzidou & Ch. Papatheodorou (Eds.), *Poverty and social exclusion* (pp. 115–159). Athens: Exandas.]

Τσιάκαλος, Γ. (2002). Ανθρώπινη αξιοπρέπεια, κοινωνικός αποκλεισμός και εκπαίδευση στην Ευρώπη. Στο Γ. Τσιάκαλος, *Η Υπόσχεση της Ηπαιδαγωγικής* (pp. 177–196). Θεσσαλονίκη: Παρατηρητής.

[Tsiakalos, G. (2002). Human dignity, social exclusion and education in Europe. In G. Tsiakalos, *The promise of pedagogy* (pp. 177–196). Thessaloniki: Paratiritis.]

Χατζησαββίδης, Σ. (2007). *Ετερότητα στη σχολική τάξη και η διδασκαλία της ελληνικής γλώσσας και των μαθηματικών. Η περίπτωση των τσιγγανοπαίδων*. Βόλος: ΥΠΕΠΘ & Πανεπιστήμιο Θεσσαλίας.

[Hatzisavvidis, S. (2007). *Diversity in the classroom and the teaching of Greek and mathematics. The case of Gypsy children.* Volos: Ministry of Education & Panepistimio Thessalias.]

English

Alderson, P. (2008). *Young children's rights: Exploring beliefs, principles and practice.* London: Jessica Kingsley.

Aronowitz, S. (1981). *The crisis in historical materialism: Class politics and culture in Marxist theory.* New York: Bergin Publications.

Fraser, N. (1989). Talking about needs: Interpretive contests as political conflicts in welfare-state societies. *Ethics, 99*(2), 291–313.

Fraser, N. (1993). Clintonism, welfare and the antisocial wage: The emergence of a neoliberal political imaginary. *Rethinking Marxism: A Journal of Economics, Culture & Society, 6*(1), 9–23.

Fraser, N., & Gordon, L. (1994). A genealogy of dependency: Tracing a keyword of the U.S. welfare state. *Signs, 19*(2), 309–336.

Freire, P., & Macedo, D. (1987). *Literacy: Reading the word and the world.* Westport, CT: Bergin & Garvey.

Giddens, A. (1994). *Modernity and self-identity: Self and society in the late modern age.* Cambridge, UK: Polity Press.

Giddens, A. (1998). *The Third Way: The renewal of social democracy.* Cambridge, UK: Polity Press.

Harvey, P., & Lind, J. (2005). *Dependency and humanitarian relief. A critical analysis.* London: Overseas Development Institute.

Honneth, A. (2003). Redistribution as recognition: A response to Nancy Fraser. In N. Fraser & A. Honneth (Eds.), *Redistribution or recognition? A political-philosophical exchange* (pp. 110–160). London: Verso.

Levitas, R. (1996). What is social exclusion? In D. Gordon & P. Townsend (Eds.), *Breadline Europe: The measurement of poverty* (pp. 357–383). Bristol, UK: Policy Press.

Lind, J. (2005). *Relief assistance at the margins: Meanings and perceptions of dependency in Northern Kenya.* London: Overseas Development Institute.

Naples, N. (2009). Crossing borders: Community activism, globalization, and social justice. *Social Problems, 56*(1), 2–20.

Oliver, M. (1990). *The politics of disablement: A sociological approach.* London: Macmillan.

Oliver, M. (1996). *Understanding disability: From theory to practice.* London: Macmillan.

Papadimitriou, D., Mamarelis, A., & Niarchos, G. (2011). The socio-economic situation of the Roma in Greece. Country Report: Greece. In W. Bartlett, R. Benini, & C. Gordon (Eds.),

Measures to promote the situation of Roma EU citizens in the European Union (pp. 142–165). Brussels: European Parliament.

Rowlands, J. (2010). Empowerment examined. *Development in Practice, 5*(2), 101–107.

Skliar, C., & Dussel, I. (2011). From equity to difference: Educational legal frames and inclusive practices in Argentina. In A. Artilles, E. Kozleski, & F. Waitoller (Eds.), *Inclusive education* (pp. 185–201). Cambridge, MA: Harvard Education Press.

Solomon, B.B. (1987). Empowerment: Social work in oppressed communities. *Journal of Social Work Practice: Psychotherapeutic Approaches in Health, Welfare and the Community, 2*(4), 79–91.

Swadener, B., Tressou, E., & Mitakidou, C. (2001). Involving preservice teachers in a program for ROM (gypsy) children in northern Greece: Lessons in child advocacy. In I. Berson, M. Berson, & B. Cruz (Eds.), *Cross cultural perspectives in child advocacy: Research in global child advocacy* (Vol. 1, pp. 189–212). Greenwich, CT: Information Age.

Townsend, P. (1987). Deprivation. *Journal of Social Policy, 16*(2), 125–146.

Townsend, P., & Gordon, D. (Eds.). (2002). *World poverty: New policies to defeat an old enemy.* Bristol, UK: Policy Press.

Townshend, J. (2009). Giddens's "third way" and Gramsci's "passive revolution." In M. McNally & J. Schwarzmantel (Eds.), *Gramsci and global politics: Hegemony and resistance* (pp. 156–172). New York: Routledge.

United Nations. (1948). *Universal declaration of human rights.* Retrieved April 20, 2013, from http://www.un.org/en/documents/udhr/index.shtml

Child-Rights Approaches
in the Early Years

A Rights-Based Approach to Observing and Assessing Children in the Early Childhood Classroom

Kylie Smith

The 1989 United Nations Convention on the Rights of the Child (UNCRC) stated that children have the right to participate in decision making and to express their views about things that concern them. The United Nations General Comment No. 7, *Implementing Child Rights in Early Childhood* (2005), encouraged researchers, educators, and policymakers to seek the views of children under 5 years of age and to take these views seriously. While momentum is growing for this work with older children, there has been little work on what it means for children in their earliest years, particularly under 5 years of age.

This chapter will explore a rights-based approach to observation and assessment of children's learning and development in early childhood education. A rights-based approach draws on the articles in the UNCRC (1989) as guiding principles to theory and practice. Using my case study from an Australian early childhood centre, the chapter will examine what happens when we, as teachers, ask children about learning and engagement from their perspective. I illustrate that children's voices shine a different light on how we see and assess (and support) children, thus providing newer insights into the subjectivities of our gaze.

My Multiple Images of the Child

Exploration of diverse images of the child supported my thinking about alternative approaches to observation and assessment of young children with a focus on rights. Three images were particularly persistent. The first and most dominant one was the "child as innocent," which emerged from theorists grounded in humanism such as Rousseau (Moss & Petrie, 2002). This image presents the innocent child, who needs protection, care, and nurture. With little or no capacity to contribute to observation and assessment, the child is merely portrayed as an incomplete adult who cannot speak or act on her/his own behalf (MacNaughton, 2003; Moss & Petrie, 2002; Smith, 2003). The second image, "child as participant," proposes that children can participate in decisions about their lives, but only when adults regard them as competent, usually developmentally able (Lloyd-Smith & Tarr, 2000). Although this image acknowledges a skilful child, the child is seen as an "apprentice" to a "master"—the early childhood educator. The third image conceptualises the "child as an active citizen." This image is the result of over 20 years of sociological work that acknowledges the child as a competent meaning maker who has valid and important knowledge about the world that is different from—not inferior to—adult knowledge (Alderson, 2008; Diaz Soto, 2005; Lundy & McEvoy, 2009; MacNaughton & Smith, 2009; Perry & Dockett, 2011). Each of these images connects to children's rights, particularly in regard to the child's right to protection and participation.

Figure 5.1 My Multiple Images of the Child

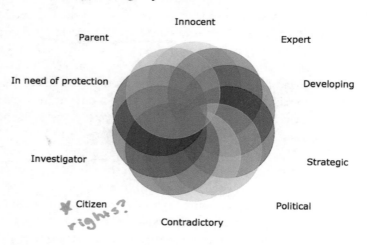

I began to engage theoretically and practically with these images of children in my work with young children and families as a novice early childhood educator and then later in my doctoral work. My doctoral work gave me a way of talking about the things that made me uncomfortable with the three dominant views of the child. I became aware of such images of children overlapping and merging at different times. I visualized every child, as Figure 1 illustrates, as being multiple: she could be innocent, expert, developing, a parent, teacher, rights bearer, and so forth.

My earlier unified, singular image of childhood and children became ruptured. I began to include the many facets of the children's experiences and roles, including their strengths and vulnerabilities, as well as my own subjectivities, my shortcomings, and my successes. I found that my singular image of children only resulted in eliminating their possibilities for participation. I felt that this was especially evident within my early childhood service, as we often saw children under 5 years of age as young, innocent, and not yet competent, and didn't articulate children's rights in everyday practice. I decided to engage deeply with my current awareness. Reading the work of Gilles Deleuze and Felix Guattari (1987) on rhizomes supported my exploration into the multiplicity of childhood and children. Deleuze and Guattari (1987) examined multiplicity as diversity rather than quantity: A multiplicity has neither subject nor object, only determinations, magnitudes, and dimensions that cannot increase in number without the multiplicity changing in nature (p. 8).

Rhizomes are about mapping new or unknown lines and entry points, not tracing which records old lines or patterns (Alvermann, 2000; Deleuze & Guattari, 1987). To examine this mapping and the complexity, a tracing is placed over the top so that deviations, breaks, or ruptures can be identified; what the effects of these can be are examined within the text (Alvermann, 2000)....the rhizome pertains to a map that must be produced, constructed, a map that is always detachable, connectable, reversible, modifiable, and has multiple entryways and exits and its own lines of flight (Deleuze & Guattari, 1987, p. 21).

This work helped me think about observation and assessment differently. Two questions that I began to consider were: Should I be worried about the amount of observations and assessments? Or should I be exploring diverse ways to analyze what I see and how I understand the child? I wanted to create ruptures in my understandings of children to "create a new line of flight" or a new way of seeing and assessing the children.

My Ruptures in Engaging with Children

Upon completion of my doctoral studies in January 2004, I began to divide my full-time employment at the University of Melbourne between two sites: I worked 3 days a week at the Swanston Street Children's Centre as an early childhood educator and co-director, and at the Centre for Equity and Innovation in Early Childhood as a research fellow for the remaining 2 days of the working week. I strategically and politically chose to do this because I wanted to continue to explore the intersections of research and practice, to evidence how they do and can inform each other.

While working as a research assistant on Glenda MacNaughton's Australian Research Council–funded project called Preschool Children's Constructions of Cultural and "Racial" Diversity with Karina Davis between 2004 and 2006, I began to question how I enacted children's right to participate in observation and assessment in the everyday classroom. These questions about classroom observation and assessment practices were prompted by the discussions and reflections we had as we developed and implemented protocols to ethically engage with children between the ages of 3 and 5 participating in the project.

We established four key protocols for ethical engagements with children. These included:

1. children being asked each time they participated in a research activity if they wanted to participate in research activities and whether they approved of these activities being recorded;

2. children being asked to select their own pseudonyms;

3. children being asked for permission to use their words or work. Even when this was agreed, we took copies of the work so that children retained their original work. We felt that this acknowledged children's ownership of their words and their artwork; and

4. children being requested to check whether we had recorded their words and ideas correctly. We agreed and informed the children and the participating early childhood services that we would come back with our recordings of our observations.

We believed that these protocols were based on our images of the "child as citizen," built on the conceptualization of the child as being multiple, a competent meaning maker with a right to have a say about matters affecting him or her, yet vulnerable in research spaces that are predominantly dictated by adults.

As a research assistant on this project, I went into two early childhood classrooms each week across a 12-month period. Sitting in these classrooms, which were mirrors of my own classroom, I began to critically reflect:

- Why do I follow the protocols as a researcher with the children participating in research to enact ethical engagement and children's rights, yet as a teacher I don't do any of this?

- How might these protocols support me to think differently about children's participation in the everyday classroom in my everyday teaching strategies?

These questions created a rupture in conceptualizing observation and assessment in theory and practice for me. I decided on that day that I would ask children whom I worked with in the children's centre if I could observe and write about their learning and development. The following week, as I walked back into my classroom, I talked with my co-educators and the children about my questions and the contradictions between what I do in research and what I do in the classroom.

I took four key steps. First, I read literature; second, I looked at policy; third, I used the UNCRC to arbitrate and renegotiate; and last, I asked how these documents and my new concept of the child can frame rights-based educational practices to observation and assessment of children's learning and development. As a result, I became committed in exploring how the "Rights of the Child" (UNCRC, 1989), intersected with the conceptualization of the child and our classroom practices. My imaginings about the implementation of a rights-based approach to observation and assessment of children's learning were repeatedly fueled as I engaged in my early childhood classroom with children ages 3 to 5. In particular I began to enact as a teacher Article 12 of the United Nations Convention on the Rights of the Child (1989). Article 12 reads as follows: How?.

> [T]o express an opinion and to have that opinion taken into account in any matter or procedure affecting the child.

I wondered if using a rights-based lens would create a fairer way for children to be seen, assessed, and therefore understood.

I familiarized myself with a large body of work that had grown over the past 20 years and continues to grow in relation to young children's participation in research (see Su & Di Santo, 2011; Fargas-Malet, McSherry, Larkin, & Robinson, 2010; MacNaughton & Smith, 2008). I began to feel that such changing images of the child, which included multiplicity, were offering provocation and inspiration for early childhood educators to begin thinking about how young children might offer their opinions and have them taken into account, especially for early childhood curriculum development and its implementation (see MacNaughton & Smith, 2008).

My Initial Inquiry

The United Nations General Comment No. 7, *Implementing Child Rights in Early Childhood* (UN, 2005) spurred interest on the part of researchers, educators, and policymakers in seeking children's views. Up to this point, dominant participatory approaches appeared in primary and secondary schools in the form of school councils and the like. For me it provided a platform to engage with what participatory rights for children under the age of 5 looked like in early childhood classrooms, particularly in relation to existing observation and documentation. This encouraged me to begin to challenge the adult-centered curriculum development for young children in Australian educational care settings.

Rethinking How I Observe and Assess Children's Learning

I realized that for over 20 years, as early childhood educators working in Australian preschool and long day care services, we have been required to observe, document, analyze, and assess children's learning and development and to use this as a foundation for designing curriculum. Traditionally, we as educators were expected to observe, make notes, and interpret for and about individual children in order to assess their learning and development. This notion of being able to "see" learning was influenced by constructivism. I grappled with constructivism that positioned children as learners who actively built new knowledge and understanding through their interaction with their world. Thus, with images of "innocent and participant child," educators believed in presenting well-constructed and controlled physical and social environments to initiate learning that occurred through cognitive processes controlled by individual children (MacNaughton, 2003). Then there was the introduction and the influence of pedagogical documentation (Rinaldi, 1998), Learning Stories (Carr, 2001), and the Mosaic approach (Clark and Moss, 2001). The concept of listening to children's perspectives was emphasized with the inclusion of children's "voices" in observation. Although this approach seemed to position children's thoughts and ideas as being central to their everyday educational care activities, I still felt that this approach took a constructivist view of the child. In my view it continued to believe in the less-developed child and the expert adult, with principles of child participation woven tokenistically through the adult-dictated curriculum. According to Clark and Moss (2001), within this paradigm children are recognized as experts in spaces created by adults, who are trained to become attuned to listening and recording children's perspectives and providing opportunities for children to co-construct their own environments. My dissatisfaction with my practices that stemmed from these approaches to recording and analyzing children's learning in Australia continued, because they only resulted in documentations and interpretations of observations of children's play behavior by adults, with children's dialogue or conversations recorded as proof of including children's "voices." Although such adult-dictated documentation and interpretation seemed like a continuation of children's narratives that were being recorded (as part of retelling what happened), I noted with disappointment that children were rarely invited to analyze the narrative the adult had undertaken, interpreted, and assessed. Adults selected and recorded the narrative, which supported the perpetuation of the "expert" adult who constructed and recorded what is important to children and to their learning. This approach could be seen as an act of censorship rather than inclusion/consultation, with the silence of children's voices as its effect. Thus, early childhood curriculum development procedures seldom provided alternative interpretations and assessments to those made by adult educators. I felt, despite the strong recommendations of United Nations General Comment No. 7 (2005), that young children's views were silenced by adult voices in educational settings. This view is amply highlighted by Cannella, who wrote that "The most critical voices that are silent in our constructions of early childhood education are the children with whom we work" (1997, p. 10). My early childhood teaching continued with my ruptures and rethinking.

My teaching in a time of national reform

The early childhood arena in Australia shifted with the introduction of a new national reform agenda, introduced in late 2007. One of the key results of this reform was the development and implementation of Early Years Learning Framework, "Belonging, Being and Becoming" (Commonwealth of Australia, 2009), a set of guidelines designed to support early childhood practices. This is the latest document that guides and supports the early childhood field and its educational care practices. One of the key statements with which this document begins is as follows:

> Early childhood educators guided by the Framework will reinforce in their daily practice the principles laid out in the United Nations Convention on the Rights of the Child (the Convention). The Convention states that all children have a right to an education that lays a foundation for the rest of their lives, maximises their ability, and respects their family, cultural and other identities and languages. The Convention also recognises children's right to play and be active participants in all matters affecting their lives. (p. 5)

I believed from above that Belonging Being and Becoming (Commonwealth of Australia, 2009) placed children's rights in the center of early childhood practices in Australia. This appeared to be a significant foregrounding of a rights-based approach within the field of early childhood education. However, upon further examination, the rest of the document did not link articles from the UNCRC to inform daily early childhood practices. For me, this raised serious questions about what it meant in real-life, everyday practices. Being specifically interested in how a rights-based approach intercepts our observation and assessment of children's learning, I began to explore and challenge my own understandings and practices of observing and interpreting children's play and interaction in my classroom.

In what follows, I share one such challenge. I do this not to provide a recipe, but in the hope of initiating questions that kindle possibilities for us, as early childhood educators, to re-explore practicing a rights-based approach within our own contexts.

My Eyes Wide Shut

On a Tuesday afternoon in early 2007, as I was sitting outside watching the children in the 3–5 age group playing, my gaze was drawn to Linda and Troy (pseudonyms), who were playing next to the side wall. Linda (girl) and Troy (boy) were 4 years old. They had both started at the centre in the babies' room when they were 3 months old. I asked them if I could watch them and write about what they were doing and saying. They both agreed, and so I grabbed a pen and paper and wrote the conversation as it unfolded. Their play drew from the animated movie *The Adventures of Sharkboy and Lavagirl*. This movie had recently been released in Australia on DVD and was readily available in supermarkets and department stores.

The Adventures of Sharkboy and Lavagirl is about a lonely child who creates an imaginary world named Planet Drool. He creates two characters: Sharkboy, a young boy who is raised by sharks after losing his dad at sea, and Lavagirl, who can produce fire and lava, and has problems setting alight objects when she touches them. Sharkboy and Lavagirl work together to save the planet from disaster.

Linda: I'm Sharkboy.
Troy: And I'm Lavagirl.
The Author: What does Sharkboy do?
Linda: I eat people.
The Author: What does Lavagirl do?
Troy: I spread fire and lava.
The Author: Are you goodies or baddies?
Linda: We're baddies.
Troy: We are good to good people.
Linda: I eat bad people and animals and am good to good people.
Troy: I spread fire on bad people.
Linda: Sharkboy is a movie. I have Sharkboy movie at my house.
Linda and Troy were running around the back yard.
Linda: Come on Lavagirl!
Troy: O.K. Come back to the house now!
Linda: Hurry up Lavagirl let's go home.
Troy: O.K. Let's go to the rocket ship.
Linda: O.K I'll drive. 54321 zero blast off!
Five minutes later Linda and Troy invited me into their rocket ship. Troy said:
Troy: You're a pretend boy.

In my doctoral work I argued that to begin to gain insight into the multiplicity of who a child is and how she understands the world, it is important to use multiple theoretical perspectives (Smith, 2003). I was drawn to their play because I had been reading feminist writing by bel hooks (2000), and my gaze immediately positioned a gendered lens over the scene. I was interested in the gender discourses in operation.

The critical reflection questions that flowed from my first analysis with the use of my gendered lens were: How might I see gender operating here? What made it possible for Troy to take on the role of a girl and Linda the role of a boy? The children under my gendered scrutiny were Linda, a girl, and Troy, a boy. At that time, I reminded myself of bell hooks's (2000) theory about man-affirmed women and her assertion that women can practice their gender and sexuality in varied ways, but only if they have the approval of men. I questioned further: Can Linda take on the role of boy because Troy lets her? Is it because of their parents' politics in how they talk about what boys and girls can do and who they can be? Can Linda take on the role of boy because she engages in different (male-dominated) storylines with her two brothers? Were Linda and Troy able to explore being a boy or girl differently because the characters were in a movie, and so Linda wasn't being a "real boy" and Troy wasn't being a "real girl"? How might popular culture create spaces for children to take up non-stereotypical gender roles?

With my emphasis on multiple analyses and interpretations to engage with the complete child, I drew on Lev Vygotsky's work for my second analysis. Vygotsky (1978) argued that children become knowledgeable and are able to give meaning to their world by negotiating with others. Moreover, Vygotsky regarded such "make believe play" (the type of role play behaviours that Linda and Troy were enacting) as a space to influence the zone of proximal development. He wrote:

> [Make believe] play creates a zone of proximal development in the child. In play, the child always behaves beyond his average age, above his daily behaviour; in play it is as though he were a head taller than himself. As in the focus of a magnifying glass, play contains all developmental tendencies in a condensed form and is itself a major source of development. (Vygotsky, 1978, p. 102)

My mind immediately raced with the following question: Were Linda and Troy learning to act with internal ideas rather than as a response to stimulus to external materials in the playground?

Vygotsky (1978) argues that "make believe play" provides important preparation for cooperation and participation in social life. Using Vygotsky's theories, I concluded that Linda and Troy were playing collaboratively, sharing ideas, demonstrating that they could listen to each other and create a storyline together. Linda and Troy were able to confidently develop roles for themselves through engaging with each other and engaging with the social world through popular culture. This event also provided me with an insight into Linda's numeracy skills, as she counted backward from 5 to zero.

Guided by my imaginings about what a rights-based observational documentation would seem like in practice, I wrote my interpretive conclusions in the afternoon and exchanged what I had written with Linda and Troy. I began:

The Author: The question I'm really interested in Linda is why you were the boy and Troy was the girl.

Linda: Well Troy wanted me to be Sharkboy but I didn't want to because I just wanted to be Lavagirl but he just made me.

Until this moment, I was quite confident that I was adept at using multiple theories to unpack recorded observations of children's play behaviors, and that this provided a complete understanding of what was happening. I understood Linda as having developed language skills and social skills that enabled her to negotiate with Troy around the character and role she wanted to play. They played out this storyline for at least 40 minutes and seemed to be enjoying the game. I failed to recognize that children are also political and strategic. Linda's statement created ruptures in my understanding of what was happening in that moment and raised questions about other observations and assessments I had made in the past. It sparked further questions. Did Linda accept the role of boy and give up her desire to be Lavagirl because she wanted to play with Troy? If she had refused to be Sharkboy, would Troy have then not wanted to play? Has Linda learned that she has to give up particular ideas or storylines to be part of the group or a game? How does my observation skim the surface of what is happening? What were the power relationships and the political and strategic negotiations that where taking place under the surface between Troy and Linda? And, most importantly, if I had not gone back and talked to Linda, would I have ever seen the other possible reasons for the roles and story that Linda and Troy engaged in?

Feminist poststructuralist theorists such as Davies (1993) and MacNaughton (2003) argue that identity is multiple, contradictory, shifting, and dynamic. Feminist poststructuralist theorists position the child as an active agent forming her own identity that is experienced, explored, and practiced through social categories of gender, class, race, culture, and ability. Performing identities is influenced and effected by desire, inclusion, and acceptance within the social context (Davis, 1993; Hughes & MacNaughton, 2001). For example, Troy will play "fighting games"—shooting and "killing" baddies to gain entry with a group of boys in the classroom, but when I enter the space he will stop the game and change his play when he sees me. (I often redirected children's "fighting games," marking them as inappropriate and action that hurts people.) Troy strategically moves between and within play and relationships so that he has approval and acceptance from the different people he encounters in the classroom.

At this stage my mind was spinning, and my heartbeat accelerated. I then went back to Troy to have a further conversation with him. I read the observation to Troy and then said:

> The Author: I'm really interested in why you were the girl and Linda was the boy.
> Troy: Because I wanted to be Lavagirl.
> The Author: Why did you want to be Lavagirl?
> Troy: Because I like her.
> The Author: Why do you like her?
> Troy: Because she has fire.

My confusion became compounded, not just because their meanings were different than mine, but because I felt less developed, less skilled, and less knowledgeable about Linda and Troy's worlds and the meanings they attached to the story. I felt compelled to go back and learn about Lavagirl and Sharkboy. I had to know what "special" powers each of these characters had, and I believed that would enable me to add another interpretation to Linda and Troy's play behavior. Was having fire and lava and being able to burn baddies more powerful and desirable than merely eating baddies?

Looking back, I realize that even as I used multiple theoretical lenses, I was searching for an answer or a truth about who each child was. Valerie Walkerdine (1990) describes the gaze of the teacher to know each individual child as "an impossible fiction" (p. 22). In my undergraduate training I had been taught that observation was a way of understanding the whole child. I believed that if I just undertook enough observations or found the right observation and assessment template or technique, I would "see" and "understand" who the child was. Walkerdine's words and my experience with Linda and Troy illustrated for me that my gaze is subjective and partial and that my observations and assessment will provide some insight into what is happening for a child, although I can never know everything. When I invite other interpretations of an observation (e.g., children's perspectives), I can begin to develop multiple understandings of the child, as discussed by Deleuze and Guattari (1987).

My copy of Gunilla Dahlberg, Peter Moss, and Alan Pence's book *Beyond Quality in Early Childhood Education and Care* (1999) is dog-eared and worn from use, yet I had forgotten their words of caution about adults (early childhood educators like me) imposing our knowledge on children, as such imposition can diminish children's ways of knowing and being:

> This is part of a wider ethical project of establishing a culture where the children are seen as human beings in their own right, as worth listening to, where we do not impose our own knowledge and categorizations before children have posed their questions and made their own hypotheses. (Dahlberg, Moss, & Pence, 1999, p. 137)

My new line of flight for a rights-based approach to observation and assessment in the everyday classroom

Thus, going back and having conversations with Linda and Troy created ruptures in how I see and assess children and the part that they play in this. These ruptures highlighted to me the complexity, multiplicity, contradictory, contingent, and shifting ways that children learn, develop, and relearn. Most of all, they change how they understand themselves, the world, and others. I knew that my principle of multiplicity examined the complexity of how a person speaks and acts and, further, how the listener hears and sees these words and performance. Moreover, in this case multiplicity to me was not about quantity, just an increase in the number of observations. I was aware that multiplicity challenged notions of universal truths and questions, and the possibility of measuring or gauging any event.

Yet this episode only reinforced my lack of knowledge, development, and skills in including children's analysis of their learning and development, which I had earlier believed was attainable. I again reinforced my learning about multiplicity.

> A multiplicity has neither subject nor object, only determinations, magnitudes, and dimensions that cannot increase in number without the multiplicity changing in nature. (Deleuze & Guattari, 1987, p. 8)

I still struggle to make meaning of my ruptures related to the above narratives and retold narratives. The observation in this chapter—the changing nature of the analysis, the children's and my perspectives—is that very multiplicity, which is neither unitary nor universal. New text (in this case children's text) created a break or rupture to illuminate my questions and complexities within the text and created new "lines of flight" (Alvermann, 2000; Davis, MacNaughton, & Smith, 2009; Deleuze & Guattari, 1987). Remapping my analysis alone would not create the same ruptures. It would create interpretations from an adult perspective and silence children's knowledge and experience.

This event changed my classroom observation and assessment practices. I now ask the children if I can observe their play. I explain to them why I want to observe the event or activity and what I will do with the information. I read back to the children what I have written about them and ask their views and ideas about how they understood the event or activity and then record their views (analysis) of the observation. I ask permission from the child to copy the document and place it in the child's journal or portfolio. As I write this, I can hear the questions and concerns that have been raised by other educators with me, which as a reader you may be thinking or screaming as you read my thoughts.

- If you always ask children permission to undertake an observation, then you will disrupt children's play.

- Children will change their behavior if they know you are watching them.

- What if children always say no? You have to have observations on each child as a regulatory requirement.

- Children are too young to analyze their own learning.

- You are placing too much pressure on young children. They just want to play.

I am unable to reconcile myself with reverting to practices that to me seemed to silence children's views and their interpretations of their play. This may be a result of all the literature, paradigms, and knowledge that stem from a rights-based approach, which I am attached to. While I don't claim to have all the answers to these questions and concerns, my thinking and discussions with my colleagues at this moment are these:

- I believe it's OK to disrupt play if you ask permission before and after the event and consciously negotiate this with children. Ask them what they would prefer that you do and decide the best strategies *with* the children rather than deciding *for* the children.

- Yes, children and adults do change their behavior when they are being watched. In their research, Sheralyn Campbell (2001) and Miriam Guigni (2003) discuss "secret children's business," where children change their discussion and/or behaviors when a teacher comes into their space. Campbell (2001) and Guigni (2003) argue that children are strategic and political and are able to move between children's and teachers' discourses to gain entry and approval.

- There are times when I need to observe a child because I am concerned about the child's development or safety, or in connection with a report for activities such as funding applications for assistance. In these instances I talk with the children to let them know why and what's happening, and the purpose of my discussion and the observation and assessment that follow. I believe children have a right to provision and protection as well as participation.

- I believe that young children can be social actors and competent meaning makers. The children are also developing, and by engaging with these activities, the children's capacity to claim their rights and their views is being given its due.

- I believe young children have the capacity to say no when they don't want to participate, and I have experienced this. Further, including children's views in observation and analysis is not about chasing children around the classroom the whole day. I would argue that we don't or shouldn't spend every moment in the classroom observing and assessing children.

I Have No Conclusion but a Continuing Journey

I remind myself how Nicholas Rose (1989) cautions us that children today are being observed more than at any other time, and it is important that we consider how their participatory rights are enacted in this process. In Australia we now have a national framework—Belonging, Being and Becoming (Commonwealth of Australia, 2009)—that places children's rights in the foreground. Our challenge is not to let this document gather dust, but to use it as a tool to support early childhood educators in advocating and implementing children's rights in the everyday classroom. I stress again that what I have shared here is not meant to provide a recipe but to ~~stimulate reflection, action, and advoca~~cy. Through my experiences and contemplations with Linda and Troy, I felt that children provided important insights into what was happening in their world, and that this shifted and changed the ways in which I saw and assessed them. But this is not the end of my journey. It is instead a "new line of flight." I am still grappling with the following questions about a rights-based approach to observation and assessment:

- How can I explore what participation in observation might look like in practice with children under 2 years of age?

- How can I explore cultural understandings of participation when verbalizing ideas and views may not be appropriate?

- How might I engage with parents to shift my thinking further?

- How can I explore what observation and assessment will look like for linguistically diverse children?

- How can I explore what observation and assessment will look like for children with diverse abilities?

- How can I respect and recognize how children's non-participation can be an act of resistance and silence as a form of participation?

These questions are constantly in the foreground of my reflections, so I am vigilant in recognizing how my attempts to enact rights will privilege some children and silence others. This drives me to develop rights-based approaches to observation and assessment (and early childhood education in general) *with* children rather than making decisions *about* children.

References

Alderson, P. (2008). Children as researchers: Participation rights and research methods. In P. Christensen & A. James (Eds.), *Research with children: Perspectives and practices* (pp. 276–290). London and New York: Falmer Press.

Alvermann, D. (2000). Researching libraries, literacies and lives: A rhizanalysis. In E. St Pierre & W. Pillow (Eds.), *Working the ruins: Feminist poststructuralist theory and methods in education* (pp. 114–129). London: Routledge.

Campbell, S. (2001). The definition and description of a social justice disposition in young children. Unpublished doctoral dissertation, The University of Melbourne, Melbourne, Australia.

Cannella, G. (1997). *Deconstructing early childhood education: Social justice & revolution*. New York: Peter Lang.

Carr, M. (2001). *Assessment in early childhood settings: Learning stories*. London: Paul Chapman.

Clark, A., & Moss, P. (2001). *Listening to young children: The mosaic approach*. London: National Children's Bureau.

Commonwealth of Australia. (2009). *Belonging, being & becoming: The early years learning framework for Australia*. Barton, ACT: Commonwealth of Australia.

Dahlberg, G., Moss, P., & Pence, A. (1999). *Beyond quality in early childhood education and care*. London: Falmer Press.

Davies, B. (1993). *Shards of glass: Children reading and writing beyond gendered identities*. North Sydney, NSW: Allen & Unwin.

Davis, K., MacNaughton, G., & Smith, K. (2009). The dynamics of whiteness: Children locating within/without. In G.M. MacNaughton & K. Davis (Eds.), *Race and early childhood education: An international approach to identity, politics, and pedagogy* (pp. 49–66). London: Palgrave Macmillan.

Deleuze, G., & Guattari, F. (1987). *A thousand plateaus: Capitalism & schizophrenia*. London: Athlone Press.

Diaz Soto, L. (2005). Children make the best theorists. In L. Diaz Soto & B.B. Swadener (Eds.), *Power & voice in research with children* (pp. 9–20). New York: Peter Lang.

Fargas-Malet, M., McSherry, D., Larkin, E., & Robinson, C. (2010). Research with children: Methodological issues and innovative techniques. *Journal of Early Childhood Research, 8*(2), 175–192.

Guigni, M. (2003). *Secret children's business: The black market for identity work*. Unpublished honours thesis, The University of Western Sydney, Sydney, Australia.

hooks, b. (2000). *Feminism is for everybody*. Cambridge, MA: South End Press.

Hughes, P., & MacNaughton, G. (2001). Fractured or manufactured: Gendered identities and culture in the early years. In S. Grieshaber & G. Cannella (Eds.), *Embracing identities in early childhood education* (pp. 114–132). New York: Teachers College Press.

Lundy, L., & McEvoy, L. (2009). Developing outcomes for educational services: A children's rights–based approach. *Effective Education, 1*(1), 43–60.

MacNaughton, G. (2003). *Shaping early childhood, learners, curriculum and context*. Maidenhead, UK: Open University Press.

MacNaughton, G., & Smith, K. (2008). Engaging ethically with young children: Principles and practices for listening and responding with care. In G. MacNaughton, P. Hughes, & K. Smith (Eds.), *Young children as active citizens: Principles, policies and pedagogies*. London: Cambridge Scholars Publishing.

MacNaughton, G., & Smith, K. (2009). Children's rights in early childhood. In M.J. Kehily (Ed.), *An introduction to early childhood studies* (2nd ed.). Maidenhead, UK: Open University Press/McGraw-Hill.

Moss, P., & Petrie, P. (2002). *From children's services to children's spaces: Public policy, children and childhood*. London: Routledge-Falmer.

Perry, B., & Dockett, S. (2011). "How 'bout we have a celebration!" Advice from children on starting school. *European Early Childhood Education Research Journal, 19*(3), 373–386.

Rinaldi, C. (1998). Projected curriculum constructed through documentation—*Progettazione*: An interview with Lella Gandini. In C. Edwards, L. Gandini, & G. Forman (Eds.), *The hundred languages of children, the Reggio Emilia approach—Advanced reflections* (pp. 113–126). London: Ablex.

Rose, N. (1989). *Governing the soul*. New York: Free Association Books.

Smith, K. (2003). *Reconceptualising observation in the early childhood curriculum*. Unpublished doctoral dissertation, The University of Melbourne, Melbourne, Australia.

Su, W., & Di Santo, A. (2011). Preschool children's perceptions of overweight peers. *Journal of Early Childhood Research, 10*(1), 19–31.

United Nations. (1989). *United Nations Convention on the Rights of the Child*. Geneva: United Nations.

United Nations. (2005). United Nations Convention on the Rights of the Child. *General comment No. 7, Implementing child rights in early childhood*. Retrieved August 22, 2006, from http://www.unhchr.ch/tbs/doc.nsf/(Symbol)/CRC.C.GC.7>En?OpenDocument

Vygotsky, L.S. (1978). *Mind in society: The development of higher mental processes.* Cambridge, MA: Harvard University Press.

Walkerdine, V. (1990). *Schoolgirl fictions.* London: Verso.

CHAPTER SIX

"You're Not Listening to Us"

Explicating Children's School Experiences to Build Opportunity for Increased Participation Within School Communities in the United States

Lacey Peters & Lisa Lacy

Introduction

"First, we play, and when the bell rings, we go inside and learn. After you are done doing it, you go to different places like Spanish and music and art." This comment was made by a young student at the beginning phases of her first formal school experience in kindergarten. In the United States, numerous policies and provisions are in place to ensure that children, regardless of their race, ethnicity, gender, abilities, or social status, are afforded equitable opportunities to engage in relevant, quality, and fulfilling educational experiences. In early childhood, for instance, policymakers, educators, and other members of the early childhood community have emphasized the importance of early learning, and initiatives to increase the number of children who enter kindergarten "ready to learn" are becoming more widespread. Policy initiatives such as the National Educational Goals Panel; Good Start, Grow Smart; and Pre-K Now are influential in the effort to promote publicly funded programs for children and families, therefore increasing the accessibility of early educational experiences for young people.

Special education policy also has a dominant influence on the learning experiences of children identified as having delays or disabilities. The Individuals with Disabilities Education Act (IDEA), for example, has governed the education of students with disabilities for more than 3 decades (Shogren, 2011). Moreover, the Least Restrictive Environment Act (LRE) stated that all students, regardless of dis/ability, were to be educated in the general education classroom. Although many educators contest the spirit of the LRE mandate, the majority of students with disabilities are educated in inclusive education settings (Florian, 2007). To this end, children with dis/abilities are often placed with teachers who may not be trained or do not feel competent to meet the educational goals and objectives of students with dis/abilities. As the population of over 6 million students with disabilities continues to rise (U.S. Department of Education, 2007), educators need to examine how instructional practices, which are intricately woven into the educational fabric that determines academic success, benefit individuals with learning disabilities and children with chronic illnesses, not to mention all people participating within the cultures of school.

Moreover, efforts to increase public investment in education have become a driving force in early childhood and elementary education, and, with this in mind, capitalistic and neoliberal politics have a strong influence over the approaches used to structure children's participation in schools. For instance, movements to create continuity between systems of pre-kindergarten and kindergarten have shifted practices in child care and preschool settings. More specifically, where there was once an emphasis on play-based, emergent curriculum, there is now a push for "playful" learning and direct instruction (Hirsh-Pasek, Golinkoff, Berk, & Singer, 2009). Further, school curricula are increasingly grounded in "empirically based" instructional strategies, and performance-based assessments are used to measure students' success in school, emphasizing the acquisition of discreet skills and knowledge over the deeper and more nuanced, less measurable skills that are equally important to a child's schooling. Consequently, the potential for children and youth to contribute to the decision-making processes that have influence over their school careers is minimized.

Regardless of the scope or discipline of the aforementioned policies and trends, an element that connects each to the broader system of education is that family involvement and participation are considered integral components in ensuring that children fully benefit from the decisions made for or about their life experiences in schools. However, as programs place emphasis on the importance of family involvement, adult voices and perspectives typically prevail in the discourses used to set the tone for younger people's school experiences, and the viewpoints of children and youth are commonly undervalued or disregarded—due in part to perceived limitations based on age or dis/ability. Acting in the "best interest of a child," adults make important judgments for, or on behalf of, children with regard to their educational experiences. For example, decisions are made about school placement, curricular or pedagogical preferences for individual learners, effective instructional approaches, and appropriate accommodations or supports provided in classroom and school communities, along with general considerations intended to influence or enhance children's opportunities to fully participate in school-based activities.

As researchers interested in consulting and collaborating with children, we take issue with dominant policies and practices used in the United States to reify or perpetuate children's position as passive or peripheral participants within the systems of schooling, and we use our work to challenge commonly held assumptions about the capacities of children to contribute to the decisions made for and about their educational experiences. More broadly, we call into question the extent to which children comprise or contribute to the "public" arena in the United States, with the intention of building dialogue on the potential for children and youth to engage more actively in their life worlds, particularly in school.

Situating Child Rights–Based Research in the United States

The United States remains one of the only countries with a population of over 1 million that has yet to ratify the United Nations Convention on the Rights of the Child (UNCRC). UNCRC opponents in the United States often raise the concern that an emphasis on children's rights will restrict parental and other adult rights and roles—or threaten power relations between adults and young people. Nonetheless, while children's rights–based movements have yet to gain broad, national support, we use the UNCRC to ground our work and examine how children's rights perspectives can enrich important educational experiences for younger people. Whereas UNCRC consists of 54 articles, each as significant as the next, Articles 12 and 13 are of critical importance to this chapter. Article 12 states:

> States Parties shall assure to the child who is capable of forming his or her own views the right to express those views freely in all matters affecting the child, the views of the child being given due weight in accordance with the age and maturity of the child.

Article 13 declares:

> The child shall have the right to freedom of expression; this right shall include freedom to seek, receive and impart information and ideas of all kinds, regardless of frontiers, either orally, in writing or in print, in the form of art, or through any other media of the child's choice.

Similar to the UNCRC, the Convention on the Rights of Persons with Disabilities (CRPD), adopted by the UN General Assembly on December 13, 2006, outlines provisions for children to participate more inclusively in a variety of social contexts within and across communities. More to the point, the CRPD recognizes that children with dis/abilities can experience more challenging life situations and be excluded or marginalized from social life to a greater extent due to the intersection of dis/ability, age, gender, and other cultural factors. Article

7 of the CRPD specifically outlines rights for children with dis/abilities as they pertain to equality, inclusion, and participation. For instance, a stipulation within Article 7 of the convention states:

> States Parties shall ensure that children with disabilities have the right to express their views freely on all matters affecting them, their views being given due weight in accordance with their age and maturity, on an equal basis with other children, and to be provided with disability and age-appropriate assistance to realize that right.

An attempt to ratify the CRPD was just recently defeated in the United States as members of Congress quashed legislation that would have enacted obligations within the treaty to more fully acknowledge the rights of persons with disabilities. Those who oppose the ratification of the CRPD voice opinions similar to those held by individuals who oppose the ratification of the UNCRC. In an effort to gain insight into the objections to the ratification of both the UNCRC and the CRPD, we turn to literature that examines discourse surrounding the disapproval of the UNCRC specifically. For instance, Smith (2011) states:

> The UNCRC provides an internationally accepted standard of basic human rights for children. It is a document of reconciliation which treats parents and children with respect, and recommends a partnership between parents, children, and the institutions of the state. (p. 12)

While Smith's argument specifically emphasizes the formation of partnerships as encouraged in the UNCRC, we assert that it is more appropriate to scrutinize the mutuality between the people's roles as duty-bearers and rights-bearers when striving to enact stipulations within the UNCRC. More to the point, the perceived changes with regard to cultural practices and routines used to define the adult-child relationships generate a point of contention in the United States. Further, while the act of listening to children may seem like a natural or simple practice, the nature of how younger people are listened to, and the extent to which their perspectives are given "due weight," is inhibited by social barriers and complicated by ethical tensions rooted in dominant perspectives on children and childhoods.

An explanation for the lack of support for children's rights to participation in the United States stems from a lack of consensus on whether children should be afforded rights in general, much less rights other than those considered to be constitutional rights. It is not unusual for children to be perceived as passive participants until they reach an "age of majority." Cheney, in her study carried out in Uganda (2007), uses the concept of children experiencing "deferred citizenship" and being viewed more as the future of a nation and less as the present. Similarly, the rhetoric of children as "citizens of the future" is used in the United States to describe younger people's roles in communities and cultural contexts, when in fact we ought to acknowledge children's full citizenship now.

Walker, Brooks, and Wrightsman (1999) explain that there is a strong tendency for adults in the United States to acknowledge children's rights to protection or nurturance (acting in the "best interest of the child") over younger people's rights to self-determination. While there is a strong belief in the United States that children have rights to protection and provision, an interesting question is raised as to why they are not afforded rights of participation. One justification manifests in an ideological sense in that children are typically perceived to be subjects in society, acting as passive participants within families and communities. Therefore, adult perceptions of children's competence largely define younger people's roles and responsibilities within social contexts of their life worlds. Maria Lahman (2008) reminds us of a prevailing assumption about younger people when she writes, "Childhood as conceived by adults is a word or world fraught with stereotypes and polarization" (p. 282). Adult assumptions about children as inexperienced, less capable, or underdeveloped human beings makes it difficult to bring children's ideas and assumptions to the fore, as well as for them to be taken seriously as they share their perspectives on their own life experiences. In addition, notions of children and childhoods are derived from adults' memories of being children themselves, creating ideological biases (Mandell, 1988) that have influence over the ideas constructed and perpetuated with regard to younger people's abilities to function as contributing members of society. Moreover, developmentalism is prevalent in discourse on human growth and learning. In addition, the influence of "ages and stages" philosophies on children and childhood have reified adult viewpoints on the capacities for young people to contribute to and fully participate in society and culture. In this chapter we argue that children, regardless of their age or ability, are citizens in their own right and therefore should be provided the opportunity to engage with policy, programming, and practice so that they are more informed and engaged members of society. MacNaughton, Hughes, and Smith (2007) underscore this point when they write: "Consulting young children respectfully about the matters that affect them encourages and assists them to develop the knowledge, skills, and confidence they need to become active citizens who can participate actively in public decision making" (p. 465).

The Potential of Giving Children's Views "Due Weight"

Although younger people spend minimal time in school as compared to home and community settings, classroom environments provide spaces for children and youth to engage in social and democratic practices that align with broader cultural and sociological rules and routines. As such, adults hold a formative role in creating openings and opportunities (Shier, 2001) for children to participate in decision-making processes within the context of education. Maxim (2010) asserts that adults can build children's "citizenship awareness" in classrooms by structuring activities that foster participation. Establishing rules with children, adopting authoritative guidance and discipline strategies, and engaging young students in civics activities are all examples of practices employed in democratic learning communities. With this being said, it is also important to point out that movements to bring children's perspectives into the broader political realms of education are fraught with complications and limitations, due in part to the contentious nature of acknowledging children's rights, as previously discussed. Yet, as former teachers and now current researchers, we are coming to realize the various ways in which children can, and do, make significant contributions to the decision-making processes impacting their life worlds. In relation to the kindergarten transition, adults can use children's opinions about acclimating to new school settings to inform the planning of transition experiences and to enrich the activities used to facilitate children's entry into formal school. In fact, researchers the world over have studied younger people's thoughts and opinions on "starting school," with the intention of examining the implications of the decisions adults have made for and about younger people's experiences transitioning into primary or elementary school environments (see, e.g., Brooker, 2002; Dockett & Perry, 2005; Einarsdottir, 2011; Loizou, 2011; Lundy, McEvoy, & Byrne, 2011; Mirkhil, 2010; Peters, 20003; Peters, 2012; Yeo & Clarke, 2005). These studies highlight the critical nature of building shared understandings (Rogoff, 2003) between children and adults by revealing the power younger and older people can utilize through the exchange of ideas and assumptions about cultures of schooling.

Within the context of special education, children with dis/abilities are often viewed through a deficit lens, perceived through a binary of *competent or disabled* (Collins, 2003). A social-cultural approach to dis/ability lends itself to "the interactional relationship between people and their institutional environment" (Artiles, 1998, p. 34). In other words, it is through a social-cultural, symbolically mediated environment that the form of dis/ability takes shape. Students with disabilities are often viewed as "different or deficient" within the social context of schools. With this in mind, we ask the question: In an environment in which a child's abilities should be considered first and foremost, how are children with dis/abilities given space for self-determination in a system that has categorized them as a certain "type" of either/or student?

It is also important to consider the roles and responsibilities of those who become older allies (e.g., adolescents or adults) of children identified as being less than able to participate because of physical, mental, or behavioral disabilities, or have been diagnosed with a chronic illness. In accordance with dis/abilities literature that has emphasized voice, self-determination, and empowerment for decades (Baglieri, Valle, Connor, & Gallagher, 2011), we contribute to the ongoing conversations taking place that examine the benefits of creating classroom communities where students can become collaborators in their own educational experiences.

Overview of the Chapter

In this chapter we elaborate on our experiences working with children, outlining the procedures used to support our work collaborating and consulting with younger people. Specifically, we discuss findings from our research that reflect children's perspectives engaging in formal education, as both new participants within school settings as well as participants commonly described as having "special needs" within classroom environments. With this information, we hope to instill a better understanding of how children's perspectives can be integrated into adult-oriented discourse on education. Further, considering that the United States has yet to ratify the UNCRC, we use this opportunity to garner broader support for children's rights and participation, exploring the potentials and possibilities that manifest when acknowledging that children's rights matter.

Giving Deeper Meaning to Children's Perspectives

Our work is informed by a number of ideas nested within children and childhood studies (see Prout & James, 1997; Qvortrup, 1987; Walkerdine, 1993). We also draw from disabilities studies to frame the work that draws out children's viewpoints on living with, or being identified as having, a delay or disability. Tisdall (2012) intersects childhood studies and disability studies in order to underscore bodies of knowledge that seek to demarginalize children and people with disabilities. Tisdall writes:

> Like children versus adults, disabled people have been positioned theoretically as being non-able bodied, with the comparison continuously against a mythical gold standard of "normal"—failing to recognise, for example, that most people have impairments at some point in their lives and capacities vary widely. People with learning difficulties have experienced exclusion, as have children, because they are deemed insufficient within the educational system, protectively or paternalistically placed in segregated or "integrated" schools. (p. 183)

Scholar activists working to promote younger people's agency not only highlight the potentials of children's participation within the social context of education, but also contribute to the efforts being made to challenge ideas that normalize children and people with disabilities. In the United States, there is an increasing number of research and civic engagement projects carried out at a micro-level, or within localized contexts, to promote agency among children and youth groups. For example, Hall and Rudkin (2011) collaborated with children in an early childhood setting as a means to ensure that preschoolers were provided opportunities to make decisions in the classroom on a daily basis. Referring to children as "community protagonists," the authors describe ways in which adults can embed routines grounded in children's rights in daily activities that establish "supportive social learning environments" for young people. It is important to point out the roles adults take on as duty-bearers, allies, partners, or liaisons within the children's rights movement. Hall and Rudkin write: "Adults committed to nurturing children as community protagonists help children exercise their rights and assume responsibilities to the greatest extent possible. They also ensure that what is possible, continually expands" (2011, p. 58).

People with disabilities are also spearheading initiatives to promote the rights of individuals living with diagnoses or labels that often overshadow their abilities and personhood (Anastasiou & Kauffman, 2011). For instance, Kids as Self Advocates, a youth-organized group in the United States, works to educate and spread positive information to people their own age to challenge commonly held assumptions about people with disabilities. In addition, a primary mission of the group is to establish connections with adults and to consult with them so that health care professionals, policymakers, and other community members have more nuanced (and possibly more accurate) understandings of what it is like to live with a disability. Whereas children with dis/abilities are often seen through a deficit lens, initiatives such as these challenge adults to act as stronger advocates, allies, partners, or interlocutors.

As such, this work informs our efforts to broaden the scope of children's participation and expand the opportunities for younger people to contribute to decision-making processes that transpire throughout their school experiences. In addition, we look to sociocultural theories and use ideas within this framework as tools for building dialogue with children. Moreover, particular concepts are instrumental in realizing the potentials associated with affording younger people's perspectives "due weight," subsequently positioning children as more active participants in school and community contexts. An example is promoting guided participation (Rogoff, 2003) wherein children are considered to be active—rather than peripheral—participants in the routines that guide their educational experiences. We argue that attempts to provide young people with a chance to contribute, directly or inadvertently, to the decision-making processes that guide their life worlds will enrich their educational experiences and increase their agency in society.

Discovering Pathways to Participating in Children's Rights–Based Research

In the following sections we present perspectives of younger people situated along different spaces within the educational milieu in the United States to seek out possibilities that emerge when adults conscientiously take children's perspectives into consideration. Lacey draws from her research on the transition to kindergarten to foreground the voices of kindergarten-age children participating in new routines that comprise practices centered on "doing school" throughout younger people's first years in primary education. Lisa, a veteran teacher and now a researcher, reflects on how she used children's rights–based approaches in her classroom to act as an ally for children identified as having delays or disabilities. Lisa is currently interviewing some of her former students, now aged 9–12 years—all of whom are identified as having a delay, disability, or chronic illness—about their experiences living with a label or diagnosis.

We blend our perspectives and experiences to bring attention to the various ways that adult-oriented decisions impact children's experiences in school. While Lacey's research focuses on children's first formal school experiences, and Lisa's emphasizes children's day-to-day experiences in the system of special education, a common thread within our work is the fact that people experience significant transitions at many points throughout their time in school, whether they happen once in a lifetime, represent a significant milestone, or occur on a daily basis. For instance, the start of kindergarten symbolizes an important milestone for many children in the United States, and many think of the entry into formal school as a "rite of passage," one that grants children greater independence and autonomy within the system of education. Children with cognitive or emotional disabilities or chronic illness not only often face challenging situations that affect their daily lives but also often struggle to establish identity, as they have to constantly negotiate trying to fit into a "normal" school identity with their peers.

Gaining Access to Children's Perspectives

The processes we employed to elicit children's perspectives teach us about the challenges that child rights advocates face when promoting the message that children's voices matter. Lacey worked in collaboration with a team of researchers to plan and implement a large-scale qualitative project consisting of child interviews with the intent of answering the question "What is it like being four, turning five, in Arizona?" As one might imagine, the conversations with children during these interviews covered a wide range of subjects: topics relating to family, their favorite things, going to the doctor, community-based activities, and school or early learning. While the data set from the larger study provides a wealth of information on younger people's experiences of being children, Lacey focused her independent research on analyzing children's viewpoints derived from their engagement with routines associated with becoming a "kindergartner." Lacey relied primarily on written transcripts to gain insight into children's perspectives on going to kindergarten but also used audio recordings of the interviews to listen more closely to what children had to say. With this in mind, and knowing that children communicate in "a hundred different languages" (Edwards, Gandini, & Foreman, 1998), Lacey struggled to resolve ethical tensions that emerged as she realized she was missing essential components of children's expressions and utterances about their lives. As an example, while steps were taken to ensure that children were provided opportunities to consult and collaborate with adult researchers, their direct participation ended at the planning and implementation phases of the large-scale interview project. Procedures to ensure validity with children serving as collaborators, such as "member-checking" (Lincoln & Guba, 1985), were not carried out, and therefore the thick, descriptive accounts of the participants' life experiences are mediated in large part by Lacey's views on children and childhoods, rather than being examples of children's "unmediated perspectives" (Swadener & Polakow, 2011). This is not to discount children's perspectives or the analysis of children's perspectives; rather, it reveals an opportunity to collaborate to a greater extent with children as co-researchers.

Moving forward and building on this project, Lisa is engaging in preliminary research that will draw out the "life worlds" of children participating in the system of special education. One of her primary goals is to better understand the impact people's assumptions about children identified as having delays and disabilities has on younger people's sense of self. As Lisa continues to engage with this research, she is realizing the ways in which she utilized a children's rights–based approach in her instructional practice as a special educator. More specifically, working with elementary-age students in a cross-categorical, pullout classroom, Lisa witnessed firsthand how hard it can be to listen to students and afford their concerns "due weight." Students would visit her for a specific amount of time according to their IEP goals and objectives. Although academic learning was emphasized, Lisa also created a space responsive to her students' individual social-emotional needs. She wanted not only to honor her students' words but also to instill a sense of self-advocacy within the peer culture of her classroom. The insight she provides showcases the ways in which she interacted in a complex system wherein she navigated the roles of child and family advocate and district employee, struggling to find her own sense of agency and autonomy required to fully acknowledge children's rights and voices. In turn, her experiences as a teacher are used to give deeper meaning to children's responses to questions she posed during her interviews with two children. The emergent themes from her research also indicate that children are afforded little opportunity to express their views on their future lives, which in turn implicates a common misnomer about children's capacities to think outside of the "here and now."

With this said, we now turn our attention to the voices of children. As we explicate their viewpoints, we consider dominant themes that emerged in our conversations, those that center on matters relating to participation, agency, and identity. It is important to acknowledge that while a purpose of this chapter is to foreground the voices of children, we recognize there are varieties of children and childhood that comprise society. The voices of younger people in this chapter are not meant to represent a single group of children but are used instead to provide a window onto the different ways children can, and do, think and talk about their life experiences.

Viewing Children's Life Worlds through Participation, Agency, and Identity

Structuring Participation

Children coming into school environments and those who participate in any classroom community must learn to follow a set of predetermined rules and routines usually established by adults and influenced by the larger systems of education. In many schools in the United States, kindergarten classrooms are described as being more structured learning environments that require children to exhibit skills that showcase independence and self-control. More specifically, teachers and other adults structure children's participation in schools by highly routinizing and regimenting daily activities, thus creating more standardized learning environments. As such, children's conversations about school are largely focused on "work" as well as the guidance and discipline strategies used to ensure that adults and children alike maximize instructional time. When asked to describe kindergarten, a child explained, "I don't really know, but you play—that's all you do, and you do homework, and you go to review centers and you do lots of work. You've got to do your words." In a different interview, another child brings our attention to "work": "First in the morning, in the a.m. class, I always do work, lots of work, and then we go out for recess." In addition, when asked to describe his teacher, a child emphasized work, stating: "When I'm not working [my teacher] tells me to get to work."

For students identified as having a dis/ability, classrooms can consist of multiple environments, meaning children must build multiple understandings of the rules and routines embedded within each of the spaces. For instance, some students receive their education in the general education classroom, while others with disabilities may spend a portion or half of their school day in a special education classroom. With regard to Lisa's experience as an elementary special education teacher, students needing "pullout" services visited her classroom to receive academic, emotional, and social support. Throughout her tenure, Lisa developed strong relationships with many of her students and as a result found herself marginalized along with the young people she taught. Later in this chapter, Lisa recounts a situation wherein she problematizes an interaction that took place in a classroom between an individual she worked with and a general education teacher.

Children's Agency in Classroom Contexts

The effects of accountability-based movements in the system of elementary education have trickled into early childhood settings, reconfiguring the practices used to facilitate children's first school experiences and ultimately impacting children's agency and autonomy in classrooms. Children participating in the system of special education are impacted by the demands of accountability and education reform in a similar manner.

One of the students Lisa spoke with is a person living with the chronic disease of sickle cell anemia. As we bring forward this child's views on his "life world," Lisa explains her interpretations of his daily interactions with a general education teacher, the power dynamics that facilitated those interactions, and her role in advocating for the rights and perspectives of the student.

Carl's illness kept him out of school for extended periods of time, making his teacher suspect when he complained about not feeling well in school. His former teacher assumed that he was faking, wanting to go home or even worse, come into my room, a place that he considers safe. I can remember one occasion where Carl's teacher, feeling frustrated at his classroom behavior, announced to the classroom, "Carl you are not going to Ms. Lacy's room, you are faking that you don't understand the assignment."

This reflection exemplifies an ongoing struggle Lisa and Carl faced when interacting with Carl's general education teacher. While Lisa promoted a classroom community that honored children's self-advocacy and agency, in this instance she had to teach Carl that staying quiet and dismissing his teacher's mistrust would be the best response to her interpretation of his illness. Whereas his teacher might have intended to redirect Carl differently, we posit that this response is indicative of the complexities of the teaching profession in terms of working in a system of accountability, but also reveals how working within such a system limits the opportunities teachers can maximize in acknowledging younger people's points of view. Carl's classroom experience with his teacher shows how students' voices are often marginalized and silenced on a routine basis.

Carl's experience is not unique. Lacey also noticed that the kindergarten children she interviewed would make references to the dynamics of their classroom community and the hierarchies established that consequently position children at the periphery. The following excerpt provides some insight into children's understanding of the predisposition for teachers or adults to be the primary authority in classrooms:

Interviewer: What else do you like to do?

Dakota: Paint, draw, and paint. Well painting is mostly something that I mostly don't do much at school.

Interviewer: Why do you think that is?

Dakota: I don't know. Well, it's just what my teachers think.

Through the analysis of children's conversations about guidance and discipline strategies used in classrooms, Lacey critically examined the child participants' allusions to the power relations influential in shaping children's participation in schools. In addition, she raised concerns about the tendency for children to form, or perpetuate, exaggerated interpretations or reproductions about the consequences they face after it has been determined that they have misbehaved in class. Children interviewed described real and imagined spaces in schools they (or their peers) visit when they get into trouble. Specifically, students mentioned going to the principal's office, the "naughty nose wall," and "jail." Some children elaborated on the situations that play out in the principal's office. One child participant said, "You go to the principal's when you have no colors and then the principal calls the policeman and then you go to jail." This boy went on to explain, "The policeman says you stay in jail for like a thousand days." Another child provided the following description:

> They go to the principal and she sends your mom, and then you get a note and then she said, "you spit on the person, and you pushed the person, and you hit the person, and you didn't take a nap, and you did everything bad."

We use Corsaro's (2005) notion of childhood symbolic culture to call into question the stories children create, or reproduce, about the routines used in classrooms for disciplinary purposes. Corsaro (2005) argues that "children quickly appropriate, use, and transform symbolic culture as they produce and participate in peer culture" (p. 116). We argue that adults capitalize on children's imagined stories about the consequences they could experience, and instead of interrupting children's thoughts about discipline (such as going to jail), adults use these ideas to maintain power and control.

Exploring Identities

The process of "doing school," whether as a kindergartner or a seasoned student, is comprised of set routines that influence the formation of children's identities. Wenger (1998) describes the formation of identity as an embedded aspect of participation grounded in learning, membership, and belonging. In many cases, children's roles and membership within educational contexts are established even prior to their interactions with teachers, peers, and other members of school communities.

Identity transformation for children in schools takes shape in many ways. During the interviews Lisa conducted, she asked the question, "What do you wish for?" Lisa described the response the interview participant provided. She writes:

> She paused for a moment and brushed her hair out of her face, and gave me what appeared to be a nervous smile and said, "my own bedroom." She continued, "When I get home I have to put my books away and help my mom with the new baby, and make

sure my little brother is staying out of my mom's way. I don't always have time to do my homework, my teacher gets mad." These words came out slowly between heavy sighs, one after the other. Slowly. She looked around the room as if to make sure no one was listening to her reveal a family secret. She hung her head down and whispered, "Can I do my homework with you before school, so I don't get in trouble anymore? I don't want trouble. I want my teacher to like me."

Lisa then provided a narrative account of Carl's response to the question "What do you wish for?" She writes:

> Carl took a deep swallow and looked at me, and said, "What did you say?" I repeated the question. We both sat in the stillness of the room. I waited patiently for Carl to speak, observing his body movements. He moved his eyes up and down looking sideways, wiggled his fingers, and adjusted his body to a slouched position in his chair. I waited. He looked at me and opened his mouth ever so slowly, and said, "Ms. Johnson, no one has asked me that before." I thought those were powerful words. As we both sat there, I wondered if we, as educators, ask open-ended personal questions to children often enough. Later Carl responded to that question by me stating, "I don't know." I continued, "Do you want to add anything else?" Carl laughed, "No."

Carl's use of the phrase "I don't know" is representative of another interesting phenomenon that emerges in interviews with children: the prevalence of the phrase "I don't know." When analyzing the interviews conducted with pre-kindergarten- and kindergarten-age children, Lacey noticed the repetition of this phrase across the transcripts. The following excerpt is an example.

> *Interviewer*: Can you tell me a little bit more about what you think kindergarten will be like next year? You said your sister tells you stuff, right? What does your sister say about kindergarten? Does she like kindergarten? Did she have fun at kindergarten?
>
> *Kendall*: Yes.
>
> *Interviewer*: Oh. Are you scared? No? That's good. Are you excited for kindergarten?
>
> *Kendall*: Uh huh.
>
> *Interviewer*: Have you been to visit your kindergarten?
>
> *Kendall*: No.
>
> *Interviewer*: Are you going to? Do you know about kindergarten?
>
> *Kendall*: No....
>
> *Interviewer*: Oh, you don't think so? Well, you never know, maybe kindergarten will be just as fun and they'll have new games. What do you think you'll learn at school?
>
> *Kendall*: I don't know.
>
> *Interviewer*: What do you think kindergarten will be like?
>
> *Kendall*: I don't know.

We call attention to this excerpt because it is representative of a type of ambiguity embedded within children's responses to interview questions and their reactions to being in interview situations, and may also signify the root of a deeper issue concerning their participation in research, as Carl alluded to—adults don't typically ask children these types of questions. In her analysis, Lacey unpacked several explanations for why children tended to say "I don't know" repeatedly during an interview. Oftentimes the children said "I don't know" to indicate they were bored, uninterested, or unwilling to participate wholly in the conversation with the adult researcher. "I don't know" was also used as a means to communicate feelings of uncertainty or discomfort when talking about kindergarten. Children also used the phrase because they seemingly did not know, point-blank, what would happen in kindergarten, or were not sure how to respond to the interviewer's prompts. It is at this point that Lacey began to wonder about the different ways adults were structuring children's participation in transition activities. Rogoff (2003) asserts: "Structuring occurs through choice of which activities children have access to observe and engage in, as well as through in-person shared endeavors, including conversations, recounting of narratives, and engagement in routines and play" (p. 287). More to the point, Lacey began to question whether children had an awareness that they were engaging in transition activities, or activities intended to promote "readiness" for kindergarten. At present, the questions are left unanswered, but this line of inquiry leads to many more curiosities. When are adults listening to children? How are adults listening to children? In what contexts are adults listening to children? Finally, what would the transition to kindergarten look like if children's voices mattered?

In a similar vein, Lisa also came to realize that her conversations with children in her classroom typically centered on routine topics such as "What do you want to be when you grow up?" or "What kinds of activities do you like to do at home?"—questions that seem important but in retrospect are shallow and nonrevealing of the inner voice of students. When Lisa asked Carl a deeper question that allowed him to probe ("What do you wish for?"), he had trouble answering the question, saying that he had never been asked that question before. With this in mind, we surmise that in order for children's voices to be heard, and for those voices to create impact within their learning environments, deeper questions must be asked that afford children the opportunity to examine their own identities and voices in situated environments such as school.

When closely examined, the excerpts from our interviews allude to the tendency for children's views to become masked, or submerged, through the daily rituals of school and home. Further, as we scrutinize the information provided by children and "listen" to their voices, many more questions remain with regard to bringing forth children's rights–based research in the United States. We can't help but wonder how the dynamics of classroom or learning communities might be different if children's rights mattered. We ponder the different ways children's perspectives can "authentically" contribute to the ongoing discourses of education and education reform. In some ways we use the metaphor of a cauldron waiting to boil over to describe the importance of providing younger people with the time and space to serve as "community protagonists," co-researchers, collaborators, or consultants with adults. So many of children's thoughts are internalized as they muddle through the realities of being a younger human being in school, yet we believe that, given the opportunity, they will reveal their most salient ideas, opinions, and viewpoints. In closing, we explore the benefits, as we see them, of building continuous dialogue with children about their life worlds, particularly in relation to their perceptions of the adult-oriented rules and routines established in school settings.

Potentials and Possibilities

One of the most important things we are learning in conducting research with children is the fact that children's voices, and the things that concern or trouble them, are as diverse as children themselves. And while we recognize that there is not one type of child or childhood, the collective stories of how younger people view themselves as learners and people can offer valuable insights for educators and policymakers. More specifically, younger people's interpretations of their membership and participation in school communities can better inform educational policymakers as to what types of school curriculum matter most to children.

As "pupil voice" gains currency with researchers (Lundy, 2007), children's rights advocates in the United States need to make a case for the inherent value of children's perspectives. To quote Swadener (2008): "When attempting to understand and advocate for children in a context of social and global justice, material and social circumstances must be understood in the context of concrete daily realities, across various environments" (p. 51). We are taking important steps toward expanding the scholarship that conveys the power in acknowledging children's rights to participation by recognizing the need to promote the personhood and agency of our youngest citizens, including children identified as having a dis/ability or chronic illness. At the same time, we recognize that there is much work to be done with regard to establishing children's rights–based research as an obligatory approach (Shier, 2001) to consulting and collaborating with young children. Considering that adults project their "aged" interpretations of school experiences on young learners, we call for a reconceptualization of children's early experiences in school, or within the system of special education, particularly one that is duly reflective of younger people's viewpoints on acclimating to, and participating in, classroom communities. With this being said, we contend that adults could better respond to the needs of young people if more conversations ensued *with* children about their participation in classrooms and/or school routines.

References

Anastasiou, D., & Kauffman, J.M. (2011). A social constructionist approach to disability: Implications for special education. *Council for Exceptional Children, 77*(3), 367–384.

Artiles, A. (1998). The dilemma of difference: Enriching the disproportionality discourse with theory and context. *The Journal of Special Education, 32,* 32–36.

Baglieri, S., Valle, J.W., Connor, D.J., & Gallagher, D.J. (2011). Disability studies in education: The need for a plurality of perspectives on disability. *Remedial and Special Education, 32*(4), 267–278.

Brooker, L. (2002). *Starting school: Young children learning cultures.* Buckingham, UK: Open University Press.

Cheney, K. (2007). *Pillars of the nation: Child citizens and Ugandan national development.* Chicago: University of Chicago Press.

Collins, K.M. (2003). *Ability profiling and school failure: One child's struggle to be seen as competent.* Mahwah, NJ: Lawrence Erlbaum.

Corsaro, W.A. (2005). *The sociology of childhood* (2nd ed.). Thousand Oaks, CA: Sage.

Dockett, S., & Perry, B. (2005). "You need to know how to play safe": Children's experiences of starting school. *Contemporary Issues in Early Childhood, 6*(1), 4–18.

Edwards, C., Gandini, L., & Foreman, G. (Eds.). (1998). *The hundred languages of children: The Reggio Emilia approach—Advanced reflections.* Greenwich, CT: Ablex.

Einarsdottir, J. (2011). Icelandic children's early education transition experiences. *Early Education and Development, 22*(5), 739–756.

Florian, L. (2007). Reimagining special education. In Dr. L. Florian (Ed.), *The Sage Handbook of Special Education* (pp. 1-20). Thousand Oaks, CA: SAGE.

Hall, E.L., & Rudkin, J.K. (2011). *Seen & heard: Children's rights in early childhood education.* New York: Teachers College Press.

Hirsh-Pasek, K., Golinkoff, R.M., Berk, L.E., & Singer, D.G. (2009). *A mandate for playful learning in preschool: Presenting the evidence.* New York: Oxford University Press.

Lahman, L. (2008). Always othered: Ethical research with children. *Journal of Early Childhood Research, 6*(3), 281–300.

Lincoln, Y., & Guba, E. (1985). *Naturalistic inquiry.* Beverly Hills, CA: Sage.

Loizou, E. (2011). Empowering aspects of transition from kindergarten to first grade through children's voices. *Early Years, 31*(1), 43–55.

Lundy, L. (2007). "Voice" is not enough: Conceptualising Article 12 of the United Nations Convention on the Rights of the Child. *British Educational Research Journal, 33*(6), 927–942.

Lundy, L., McEvoy, L., & Byrne, B. (2011). Working with young children as co-researchers: An approach informed by the United Nations Convention on the Rights of the Child. *Early Education and Development, 22*(5), 714–736.

MacNaughton, G., Hughes, P., & Smith, K. (2007). Young children's rights and public policy: Practices and possibilities for citizenship in the early years. *Children & Society, 21*(6), 458–469.

Mandell, N. (1988). The least adult role in studying children. *Journal of Contemporary Ethnography, 16*(4), 433–467.

Maxim, G.W. (2010). *Dynamic social studies for constructivist classrooms.* Boston: Pearson.

Mirkhil, M. (2010). "I want to play when I go to school": Children's views on the transition to school from kindergarten. *Australasian Journal of Early Childhood, 35*(3), 134–139.

Peters, L. (2012). *"When the bell rings we go inside and learn": Children's and parents' understandings of the kindergarten transition.* Unpublished doctoral dissertation, Arizona State University, Tempe.

Peters, S. (2003). "I didn't expect that I would get tons of friends…more each day": Children's experiences of friendship during the transition to school. *Early Years, 23*(1), 45–53.

Prout, A., & James, A. (Eds.). (1997). *Constructing and reconstructing childhood: Contemporary issues in the sociological study of childhood.* New York: Routledge.

Qvortrup, J. (1987). Introduction: The sociology of childhood. *International Journal of Sociology, 17*(3), 3–37.

Rogoff, B. (2003). *The cultural nature of human development.* New York: Oxford University Press.

Shier, H. (2001). Pathways to participation: Openings, opportunities and obligations. *Children and Society, 15,* 107–111.

Shogren, K. A. (2011). Culture and self-determination: A synthesis of the literature and directions for future research and practice. *Career development for exceptional individuals, 34*(2), 115–127.

Smith, A. (2011). Respecting children's rights and agency: Theoretical insights into ethical research procedures. In D. Harcourt, B. Perry, & T. Waller (Eds.), *Researching young children's perspectives: Debating the ethics and dilemmas of educational research with children* (pp. 12–25). New York: Routledge.

Swadener, B.B. (2008). Children's rights, voices, and allies: Stories from Kenya and the USA. *International Journal of Equity and Innovation in Early Childhood, 6*(1), 43–55.

Swadener, B.B., & Polakow, V. (Eds.). (2011). Introduction to Special Issue: Children's rights and voices in research: Cross-national perspectives. *Early Education and Development, 22*(5), 1–7.

Tisdall, E.K.M. (2012). The challenge and challenging of childhood studies? Learning from disability studies and research with disabled children. *Children & Society, 26,* 181–191.

United Nations. (1989). *Adoption of a Convention on the Rights of the Child* (U.N. Document No. A/44/7366). New York: United Nations.

U.S. Department of Education. (2007). *Guide to U.S. Department of Education programs.* Washington, DC: Office of Communications and Outreach.

Walker, N.E., Brooks, C.M., & Wrightsman, L.S. (1999). *Children's rights in the United States: In search of a national policy.* Thousand Oaks, CA: Sage Publications.

Walkerdine, V. (1993). Beyond developmentalism. *Theory Psychology, 3*(6), 451–469.

Wenger, E. (1998). *Communities of practice: Learning, meaning, and identity.* New York: Cambridge University Press.

Yeo, L.S., & Clarke, C. (2005). Starting school—A Singapore story. *Australian Journal of Early Childhood, 30*(3), 1–8.

CHAPTER SEVEN

Renarrativizing Indigenous Rights–Based Provision Within "Mainstream" Early Childhood Services

Jenny Ritchie & Cheryl Rau

Aotearoa[1] New Zealand is a small island country in the southern hemisphere with an Indigenous population, the Māori, comprising approximately 15% of the total population of 4.4 million, and 22% of the school population (Statistics New Zealand. Tatauranga Aotearoa, 2012). In 1840, Māori chiefs and the British Crown signed the Treaty of Waitangi/ *Tiriti o Waitangi*, which in exchange for the allowance of British settlement, confirmed that Māori would retain their lands and everything of value to them, including their belief systems and language (Orange, 1987). Unfortunately, the incoming British settlers largely ignored these commitments in their determination to obtain land for their own purposes. They not only alienated Māori from their *whenua* (traditional lands), but through their usurpation of "democratic" processes also greatly impacted the intergenerational transmission of traditional knowledges and language (Walker, 2004). Through Māori determination and persistence, the last quarter of the 20th century saw a gradual recognition of Māori rights of retaining their language and gaining restitution for losses of lands and resources. As a response to a claim by Māori to the Waitangi Tribunal (Waitangi Tribunal, 1986), the Māori Language Act of 1987 recognised *te reo* Māori as an official language (New Zealand Parliament, 1987). The educational system, which had historically played a predominant role in the invalidation of the Māori language, began to make passing nods in the direction of Māori aspirations. The early childhood care and education sector, however, was progressive in acknowledging the obligations contained within Te Tiriti o

Waitangi, and in 1996, the first national early childhood curriculum, *Te Whāriki, He whāriki mātauranga mō ngā mokopuna o Aotearoa: Early Childhood Curriculum* (New Zealand Ministry of Education, 1996), became the first bilingual national curriculum in the country. In this chapter we provide a challenge to simplistic and individualistic notions of the "rights of the child" by providing some illustration of the complexities of *Māori* conceptualizations that demand consideration of the individual child's self-determination in relation to his or her particular genealogical/cultural/historical contexts.

The Rights of Indigenous Children

Article 29, Section C, of the United Nations Convention on the Rights of the Child states that "the education of the child should be directed to the development of respect for the child's parents, his or her own cultural identity, language and values," and Article 30 reinforces that where "ethnic, religious or linguistic minorities or persons of indigenous origin exist, a child belonging to such a minority or who is indigenous shall not be denied the right, in community with other members of his or her group, to enjoy his or her own culture, to profess and practise his or her own religion, or to use his or her own language" (United Nations, 1989).

According to the United Nations Declaration on the Rights of Indigenous Peoples, "Indigenous peoples have the right to the recognition, observance and enforcement of treaties, agreements and other constructive arrangements concluded with States or their successors and to have States honour and respect such treaties, agreements and other constructive arrangements" (United Nations, 2007, p. 13). Other articles of the United Nations Declaration on the Rights of Indigenous Peoples outline the obligations of the state parties in relation to Indigenous cultural values and languages. According to Article 14, Section 3, "States shall, in conjunction with indigenous peoples, take effective measures, in order for indigenous individuals, particularly children including those living outside their communities, to have access, when possible, to an education in their own culture and provided in their own language" (United Nations, 2007, p. 7). And Article 15, Section 1, reads: "Indigenous peoples have the right to the dignity and diversity of their cultures, traditions, histories and aspirations which shall be appropriately reflected in education and public information" (United Nations, 2007, p. 7). New Zealand was one of only four nations that initially refused to sign on to this declaration when it was adopted by the United Nations in 2007 (along with Australia, Canada, and the United States). Now only the United States stands outside of this international covenant.

These international obligations serve as a beacon to guide Aotearoa New Zealand as the nation continues to struggle with long-standing structural inequalities, the ongoing legacy of colonization. A recent report by the New Zealand

Human Rights Commission concluded that in "health, education, criminal justice, and in public services, Māori, Pacific peoples and ethnic communities are disproportionately disadvantaged by a 'one size fits all' model of provision" (Human Rights Commission, 2012a, p. 50). In another submission, the commission highlighted the significance of fluency in *te reo* Māori (the Māori language) as an identifier of "being Māori" (Human Rights Commission, 2012b, p. 22). In terms of remedies, the commission called for recognition of "Māori definitions and indicators of wellbeing, including the views of Māori children" and the "intimate link between the wellbeing of Māori children and the wellbeing of their whānau, communities and the ecosystems in which they live" (Human Rights Commission, 2012b, p. 31). In the following section we consider the extent of provision of education within the Māori language. Such provision has been identified by Māori as central to Māori culture and identity (Durie, 1997; Pere, 1982/1994, 1991).

Early Childhood Care and Education in Relation to Māori Children's Rights to Their Language

Only 21% of Māori children who attend early childhood care and education services are enrolled in *kōhanga reo* (the Māori immersion family development and early childhood education movement) (Ministry of Education, 2011). As they move into the primary (elementary) school system, fewer than 10% of children attend a school where Māori is spoken more than half of the time, and only 2% attend *kura kaupapa* (schools with a Māori philosophy and immersion in Māori language) (Ministry of Education, 2011). Despite the hard work of many Māori within the education sector and elsewhere, the language remains endangered (Waitangi Tribunal, 2010). Meanwhile, there is a shortage of quality teachers in Māori immersion education services, with fewer older, first-language speakers remaining. The Waitangi Tribunal, a national commission that investigates claims by Māori of breaches of Te Tiriti o Waitangi, recently found that "Te reo Māori is approaching a crisis point. Though it can be revived through programmes of Māori language education for children, this strategy is no longer working" (Waitangi Tribunal, 2011, p. 2). While the Ministry of Education confirms that "Every Māori learner has a right to access high quality education that attends to their identity, language and culture," it goes on to concede that "The Ministry's arrangements for Māori language in education, while well meaning, have been reactive and ad hoc" (Ministry of Education, 2011, p. 33). It could be surmised that the limited funding available for Māori language in education has been focussed on supporting Māori immersion schooling. Yet the majority of Māori learners attend "mainstream" settings where there is often minimal emphasis on ensuring Māori language provision of any quality at all, let alone the high-quality models of authentic language that are required if children are to learn a second language effectively, or to extend their use of *te reo* if it has been a language in the home. The ministry admits that it "has never had a strategy to guide the way in which it thinks about Māori language" (Ministry of Education, 2011, p. 34) and is currently working to develop such a policy. The majority of early childhood teachers do not speak Māori proficiently (Harkess, 2004), although this is strongly advocated in *Te Whāriki*, the curriculum document.

Te Whāriki and *te reo Māori*

The introduction of *Te Whāriki*, the New Zealand early childhood curriculum, contains the bold statement that "In early childhood settings, all children should be given the opportunity to develop knowledge and an understanding of the cultural heritages of both partners to Te Tiriti o Waitangi" (New Zealand Ministry of Education, 1996, p. 9). It further recognizes that "New Zealand is the home of Māori language and culture: curriculum in early childhood settings should promote te reo and ngā tikanga Māori [the Māori language and culture], making them visible and affirming their value for children from all cultural backgrounds" (New Zealand Ministry of Education, 1996, p. 42). Therefore, "The curriculum should include Māori people, places, and artifacts and opportunities to learn and use the Maori language through social interaction" (New Zealand Ministry of Education, 1996, p. 43).

In the most recent population census (2006), only 1.6% of *Pākehā* (citizens of European ancestry) responded that they could speak Māori, while 24% of Māori reported that they were speakers of their language (Statistics New Zealand. Tatauranga Aotearoa, 2010). Māori make up 9.1% of the early childhood care and education teacher workforce (Ministry of Education, 2012). This means that statistically, and in reality, early childhood care and education teachers who are fluent first- or second-language speakers of *te reo* Māori are few and far between.

Since 1996, early childhood teacher education providers have been faced with the challenge posed by *Te Whāriki* of preparing their graduates who study with them for either 1- or 3-year programs to not only understand how to apply the pedagogical complexities of this sociocultural, non-prescriptive curriculum, but also to gain sufficient proficiency in the Māori language to fulfill the admirable goals of the curriculum in relation to inclusion of *te reo* Māori (the Māori language). Student teachers who are recent immigrants to New Zealand, and whose home languages are other than English or Māori, need to acquire Māori as a third language.

Implementing *Te Whāriki*

Since the introduction of *Te Whāriki* in 1996, we have facilitated a series of research projects that have been related to the response-ability of teachers to deliver on the expectations of Te Whāriki in relation to Te Tiriti o Waitangi (Ritchie, 2002; Ritchie et al., 2010; Ritchie & Rau, 2006, 2008). Observational data collected in 1998 from 13 different early childhood centers in one New Zealand city showed teachers conscientiously, but rather instrumentally, trying to incorporate simple Māori language items such as colors and numbers into their conversation with children (Ritchie, 1999, 2002). Although they realized it was important to include aspects of Māori language and culture, they lacked the confidence and knowledge to move beyond a rather limited repertoire. The language was usually employed in a tokenistic way, without any contingency to Māori knowledges or *tikanga*. For instance, when Māori words were inserted into English sentences, there was no modelling of Māori grammar. Some teachers also used simple phrases in Māori to command children's attention or compliance. During the observations it was clear that despite the availability of resources in *te reo* Māori such as books and cassette tapes (some of which were issued to early childhood care and education settings by the Ministry of Education's publications service), there was very little use made of these resources or materials. This intentional but limited use of *te reo* was, however, more than had been reported in an earlier, pre-*Te Whāriki* study in another New Zealand city in 1992, where there was very little reported use of the Māori language (Cubey, 1992).

Our more recent studies employed narrative methodologies (Ritchie et al., 2010; Ritchie & Rau, 2006, 2008). Teachers who joined us as co-researchers in these projects did so because they were committed to pedagogies that honored *Te Tiriti o Waitangi*. It should be noted that the range of teachers involved in our studies were not necessarily representative of the wider early childhood community in terms of the extent of the expression of this commitment. Some of our teacher co-researchers were Māori. Others had already demonstrated their commitment to implementing practice that reflected the "bicultural" expectations of *Te Whāriki*, and many had participated in professional learning opportunities that aimed to enhance these particular understandings. The pedagogical enactment of these teachers was consistent with their understanding of the intrinsic connection between *te reo me ōna tikanga* (the Māori language and culture). In contrast to the earlier study, where the use of *te reo* was confined to certain limited formats, in the later studies it was clear that *te reo me ōna tikanga* were often being holistically and authentically incorporated by teachers into their everyday practice through daily routines such as *mihi* (welcoming rituals), *karakia* (spiritual incantations such as the saying of "grace" in the Māori language before meals), and frequent reference to *Atua* Māori (Māori Gods, the spiritual guardians of various domains such as forests and oceans) and *pakiwaitara* (legends and stories), which gave expression to Māori understandings of *wairuatanga* (spiritual interconnectedness). This, in turn, generated for Māori families a sense of spiritual well-being, enhancing their feelings of belonging (Ritchie, 2009).

Kei a ia ano ana tikanga, mana ano

The guiding document of the Kura Kaupapa movement, *Te Aho Matua*, identifies the upholding of the rights and *mana* (prestige, authority, power) of *tamariki* (children) as fundamental to their well-being and to pedagogies for their learning, as seen in the statement "Kei a ia ano ana tikanga, mana ano" (Tākao, Grennell, McKegg, & Wehipeihana, 2010, p. 156). In Aotearoa, the notions of *tikanga* (rights, what is culturally right), and *tino rangatiratanga* (supreme chieftainship, self-determination) were to be protected through the governance allowed to the British Crown in the signing of *Te Tiriti o Waitangi*/The Treaty of Waitangi in 1840 (Te Puni Kōkiri, 2001). Furthermore, these rights are reaffirmed in the United Nations Declaration on the Rights of Indigenous Peoples (United Nations, 2007), which, when applied in Aotearoa, means that *tamariki* Māori (Māori children) and their families have been guaranteed rights to their *whakapapa* (origins) and *reo* (language) as described in an earlier section of this chapter. The late Māori leader John Rangihau pointed out the recursive relationship between confidence and competence in the Māori language and the well-being, esteem, and power of Māori individuals and collectives (cited in Ka'ai, 2004).

Integral to a Māori cultural paradigm is the belief in an ethics imbued with recognition of the instrinsic *mana* (prestige) of every child/person, where deep respect for oneself, humankind, and the environment is influenced by *whakapapa* (origins). Māori academic Linda Tuhiwai Smith writes:

> From indigenous perspectives ethical codes of conduct serve partly the same purpose as the protocols which govern our relationships with each other and with the environment. The term "respect" is consistently used by indigenous peoples to underscore the significance of our relationships and humanity. Through respect the place of everyone and everything in the universe is kept in balance and harmony. Respect is a reciprocal, shared, constantly interchanging principle which is expressed through all aspects of social conduct. (Smith, 1999, p. 120)

Respect is critical to Māori epistemology, whereby the ethic of *mana* is interwoven within *whānau* (family), *hapū* (sub-tribes), and *iwi* (tribal) relations, guiding *tamariki* (children) and *whānau* in their enactment of past, present, and evolving relationships. Māori scholar Hirini Moko Mead (2003) prioritizes the conceptual value of *mana* as a critical element that frames how individuals, *whānau*, and groups co-exist respectfully. Mead draws upon the work of compilers of the long-standing Māori dictionary (Williams, 1971) to explain that *mana* "has a range of meanings: 'authority, control', 'influence, prestige, power', 'psychic force', and which is 'effectual, binding, authoritative'" (Mead, 2003, p. 29).

Mana directly links to *manaakitanga* (hospitality, generosity, kindness). *Manaakitanga* is significantly valued as a paradigm that ensures the well-being of people and the environment. Two words contained within the term *manaaki* (support, take care of, give hospitality to) express the relevance to Māori: the word *mana*, which incorporates personal and collective influence, life-force, and power, and the word *aki*, which means to nurture, encourage, and challenge. It is an imperative within *te ao* Māori (the Māori world) that the ethical foundations of *manaakitanga* are maintained in all encounters, that the *mana tangata* (prestige of people) is kept intact. Mead (2003) articulates that *mana* must be upheld, respected, and enhanced through interactions, situations, and events.

The Māori scholar Rangimarie Rose Pere (1982/1994) views *mana* as being subtly integrated within Māori existence. She also considers it to be a conceptual belief that reaches beyond being translated from *te reo* Māori (the Māori language). For Pere, *mana* is perceived as having multiple meaning, including "psychic influence, control, prestige, power, vested and acquired authority and influence, being influential or binding over others, and that quality of the person that others know that he or she has" (1994, p. 36). *Mana* in this context recognizes a veil of influence "which embraces people, and when worn demands and provides far more than just prestige and status" (Pere, 1994, p. 38). To *manaaki* (offer hospitality, demonstrate generosity) is to uphold the prestige and well-being of both individuals and the collective. It is an obligation to kinship, genealogical ties, environment, and humankind and relies upon the qualities of *ngākau mārie* (having a peaceful heart) in order to resonate. In situations where *manaaki* is not enacted, it can diminish the *mana* of *tamariki*, *whānau*, *hapū*, and *iwi* (Durie, 1997). In these circumstances there are negative implications for *tamariki* and *whānau Māori*, who may feel uncomfortable and excluded.

Te Whāriki and *Ngā Taumata Whakahirahira*

The New Zealand early childhood curriculum *Te Whāriki* (Ministry of Education, 1996), is a *Te Tiriti*–based curriculum, being grounded in recognition of *Te Tiriti o Waitangi*, with a *te ao* Māori framework that includes "*Ngā Kaupapa Whakahaere*" (Principles) and "*Ngā Taumata Whakahirahira*" (Strands), outlined in Part B of the document (pp. 31–38). Ngā Taumata Whakahirahira includes five areas: *Mana Atua*/Well-being, *Mana Tangata*/Contribution, *Mana Reo*/Communication, *Mana Whenua*/Belonging, and *Mana Aotūroa*/Exploration. The *kupu* Māori (Māori words) hold their own integrity and meaning; the English text within the remainder of the document is not a translation of Part B. In this section of the chapter we discuss the significance of *mana* in each of the five Ngā Taumata Whakahirahira contexts listed above.

Mana Atua celebrates resonating one's uniqueness, one's spirituality. It emphasizes the importance of enabling growth, the fullest extent of the child's well-being, including uniqueness and spiritual development. The godliness that resides within the child is highlighted, the source of this truth derived from the past. The *mauri* (life force) is central to Māori positioning and thinking, all things being sacred. "Whakamanahia te tipu o tona whakapono i roto i ai a" (Ministry of Education, 1996, p. 35) refers to upholding the child's sense of self-knowledge. The importance of Māori cosmology, in understanding the way in which Māori whakapapa is generated from the gods so that the life principle of the people begins in the womb and is the foundation of thought, recognizes the interconnectedness of the physical and the spiritual as an integral understanding. The role of the educator is pivotal to ensuring that the *tamaiti* (child) is immersed in experiences that enrich and acknowledge personal and collective mana.

> Hikitia tōna mauri! Ka tika āna mahi, ahakoa pēhea te iti, whakanuia! Ko ia anake e rongo ana i te hōhonutanga o ana whakanui. (Ministry of Education, 1996, p. 35)

> *Uplift his/her mauri! Her/his work is correct, no matter how small, celebrate it! Only he/she senses the depth of her/his being celebrated.* [authors' translations]

Mana Tangata prioritizes supporting the self-growth of children so that they stand capably to be generous and supportive, and to offer their understandings to the world. It is critical that the *tamaiti* has opportunities and experiences that acknowledge his/her origins.

> Kia mōhio ia ki ōna whakapapa, ki te pātahi o ōna whānau, ki ōna kaumatua me ōna pakeke. Kia mōhio ia ki ngā kārangaranga whānau, ki ngā tēina, ki ngā tuākana, ki ngā tuāhine me ngā tungāne, ki ōna kōkā, ōna mātua, ōna tīpuna, me ētahi atu. Kia mōhio hoki ki a Ranginui rāua ko Papatūānuku, ā rāua tamariki, me ngā kōrero mō rātou. (Ministry of Education, 1996, p. 35)

> *The child should know her/his whakapapa, connecting and responding to her/his family, elders, parents, older siblings and cousins, younger siblings and cousins, aunts, parents and so on. She/he should also know Ranginui (Sky Father) and Papatūānuku (Earth Mother) and their children, and the stories about them.*

The contribution of the *tamaiti* is enhanced through loving spirit, generous and abundant hearts. "E whakaū ana i te taura here tangata, i te mana āhua ake, me te tino rangatiratanga o te mokopuna" (Ministry of Education, 1996, p. 35) expresses the significance of unity, reaching and grasping the ropes that bind us together as people to achieve all the manifestations of *mana* and *tino rangatiratanga* (self-determination). The relevance to teachers is the need to remember that children are the seeds from Rangiatea (the original birthplace of the Māori people) and that no matter how small they might be, they are as precious as a valued greenstone ornament. Teachers should also have a calm heart.

Mana Reo emphasizes enabling the growth of language, since through language, the child's mana and well-being will grow:

> Mā te reo Māori ka kiia te mokopuna he Māori. (Ministry of Education, 1996, p. 36)

It is through the Māori language that the child speaks as Māori (states her/his identity as Māori).

Te reo (the Māori language) is a *taonga* (treasure), a window illuminating the values, beliefs, and truths of the people and through which the *tamaiti* will come to know her/his world, the Māori world, the contemporary world, the world of the future, all through this lens of *te reo* Māori.

Mana Whenua is about enabling and enhancing the uniqueness of the person's *mana*, the local marae (meeting-place, hub of each Māori community), the land of origin. When a *tamaiti* is born, her/his *whenua* (placenta) and *pito* (umbilical cord) are returned back to their whenua (land: the word *whenua* has the meanings of both land and placenta).

> Nā ēnei tikanga ka poua te mana tūrangawaewae o te mokopuna mō tōna whenua ki tōna ngākau. Ka aroha hoki ia ki te taiao. Ka noho pūmau te mokopuna ki te wairua o te whenua, ka noho pūmau te wairua o te whenua ki te mokopuna. (Ministry of Education, 1996, p. 36)

> *Through the custom of burying the placenta, the esteem of belonging to his/her home (place of standing), and of his/her land is implanted within his/her heart. S/he will have a close spiritual connectedness to the land. The child will uphold the spirit of the land, and the spirit of the land will uphold the child.*

Teachers need to research and share knowledges pertaining to Papatūānuku, the Earth Mother, and her offspring, through proverbs, stories, local legends, songs, and *haka* (traditional action songs) of the land and ensure the *tamariki* understand their role as *kaitiaki* (caretakers, guardians) of the land. The *tamaiti* should also experience the beauty of all the wonderful coverings of the Earth Mother.

Mana Aotūroa engages *tamariki* and *kaiako* (educators) in research and powers of observation, enhancing the aspects of research and knowledge of the world of nature, light, science, living things, and the wider world. *Tamariki* are to explore knowledges and understandings of the Earth Mother, Sky Father, and their children. It is important for teachers to provide opportunities for *tamariki* to experience their world through hearing, seeing, tasting, smelling, feeling—through the skin and feeling through their emotions. It is important for the *tamaiti* to know the signs regarding the planting of food, catching fish, and gathering *kaimoana* (seafood) so that *mana* is upheld for the *tamaiti*, people, and the environment.

Nga Taumata Whakahirahira provide a window into *te ao* Māori through the lens of *mana*, whereby respectful relationships are upheld, experiences are life-enhancing, prestige remains intact, and *tino rangatiratanga* (self-determination) is celebrated. It is the position of this chapter that these are very culturally specific rights that require of early childhood educators in Aotearoa a deep understanding that goes beyond generalized notions of "children's rights."

Renarrativization Possibilities

We have argued elsewhere that in our country, the discourses emanating from historical imbalances resulting from the history of colonization require renarrativization, a process whereby the proactive generation of counter-narratives can serve to validate Māori understandings, repositioning these as central to the early childhood care and education curriculum for children and families in Aotearoa (Ritchie, 2011, 2012; Ritchie & Rau, 2010). In this section we draw on examples from three recent research projects (Ritchie et al., 2010; Ritchie & Rau, 2006, 2008), acknowledging, as we do so, our deep gratitude for funding from the New Zealand Teaching and Learning Research Initiative and for the huge efforts of the teachers, children, and families who contributed so much to these studies.

At Bellmont Kindergarten Te Kupenga, an early childhood setting in the city of Hamilton that has been involved in all three of our studies, the teachers Pat and Pera have renarrativized a *Te Tiriti o Waitangi*–based partnership, Whaea Pera (Whaea is a respectful term for a mother or a female teacher). A Māori teacher at the kindergarten explained her understanding of their kindergarten philosophy in the following way:

> It's your whole being, your everything. You know your *pā* (villages), your *waka* (canoe), your *mana* (prestige), your *iwi* (tribe), *te katoa* (everything). And it's all about *mātauranga* (knowledge), but knowledge about *tamariki* (children), and that's what we said to ERO (the Education Review Office, the national organisation that reviews the practices of education settings): "In our philosophy we look at the children, and the parents. Pat and I lay this *whāriki* (woven mat) down as our foundation of learning and in that learning we bind it together like this *kete matauranga* (basket of knowledge) that they take away with them, but then in turn the parents can give something back, because they share how they feel." Pat says, "We're not just teachers, we're mothers, we're nannies, we're aunties, we're social services people, we're everything." It's all about love and trust and delivering it in that *rangimārie* (peaceful) way where it's not threatening, they can come and ask, they can *kōrero* (speak, talk). [Previously unpublished data from the Puawaitanga study]

Whaea Pera refers to knowing one's *mana*, being aware of how it is upheld through knowledge of your home village, your canoe, your tribe, and the commitment to reciprocity. Providing experiences for children and families to participate in *te ao* Māori, to contribute their *mana* to situations of learning, enriches all. At Bellmont Kindergarten Te Kupenga, the child and the family are viewed as one; to know the child is to know the family. Rangimārie (peacefulness) and aroha (love) are pivotal to the respectful relationships established at the center.

Vikki, a Māori educator who was at that time a Māori teacher at Galbraith Kindergarten in the small rural town of Ngāruawahia, highlights the relevance of respect for the *mana whenua* (local Māori, who hold the *mana* of that area), of respectful behaviour when you are from another tribal area and following *tikanga* (correct practice), that is, what she perceives is the right way to act as a *manuhiri* (visitor) living in a tribal area that is not her own:

> It's important to recognise and acknowledge *tangata whenua* (people of the land) for the *taonga* (treasures) that they have to offer to *whānau* and to *tamariki*. It's important to know how to seek guidance and knowledge in a *ngāwari* (gentle) way, not in an "I'll take this" manner. And that concept for Māori is knowing that *te reo me ōna tikanga* (Māori language and culture) are *taonga* (treasures), they're valuable and should be treated as such. As a *kaiako* (teacher) I am happy to impart what I know to *tamariki*. One thing I have been taught from my Tuhoe (a North Island tribe) upbringing is to be humble when you are in another area. There are certain processes one needs to follow. For example, the first thing with *whānau* is that you make them welcome in your *whare* (house), kindergarten, *manaaki kai* (share food), *manaaki kōrero* (share ideas), *whakawhanaungatanga* (relationship-building), making links to people and places we share, that time is making people feel like they belong, that it's a genuine *kōrero* (talk). It matters to me to make those connections. [Previously unpublished data from the Whakawhanaungatanga project]

Vikki talks deeply about the way in which Māori experience *whakamā* (shyness, embarrassment), articulating strategies to ensure that *tamariki* are not placed in situations that compromise their *mana*, so that they experience *manaakitanga* and their prestige is upheld.

> Our *tamariki* also can be very *whakamā* (shy, embarrassed), for example, [when] being put out there, asked to stand up, questioning them and expecting them to respond when actually they probably will listen but won't say anything. Now, that in itself is an important difference for many of our Māori *tamariki/whānau*. Asking our *tamariki* to look directly into the *kaiako's* face to speak to them puts the *tamaiti* into the position where they become *whakamā*, and this is looked upon as being disrespectful. Isn't it disrespectful not to know the *tamariki* and their language? For example, [the] different body language. Our *tamariki* will put their eyes down towards the floor as a sign of respect. What made a difference in connecting with *tamariki* Māori was to *kōrero* Māori (speak in the Māori language), whatever the range of Māori language the *tamariki* had. *Whakamā* is a powerful Māori concept because it helps us self-reflect, look at what we have and could have done differently to make sure we do things in a *tika* (right) way. [Previously unpublished data from the Whakawhanaungatanga project]

Vikki is applying Māori ethics, using her knowledge and understanding to ensure that relationships are maintained honorably, clearly stating that teachers need to be aware of the cultural nuances of the children in their centers, and understanding that the rights (*tikanga*) of Māori children and families are upheld when the correct (*tika*) processes are enacted.

The educators of Papamoa Kindergarten prioritize the *Te Whāriki* principle of "Whakamana/Empowerment," whereby mutual respect between *tamariki* and the environment is considered to be an important ethic of the center. They therefore provide experiences that enhance children's *mana*, along with an appreciation for the natural environment. Respectfulness is enacted through the children's engagement in beautiful environments in which the children, families, and educators take great pride, as well as through creating situations in which the *mana* of the child and the environment are simultaneously upheld, reflecting mutual respect between the two. They consider that "*Whakapapa* (genealogy) links us with the whenua (land)/moana(sea) and cultural concepts. Working with *whānau* and their *pepeha* (narratives of origin) increased connections, relationships and valuing who people are and where they come from. Children see adults talking and connecting which gives them *mana*" [previously unpublished data from Papamoa Kindergarten, Titiro project].

Katerina, a Māori teacher-educator, provides political insight into the operative power dynamics within an early childhood center, and exercising *tino rangatiratanga* to ensure a respectful reciprocal relationship is in place.

> Well, if you sit behind the desk, I'm not going to feel comfortable. If you're teaching my babies and you have the privilege of hanging out with my babies, I need you to get away from that desk and come out in front of the desk and sit down with me and just talk as two Mamas, or two women who are having a cup of tea, and like real cups of tea too. Not when you sit there and it's so stiff and formal that nobody wants to talk. (Ritchie & Rau, 2006, p. 15)

Here we see Katerina, in postioning herself as a Māori mother, challenging Pākeha (those of European ancestry) teachers to change the power dynamics by coming out from "behind the desk" to engage with her in a more welcoming way, to demonstrate *manaakitanga*, to ensure that her *mana* is kept intact. Katerina asks *Pākehā* teachers to question whether they are "actually inviting the Other in and crossing those cultural divides in a sense" (Ritchie & Rau, 2006, p. 15). These examples demonstrate some ways in which teachers who are politically and culturally aware and responsive can exercise their potential to create renarrativized spaces where concepts of *manaakitanga* and *mana* are sensitively recognized and upheld.

Concluding Thoughts

First, we need to acknowledge that the explanations given here of *kaupapa* Māori constructs, such as *mana*, and of the knowledges and meanings contained within *Te Whāriki*, are subjective and of necessity only partial, given the holistic nature of *te ao* Māori conceptualizations, as well as of the early childhood curriculum document itself. Second, our intention has been to complicate simplistic and individualistic notions of the "rights of the child" by illustrating the complexities of *te ao* Māori conceptualizations that simultaneously require consideration of the individual child's self-determination in relation to the aspirations and values of her/his whānau, hapū, and iwi (extended family, sub-tribe, and tribe).

To illustrate this aspect, Mere Skerrett (2007) highlights the implications for education settings of a commitment to *tino rangatiratanga*, as articulated within Te Tiriti o Waitangi (the Māori version of the Treaty of Waitangi) as requiring "re-visioning of the spaces [and] complex power-sharing relationships [involving] the sharing of resources" (p. 8). Beyond this institutional, structural level, she explains the combined meanings of the constituent words within the term *tino rangatiratanga*: "'rangatiratanga'—'ranga' (to weave), 'tira' (a group), [and] 'tanga' (a noun-forming suffix)" as signifying "being able to meld people, to bring them together in a united cause." Furthermore, the addition of the prefix "tino" (essentiality, the absolute self, total or complete reality), provides "a sense of togetherness of self, self realisation" (p. 8). A second interpretation she offers is that *tino rangatiratanga* may be a condensed version of the words "ranga te ira tangata"— the bringing together (or a combined meta-knowledge) of the essence (genetic pool) of people at different levels, in different times and spaces, and for different purposes in all that is humanising" (p. 8). This concept, she believes, emanates from the *whakapapa* (genealogy) transmitted across generations. Skerrett then illustrates the operation of *tino rangatiratanga* as power, purpose, pedagogy, and leadership.

In this chapter we have provided an illustration of the specific application of notions of Indigenous children's rights within the context of Aotearoa New Zealand, demonstrating ways in which conceptualizations from *te ao* Māori can inform and be applied within early childhood care and education pedagogies— pedagogies that, it is to be hoped, operate in service of *tino rangatiratanga*, upholding the *mana* of children, families, and educators.

Glossary

aki—to nurture, encourage and challenge

Aotearoa—a Māori name for New Zealand

aroha—love, compassion, empathy

Atua Māori—Māori Gods, the spiritual guardians of various domains such as forests and oceans

hapū—sub-tribe(s)

iwi—tribe(s)

kaiako—educators

kaimoana—seafood

kaitiaki—caretakers, guardians

karakia—spiritual incantations, prayers, grace

kaupapa—philosophy

kete matauranga—basket of knowledge

kōhanga reo—the Māori immersion family development and early childhood education movement *kōrero*—speak, talk

kōrero Māori—speak the Māori language

kura kaupapa—schools with a Māori philosophy and immersion in Māori language

mana—prestige, authority, power

mana tangata—prestige of people

mana whenua –authority of those who are ancestrally linked to a particular location

manaaki—to support, take care of, give hospitality to, protect

manaaki kai—share food

manaaki kōrero—share ideas through talking about them

manaakitanga—hospitality, generosity, kindness

manuhiri—visitor(s)

marae—meeting-place, hub of each Māori community

mātauranga—knowledge(s)

mauri—life force

mihi—greetings, welcoming rituals

moana—sea, ocean

ngā tikanga Māori—culturally preferred practices

ngākau mārie—having a peaceful heart, having a calm presence

ngāwari—gentle

pā—village(s)

Pākehā—citizens of European ancestry

pakiwaitara—legends and stories

Papatūānuku—Earth Mother

pito—umbilical chord

ranga—to weave

rangatiratanga—chieftainship, authority

rangimārie—peace, peaceful, peacefulness

Ranginui—Sky Father

reo—language

tamaiti—child

tamariki—children

tangata whenua—people of the land, Indigenous people

taonga—treasure, something of great value

te ao Māori—the Māori world, Māori worldview

te katoa—everything

te reo Māori —Māori language

te reo me ōna tikanga—Māori language and the culturally preferred practices it expresses

Te Whāriki—the name of the New Zealand early childhood care and education curriculum, literally, a woven flax mat

tika—correct, right

tikanga—rights, correct procedure, custom, habit, lore, method, manner, rule, way, code, meaning, plan, practice, convention

tino rangatiratanga—absolute chieftainship, authority, self-determination

tira—a group of people

Tiriti o Waitangi—Treaty of Waitangi

wairuatanga—spiritual interconnectedness

waka—canoe(s)

Whaea—a respectful term for a mother or a female teacher

whakamā—shyness, embarrassment

whakapapa—origins, geneology

whakawhanaungatanga—create a sense of relatedeness

whānau—extended family/families

whānau Māori—Māori families

whāriki—woven flax mat

whenua—land, placenta

References

Cubey, P. (1992). *Responses to the Treaty of Waitangi in early childhood care and education.* Unpublished master's thesis, Victoria University of Wellington, Wellington, New Zealand.

Durie, A. (1997). Te Aka Matua. Keeping a Māori identity. In P. Te Whāiti, M. McCarthy, & A. Durie (Eds.), *Mai i Rangiātea. Māori wellbeing and development* (pp. 142–162). Auckland, New Zealand: Auckland University Press with Bridget Williams Books.

Harkess, C. (2004). *Ethnicity in the early childhood education teacher-led workforce.* Wellington, New Zealand: Demographic and Statistical Analysis Unit, Ministry of Education. Retrieved from http://edcounts.squiz.net.nz/__data/assets/pdf_file/0010/9766/ethnicity-ece-teacher-led-workforce.pdf

Human Rights Commission. (2012a). *A fair go for all? Addressing structural discrimination in public services.* Wellington, New Zealand: Human Rights Commission. Retrieved from http://www.hrc.co.nz/wp-content/uploads/2012/08/HRC-Structural-Report_final_webV1.pdf

Human Rights Commission. (2012b). *Submission by the Human Rights Commission to the Inquiry to the Māori Affairs Select Committee into the determinants of wellbeing for Māori children.* Wellington, New Zealand: Human Rights Commission.

Ka'ai, T.M. (2004). Te mana o te reo me ngā tikanga. Power and politics of the language. In T. Ka'ai, J. Moorfield, M. Reilly, & S. Mosley (Eds.), *Ki te whai ao. An introduction to Māori culture and society* (pp. 201–213). Auckland, New Zealand: Pearson Education.

Mead, H.M. (2003). *Tikanga Māori. Living by Māori values.* Wellington, New Zealand: Huia.

Ministry of Education. (1996). *Te Whāriki. He whāriki mātauranga mō ngā mokopuna o Aotearoa: Early childhood curriculum.* Wellington, New Zealand: Learning Media. Retrieved from http://www.educate.ece.govt.nz/~/media/Educate/Files/Reference%20Downloads/whariki.pdf

Ministry of Education. (2011). *Briefing to the incoming Minister.* Wellington, New Zealand: Ministry of Education. Retrieved from http://www.minedu.govt.nz/~/media/MinEdu/Files/TheMinistry/PolicyAndStrategy/EducationBIM2011.pdf

Ministry of Education. (2012). *Education counts. Maori in ECE*. Wellington, New Zealand: Ministry of Education. Retrieved from http://www.educationcounts.govt.nz/statistics/ece2/mori-in-ece

New Zealand Parliament. (1987). *Maori Language Act 1987*. Wellington: New Zealand Parliament. Retrieved from http://www.legislation.govt.nz/act/public/1987/0176/latest/DLM124116.html?search=ts_act_Maori+language_resel&p=1&sr=1

Orange, C. (1987). *The Treaty of Waitangi*. Wellington, New Zealand: Allen and Unwin/Port Nicholson Press.

Pere, R.R. (1991). *Te Wheke*. Gisborne, New Zealand: Ao Ake.

Pere, R.R. (1994). *Ako. Concepts and learning in the Maori tradition*. Hamilton, New Zealand: Department of Sociology, University of Waikato. Reprinted by Te Kohanga Reo National Trust Board. (Original work published 1982)

Ritchie, J. (1999, Winter). The use of Te Reo Māori in early childhood centres. *Early Education, 20*, 13–21.

Ritchie, J. (2002). *"It's becoming part of their knowing": A study of bicultural development in an early childhood teacher education setting in Aotearoa/New Zealand*. Unpublished doctoral dissertation, University of Waikato, Hamilton, New Zealand.

Ritchie, J. (2009). He Taonga Te Reo: Honouring te reo me ona tikanga, the Māori language and culture, within early childhood education in Aotearoa . In S. May (Ed.), *LED2003: Refereed conference proceedings of the 1st International Conference on Language, Education and Diversity*. Hamilton, New Zealand: Wilf Malcolm Institute of Educational Research (CD-ROM ed.), University of Waikato.

Ritchie, J. (2011). Ecological counter-narratives of interdependent wellbeing. *International Journal of Equity and Innovation in Early Childhood, 9*(1), 50–61.

Ritchie, J. (2012). Early childhood education as a site of ecocentric counter-colonial endeavour in Aotearoa New Zealand. *Contemporary Issues in Early Childhood, 13*(2), 86–98.

Ritchie, J., & Rau, C. (2006). *Whakawhanaungatanga. Partnerships in bicultural development in early childhood education. Final report to the Teaching & Learning Research Initiative Project*. Wellington, New Zealand: Teaching and Learning Research Institute/New Zealand Centre for Educational Research. Retrieved from http://www.tlri.org.nz/pdfs/9207_finalreport.pdf

Ritchie, J., & Rau, C. (2008). *Te Puawaitanga—Partnerships with tamariki and whānau in bicultural early childhood care and education. Final report to the Teaching and Learning Research Initiative*. Wellington, New Zealand: Teaching and Learning Research Institute/New Zealand Centre for Educational Research. Retrieved from http://www.tlri.org.nz/pdfs/9238_finalreport.pdf

Ritchie, J., & Rau, C. (2010). Kia mau ki te wairuatanga: Counter-colonial narratives of early childhood education in Aotearoa. In G.S. Cannella & L.D. Soto (Eds.), *Childhoods: A handbook* (pp. 355–373). New York: Peter Lang.

Ritchie, J., Duhn, I., Rau, C., & Craw, J. (2010). *Titiro Whakamuri, Hoki Whakamua. We are the future, the present and the past: Caring for self, others and the environment in early years' teaching and learning: Final report for the Teaching and Learning Research Initiative*. Wellington, New Zealand: Teaching and Learning Research Initiative/New Zealand Centre for Educational Research. Retrieved from http://www.tlri.org.nz/sites/default/files/projects/9260-finalreport.pdf

Skerrett, M. (2007). Kia Tū Heipū: Languages frame, focus and colour our worlds. *Childrenz Issues, 11*(1), 6–14.

Smith, L.T. (1999). *Decolonizing methodologies. Research and indigenous peoples*. London and Dunedin, New Zealand: Zed Books Ltd and University of Otago Press.

Statistics New Zealand, Tatauranga Aotearoa. (2010). *The social report. Te pūrongo oranga tangata. Cultural identity*. Wellington, New Zealand: Statistics New Zealand. Retrieved from http://www.socialreport.msd.govt.nz/documents/cultural-identity-social-report-2010.pdf

Statistics New Zealand, Tatauranga Aotearoa. (2012). *Estimated resident population of New Zealand.* Wellington, New Zealand: Statistics New Zealand, Tatauranga Aotearoa. Retrieved from http://www.stats.govt.nz/tools_and_services/tools/population_clock.aspx

Tākao, N., Grennell, D., McKegg, K., & Wehipeihana, N. (2010). *Te Piko o te Māhuri. The key attributes of successful Kura Kaupapa Māori.* Wellington, New Zealand: Ministry of Education.

Te Puni Kōkiri. (2001). *Texts of the treaty.* Wellington, New Zealand: Te Puni Kōkiri/Ministry of Māori Development. Retrieved from http://www.tpk.govt.nz/en/in-print/our-publications/publications/he-tirohanga-o-kawa-ki-te-tiriti-o-waitangi/download/tpk-treatytexts-2001-en.pdf

United Nations. (1989). *United Nations Convention on the Rights of the Child.* Geneva: United Nations. Retrieved from http://www.un-documents.net/crc.htm. doi:http://www.cyf.govt.nz/432_442.htm

United Nations. (2007). *United Nations declaration on the rights of indigenous peoples* (A/RES/61/295: General Assembly). Retrieved from http://www.un.org/esa/socdev/unpfii/documents/DRIPS_en.pdf

Waitangi Tribunal. (1986). *Te Reo Māori Report.* Wellington, New Zealand: GP Publications. Retrieved from http://www.waitangi-tribunal.govt.nz/reports/view.asp?ReportID=6113B0B0-13B5-400A-AFC7-76F76D3DDD92: Waitangi Tribunal

Waitangi Tribunal. (2010). *Te Reo Māori. Wai 262. Pre publication report.* Wellington, New Zealand: Waitangi Tribunal. Retrieved from http://www.waitangitribunal.govt.nz/scripts/reports/reports/262/056831F7-3388-45B5-B553-A37B8084D018.pdf

Waitangi Tribunal. (2011). *Ko Aotearoa Tēnei—Factsheet 6. Te Reo Māori.* Wellington, New Zealand: Waitangi Tribunal. Retrieved from http://www.waitangitribunal.govt.nz/doclibrary/public/reports/generic/Wai0262/Wai262Factsheet6TeReoMaori.pdf

Walker, R. (2004). *Ka Whawhai Tonu Matou. Struggle without end* (rev. ed.). Auckland, New Zealand: Penguin.

Williams, H.W. (1971). *A dictionary of the Maori language* (7th ed.). Revised and augmented by the Advisory Committee on the Teaching of the Maori Language, Department of Education. Wellington, New Zealand: A.R. Shearer, Government Printer.

CHAPTER EIGHT

Restoring Indigenous Languages and the Right to Learn in a Familiar Language

A Case of Black South African Children

Nkidi Phatudi & Mokgadi Moletsane

According to BBC News, the grandmother of a well-known mother tongue activist used to speak in a language that no one understood. When they asked their mother, she would say that grandmother is speaking to God. The language was Oromo, an Ethiopian language. Grandmother landed in SA as a slave in the 1800s and had no one to speak the language with. She only reconnected with who she was by speaking the language to herself. Being far away from her land of birth, she reconnected with her past through her mother tongue, her only identity in a foreign land! (BBC News, 25 August, 2011)

Every child has the right to education in South Africa. South African policy on inclusive education is based on providing education that is appropriate to the needs of all children—whatever their origin, background, or circumstances (Donald, Lazarus, & Lolwana, 2009). This provisioning includes appropriate language if it is designed to meet the needs of all learners. *White Paper 6* of South Africa's Department of Education (2001) regards language of instruction as one of the barriers that can lead to learning difficulties.

"Barrier to learning" is defined by Donald, Lazarus, and Lolwana (2000) as any factor, internal and/or external, that constitutes an obstacle to a learner's ability to productively benefit from schooling. Donald, Lazarus, and Lolwana (2009) further mention that "the education system should meet the specific needs of such learners as inclusively as possible rather than separating, excluding or in any other way discriminating against them," especially regarding language of teaching and learning. Thus, policies and laws have been enacted to promote inclusivity. Of significance are the South African Schools Act of 1997 and the Language in

Education Policy of 1997, which brought about parity and equity insofar as the language of teaching and learning was concerned. Children can be taught in the language they understand best.

The language playing field, however, is extremely uneven in South Africa. Despite languages being accorded the same official status, they do not enjoy the same emphasis and priority in their implementation in schools. According to Skutnabb-Kangas (2004), most indigenous languages are neglected, and the preferred language of instruction is the dominant language rather than the mother tongue. Because they are taught in a second language, children in the Foundation Phase (which is a primary school level which ranges from Grade R [bridging class between preschool and primary school] to Grade 3) are adversely affected in terms of cognitive, emotional, and scholarly development (Phatudi & Moletsane, 2013). In South Africa, language rights are protected by the Constitution, and clause 29(2) entitles South Africans to receive instruction in their language of choice. However, this choice is often compromised. Laws enacted to bring equity and order to the citizens sometimes become flawed or are in conflict with what they are supposed to do.

This chapter critically explores the role of policies and enactments made in the South African education arena, with respect to the restoration of indigenous languages into mainstream teaching in the classroom. The chapter begins by situating the right to one's own language use within international discourses such as the United Nations Convention on the Rights of the Child (UNCRC) and the Constitution of the country, and detailing how that right is being implemented and interpreted by teachers in the early years of learning. A research study on Foundation Phase teachers regarding their experiences in teaching in their mother tongue was conducted, and the findings are also presented in this chapter. The study involved the use of individual interviews and classroom observations.

Context of the Study on the Experiences of Mother Tongue Instruction in the Foundation Phase

The authors conducted a research study on mother tongue and language of teaching and learning in South Africa. The purpose of the study was to understand the perceptions and daily teaching experiences of Foundation Phase teachers in a previously disadvantaged school. The other factor that inspired the authors to conduct this research was the call for proposals made by the Department of Higher Education (DHE) to the Foundation Phase departments in higher education institutions to investigate ways and means of reinstating African languages to their original position at the teacher training level. The reason for this was that more and more schools were changing their Language of Learning and Teaching (LOLT) as a result of diminishing teacher cohorts that could teach in African languages. Since the closing of colleges of education in a rationalization measure taken by the government to deal with duplication of services as a result of apartheid policies, teacher training is conducted only at universities. The universities that are responsible for teacher education are the previously White universities, where the language of instruction is either English or Afrikaans.

A qualitative study on the experiences of teachers regarding the importance and place of mother tongue instruction in schools was conducted in two primary school classrooms. The investigation was a case study grounded in interpretivist paradigm. Data was collected by means of individual interviews, classroom observations, field notes, and a literature review. The theory that grounds the study was the mother tongue proficiency model (Phatudi & Moletsane, 2012). Convenience sampling was employed in selecting the school. Two Foundation Phase classrooms in a peri-urban school in the North West Province of South Africa were participants in the study.

The study was conducted in grade 2 and grade 3 classes. Each class consisted of at least 55 learners. These classes were chosen because teachers agreed and signed consent forms to participate in the study. The results, therefore, cannot be generalized to the whole school, because only two classes participated in the study. Themes that emerged from the study were discussed, and recommendations based on the literature and the participants' experiences were made.

The authors conducted interviews and observed how teaching in the medium of African languages was mediated and how this affected learning. Lessons on English were also a subject of the study. Experiences of teachers were crucial to how they valued their mother tongue and taught it in class. The interviews were prepared in English, but one of the teachers in class asked if she could respond in Setswana. This was an indication that the teacher was more comfortable speaking Setswana than English. Fortunately, one of the authors shared the language with her, as all 7 years of her primary education were done in Setswana. An observation was also carried out on the learners' use of English and Setswana.

At the time of the study, Setswana was the language of learning and teaching. North West Province is a predominantly Setswana-speaking area in very close proximity to the big cities of Pretoria and Johannesburg. People seeking work in those cities settle in areas within traveling distance. The village and school have therefore acquired a multicultural and multilingual nature. Since the demise of the old apartheid government, people in South Africa have largely moved around freely, as the restrictions previously imposed by the apartheid government on places of abode of the indigenous people have been done away with. This has resulted in something of a dissipation of the settlement of people according to their tribal and language origin. South Africa has recently experienced an influx of people from outside the country; they come largely from the continent to settle as economic or political refugees. Speaking different languages from the indigenous ones, they have added diversity to the local mosaic.

This multicultural nature of South Africa has had an impact on how its citizens view mother tongue teaching. Debates are raging about whether African languages have a place in modern South Africa or not. This chapter deals primarily with how teachers perceive mother tongue teaching in a multilingual context. This research, in which one of the authors is engaged, is supported by the DHE (Department of Higher Education) and is funded by the European Union.

Conventions and Policies Pertaining to the Status of Languages

The law is revealing in terms of understanding the treatment of children within a legal system, but it also has contradictions and is sometimes lacking in implementation strategies. According to Fionda (2001; cited in James & James, 2004), the conception of childhood adopted within any area of law can significantly affect the way the child is treated or the way in which his or her needs and interests are met. The universality of childhood as a life-space, in conjunction with the universalizing tendencies of law, has in recent years triggered a profoundly important international discourse about childhood. Such universalizing tendencies in relation to childhood date back to the early part of the 20th century, with the promulgation of the Geneva Declaration of the Rights of the Child in 1924, followed by the UN Declaration on the Rights of the Child in 1959, and a plethora of subsequent international statements and declarations of varying levels of scope and significance (James & James, 2004). South Africa is a signatory of the UN Convention on the Rights of the Child and uses the convention as its benchmark in upholding children's rights. The South African Constitution of 1996, Sections 28 and 29, states that every citizen has a right to education. Of special significance is Section 29, clause (a), which states that learners should be taught in the language they understand best (Republic of South Africa, 1996), a significant step that ensures that education is inclusive rather than exclusive. All nine indigenous languages of South Africa have subsequently been promoted to official status. According to James and James (2004), this can be construed as directed at preparing the child for active life as an adult and developing respect for the child's own cultural and national values and those of others.

However, there seems to be some discord between the law in South Africa regarding language use and the implementation thereof in the classroom. African indigenous languages are not given the recognition espoused in policies inside the Foundation Phase classroom, as the present study revealed.

What Is Mother Tongue Instruction?

The indigenous languages of South Africa are mother tongues to almost 80% of the population. The Constitution (1996) gives recognition to all languages, including the nine indigenous languages, and has conferred "official" status on them. These nine indigenous languages are Sepedi, Sesotho, Setswana, IsiNdebele, IsiZulu, isiXhosa, Xitsonga, Tshivenda, and SiSwati. Two other languages—Afrikaans and English—were and still are official languages. The Language in Education Policy (LiEP) of 1997, which came after the advent of democracy, mandates that the first 3 years of formal education are to be in the child's mother tongue. Thus the language the child is familiar with—in other words, the language of the immediate environment—is seen as suitable for introducing the child to reading and writing. This view is in accord with research indicating that children learn better in a familiar environment that includes their language (Bullard, 2010).

Mother tongue is defined as the language the child learns from birth in his/her environment. This is the language in which the child is socialized and with which he/she identifies. It is the language of the family and the immediate environment. (Mother tongue can also be referred to as the "primary" or "first language," but in this chapter the authors prefer to use the phrase "mother tongue.") The mother tongue is likened to the "soul" of the nation. Without a mother tongue, a nation ceases to exist, and so the mother tongue has to be given its rightful place in education. Children should be taught in their mother tongue to hold on to their identity and to develop basic concepts and necessary skills for learning a second language (Ball, 2010; Cummins, 1996).

The mother tongue is credited with improving the child's self-esteem. When children realize that the language of the school is different from their home language, they may tend to place less value on their own language. This may affect their self-confidence and self-esteem. If children are to maintain and respect their heritage and culture and home community, mother tongue teaching is core to learning (Ball, 2010). Denying the child the opportunity to learn in the mother tongue constitutes a violation of a fundamental human right (Alexander & Busch, 2007).

Importance of the Mother Tongue on Foundation Phase Learners

Proficiency in the mother tongue is a prerequisite for learning a second language, as illustrated in Figure 8.1.

Figure 8.1 provides a holistic picture of the benefits of using the mother tongue from the time the child enters school until the introduction of a second language, which in South Africa is English.

When children start school, they are exposed to their mother tongue, which is the only language they have mastered and can understand. The first block of Figure 8.1 indicates the importance of the mother tongue during the first years of school. At that stage, Foundation Phase children are expected to be able to speak fluently in their mother tongue about concrete, everyday things in daily interac-

Figure 8.1: Mother Tongue Proficiency Model (Phatudi, & Moletsane, 2013)

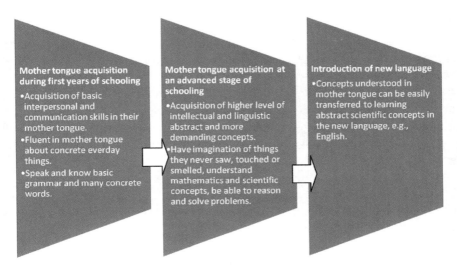

tions in their own environment with parents, siblings, and neighbors. They can see, identify, smell, and touch things they are talking about, and they get immediate feedback if they do not understand. They speak and know the basic grammar and many words. They can explain their needs in their mother tongue and have rudimentary interpersonal communicative skills. They have mastered the humor of that particular culture. This may be enough for the first grades of school, where the content for learning is within the child's real-life world.

The second block of Figure 8.1 explains that as children progress through school, they need intellectually and linguistically abstract and much more demanding concepts. They need to be able to understand and talk about things they've never seen or that cannot be seen (abstract)—for example, mathematical and scientific concepts. Children will be required to solve problems using just language and abstract reasoning (Skutnabb-Kangas, 2009). After acquiring more intellectually and linguistically advanced language, they will be ready to be introduced to the new language, which is reflected in the third block of Figure 8.1.

Declining Interest in Using Mother Tongue

Many schools in South Africa are purportedly adopting English as the medium of instruction, and not learners' mother tongue (Hoadley, Murray, Drew, & Setati, 2010). Parents have linked the choice of language of instruction with what they perceive as the best way to provide their children with the quality education that has been denied them over the years. Children are therefore registered in schools that do not offer instruction in their mother tongue. This should be understood within the larger picture of South African history. The country, newly born and re-emergent from the politics of the past, was not expected to change overnight. The apartheid government, with its discriminatory practices, had created educational class distinctions according to racial groups. The majority of the population—that is, Blacks—were subjected to an inferior education system called Bantu Education. The system was substandard in terms of teacher training and resources and did not promote self-esteem. The advent of the new democracy opened up schools to all racial groups. Children could now be registered in formerly White schools, where resources were seen as good and teachers were well trained. This initiated a migration of Black people to city schools, where English was the language of learning and teaching (Phatudi, 2013).

In an attempt to curb this migration, some Black township schools introduced English as the language of learning and teaching (LOLT), despite the fact that its proficiency in terms of teaching strategies is still not well developed and thus poses many challenges. Schools are now teaching in both the mother tongue and English without any clearly defined medium of instruction. It is not an anomaly to find a lesson in English being taught through the medium of an African language (Mashiya, 2010). African languages have not emerged unscathed, as they, too, are not offered in their original, standardized form. Various explanations for this are offered that pertain to the changing face of the communities, which are becoming increasingly multicultural and multilinguistic.

The debate about language of learning in schools has been going on for a long time. The argument has revolved around the use of English, which is seen as bringing economic emancipation and the opportunity to secure a place in the global discourse. Sufficient research on language and literacy exists to persuade even the biggest skeptic that the argument for the mother tongue is not an "either/or" argument *against* English, but an argument *for* a pedagogically sound approach to learning for all children that involves both the mother tongue and English (PRAESA [Project for the Study of Alternative Education in South Africa], 2012). It is a fact that the brain is not a container with two or more distinct compartments for each language. The transfer of knowledge and skills from one language to another, in oral and written forms, with grammar and vocabulary, differs from language to language. Once children learn concepts about print and cueing strategies for reading in one language, they can apply them to the next language they learn.

Empirical research shows that the longer indigenous learners in a low-status position have their own language as the main medium of teaching, the better their general school achievement and the more skilled they become in the dominant language—provided, of course, that they have good instruction in it, preferably by bilingual teachers (Ball, 2010; PRAESA, 2012). In addition, learning in their mother tongue will ease the process of acquiring an additional language, as concepts understood in the mother tongue can be transferred to learning abstract scientific concepts in English.

Findings on Foundation Teachers' Experiences

This section reports on how the teachers who participated in the study experienced teaching in the medium of African language (Setswana) and how this affected learning. The themes emerged from the research include:

- Preference for teaching in English instead of Setswana
- Views on the introduction of English
- Language of teaching and learning in schools
- Support given to African indigenous languages in schools

Preference for Teaching in English Instead of Setswana

The third-grade teacher expressed her desire to have English as the language of learning and teaching at the school. This sentiment was also expressed by the head of the Foundation Phase and the school head during informal conversations. They were in the process of applying for permission to switch from the mother tongue to English. The reason cited was that the profile of learners was changing rapidly. They were now faced with multilingual and multicultural classrooms, with only a few children speaking Setswana at home. However, it was confirmed that the language used outside the classroom was Setswana. According to the teacher, children's Setswana language command was not very good; thus, learning in English was suggested as an option.

In an English reading lesson, where one of the authors sat as an observer, there was substantial code-switching into Setswana. It could be said that English was taught through the medium of Setswana. The teacher attributed this to the paucity of English concepts that were understood by learners. She indicated that she often used Setswana to explain words unknown to students, a language she said they were not proficient in. "If you mix Setswana with English, they understand better," she said, contradicting the perception that Setswana was not important for making the transition to English. The lesson went on with all the explanations being made in Setswana—a language of the immediate environment—and not English.

> As I looked around the classroom, I saw a list of learners' names on the notice board. To my amazement the learners' names were in Setswana, the language of the immediate environment, an indication that parents cared about the language.

When the teacher briefly went outside the classroom, some of the students came to chat with me. They were comfortable using Setswana to communicate with me, a language I was told they were not proficient in.

Children read Setswana with relative ease and understanding. Any difficulties noted could be attributed to the teaching strategies, which did not emphasize decoding skills. Children participated actively, as they could express themselves well. Their enthusiasm in reading could never be contained; they read with understanding and self-confidence. Using the language they were familiar with gave them a sense of pride.

Views on the Introduction of English in Class

The new Curriculum Assessment Policy Statement (CAPS) of 2012 states that English shall be introduced from the first grade of schooling to the third grade as a subject. It shall be used as the language of learning and teaching from grade 4. The curriculum further supports the principle of additive bilingualism as opposed to subtractive bilingualism. The introduction of English as the LOLT in grade 4 does not have to compromise the use of the mother tongue, but the two languages should be maintained and taught together.

The teaching of English experiences major problems if faced with inefficiency. Teachers who are not trained to deal with the introduction of English and lack the necessary skills and techniques may be unable to achieve success (Nel & Müller, 2010). The sociocultural and financial positions of families also have a negative impact on English learning. Illiterate parents who cannot read or write are incapable of helping their children with learning at home (Senosi, 2004). This, coupled with the presence of teachers who are not well trained in teaching English, increases the chances of poor language learning by children.

Teacher A indicated that "in teaching Setswana in Grade 3 she also introduces English terminology. This is to prepare learners for Grade 4, where English is to be used as LOLT." Setswana is perceived as the bedrock on which English rests. Without the mother tongue it would be difficult to introduce English.

Teaching in English has its own challenges. The problem resides in its lexical and syntactical structure, which is different from that of the African languages (Henning & Dampier, 2012). Teachers who find it difficult to reconcile the structures of the two languages opt for rote learning, an approach that does not assist in building comprehension. When questions are asked, in-class learners are not in a position to answer them. In a reading lesson in Teacher B's class, the teacher read from a reader, and learners repeated after her in unison. Each sentence was read at least twice. However, learners battled to pronounce some words, although they were repeated a number of times. The following is an example of a reading lesson that went awry:

When reading "main," children pronounced it as "many," which changed the meaning of the text read. Unfortunately the teacher, who was in a temporary capacity, did not know how to deal with the problem. After going through the sentence with "main," children still said "many." This problem was never solved during my time of observation. One wonders how many words which carry meaning of a reading text are read without understanding.

(The author later suggested some strategies that could be used to deal with the problem. Children knew the word "rain," so main could be taught together with rain as word families.)

Teacher A pointed out that her children were proficient in reading in Setswana. She said that the ability to teach "depends on individual teachers, on how they facilitate reading." She agreed that children who were good readers in Setswana tended to be good readers in English. Despite the fact that she preferred English over Setswana, she conceded that her children's understanding of Setswana was far better than their understanding of English. Lessons taught in the mother tongue were better understood than those taught in English.

Language of Teaching and Learning in Schools

Contrasting conclusions are drawn by teachers regarding the teaching of English at the expense of the mother tongue. In arguing for their preference of English as the language of teaching and learning in Foundation Phase classes, teachers posit that education is meant to prepare children for full citizenship and a role as successful global players. The best way that this can be achieved, as stated by Teacher A, is "through the teaching of English from the early grades." This view of English as the language that best prepares for the future is shared by many teachers and parents. Ngugi waThiong'o (cited in Alexander, 2007) called this type of thinking "the colonisation of the mind." The African languages continue to be used peripherally at home but are kept from being used in high-status situations, as though they are taboo (Alexander, 2003).

Parents from a disadvantaged background are of the same view as teachers in preferring English-language education and assimilation for their children (Phatudi, 2012). They hope that it will be beneficial for them in the future by leading to better jobs, but parents might be deceived by ideological forces such as glorification, stigmatization, and rationalization. Ideological forces and "manufactured consent" (Herman & Chomsky, 1988; cited in Skutnabb-Kangas, 2009) may prevent parents from seeing why mother tongue–based multilingual education would do the job better than dominant-language assimilatory submersion education. Glorification of dominant languages, stigmatization of the indigenous/tribal and minority (ITM) languages, and the rationalization of the relationship between them may make ITM groups wish to shift languages and assimilate through false promises of the benefits accrued.

The strong preference for English expressed by teachers and parents is deeply rooted in the history of the country. Prior to 1994, the apartheid government of South Africa imposed the use of mother tongues only for African first-language speakers as languages of learning and teaching in schools. The policy was interpreted by Black people as a way of keeping them away from quality education. However, Heugh (2005) states that Black students' knowledge of their mother tongues assisted them in achieving good academic records. Currently, however, other forces seem to be at play in South Africa, as children are not proficient users of both their mother tongue and English (Phatudi, 2013). A population of mediocre language learners is being produced at the same time that national and international studies report findings on the poor state of language use in the country (DBE, 2012; Howie, 2006).

Support Given to African Indigenous Languages in Schools

Similarly, in the case of English and Afrikaans, the African languages are supported by the government in terms of books and the curriculum. However, the books are sometimes hard to obtain. Teachers in the 2012 study claimed that, owing to administrative constraints, the government takes longer than necessary to deliver the books. Sometimes books in a language not used at a school are delivered. Publishers also publish only schoolbooks in African languages, thus perpetuating the idea that the African languages are school-based and cannot be used for enjoyment. It is very difficult to find a good novel in an African language that can be read for leisure. Indeed, reading in African languages does not extend beyond the school environment.

In-service training for teachers is also intermittent and not wholly focused on mother tongue training. Mudzielwana (2012) reports that teachers complain that the supplementary materials for language teaching in Tshivenda are in English. Materials for facilitating teaching are in English, thus defeating the purpose of elevating the status of mother tongue teaching. The teachers in this study alluded to the absence of workshops for teachers, especially for those in multilingual and multicultural contexts. Teacher B referred to the assistance offered to schools in the neighboring province of Gauteng (meaning "the place of gold") through the use of teaching assistants. According to her, this practice, if implemented in her province, could alleviate some of the challenges related to mother tongue teaching.

As with all other curricula, the language curriculum is first written in English and then translated into the other official languages. It is not unusual to find invented terminology in the African languages curriculum, where a word in English might be unknown or not yet translated into an African language. The invented words might be known only to the author and not to the wider readership. Teacher B was concerned about the unfamiliarity of words in Setswana books. She said that children cannot relate to the terminology used in these books. When asked why she was not using the local language/words as synonyms for the unfamiliar words in the book, she replied that "lack of standardised language is problematic." Lack of dictionaries in Setswana makes the problem even more complex. This state of affairs might give the impression that the English language, with its standardized terminology, is the only language that matters, that the others can be used informally for communicative purposes at home. English is assumed to be the language that might yield better results than African languages.

Is teaching in English a solution, or is bilingual education a possibility? Alexander (2007) posits the idea of bilingual education as one approach to the dilemma the country is facing. However, adopting a subtractive bilingualism, as suggested by teachers in the schools surveyed, is tantamount to annihilating African culture. Culture is embedded within a language, and loss of language entails a loss of identity and culture. Neville Alexander's grandmother could still reconnect with her distant past by speaking in the language of her birth, even if no one understood her. Bilingual education requires proficiency in terms of speaking and using correct techniques and strategies in both the mother tongue and in English. Teacher A insisted that she uses Setswana to explain difficult English words. She blamed the education authorities for lack of adequate support to teach languages efficiently.

Bangbose (2007) warns about this constant reference to the inadequacies of language, teachers, and materials as an excuse for not teaching African languages. He cites examples of mother tongue instruction in Africa that broke new ground. If examples of the Operational Research Programme for Language Education in Cameroon (known as PROPELCA in French) and PRAESA in the Western Cape can be replicated, it could help to eliminate the stigma surrounding African languages and the perception that they are useful only in the home.

Discussion

When the mother tongue or the language of the immediate environment is accepted at school and promoted at home, the concepts, language, and literacy skills that children are learning in the majority language can be transferred to the home language (Ball, 2010; Skutnabb-Kangas, 2004). In short, the languages nurture each other when the educational and home environments permit children access to both (Ball, 2010; Skutnabb-Kangas, 2004). In particular, the mother tongue or the language of the immediate environment has the potential for developing learners' cognitive faculties, which are instrumental in learning another language, as highlighted in the Mother Tongue Proficiency Model (Phatudi & Moletsane, 2013) in Figure 8.1. This was confirmed by teacher B when she said that she uses Setswana to explain important concepts found in English.

The move away from mother tongue instruction is not only synonymous with multilingual and multicultural contexts, but also applies in those contexts where there is a predominance of one language group over the other. Ramphele (2009) cautions against the constant erosion of African languages. She mourns the fact that the African languages are hardly used in official circles, although they have been elevated to official status. She further points to the wedge that is driven between children and their cultural heritage. If children are not going to be recipients of their cultural heritage, the diversity of the nation and its languages, which needs to be upheld and respected, will disappear (Alexander, 2007). Our study revealed that children besides Setswana not being the language spoken in their homes, but widely spoken at school have vast understanding of the language thus, are dependent on the language (Setswana) to learn English. Teacher A explained that even outside the classroom, children use Setswana to communicate with each other. Teacher B further emphasized the importance of the use of Setswana. She explained that lessons taught in Setswana were far more successful than those taught in English. Although the facts speak for themselves, she was still of the opinion that children can learn better in English than Setswana, a language of the immediate community, contrary to the importance she attributed to Setswana.

The mother tongue languages do not enjoy the respect and popularity they used to before 1994. Along with the re-emergence of South Africa from obscurity and its re-admittance to the international community came the desire of South Africans to be associated with global trends, namely, being proficient in English. Despite the fact that English is spoken as a first language by just 8% of the population, it is the most widely spoken language and is used for learning in about 70% of the schools (DoE, 2010). The outcomes of learning in English have yet to be determined. The pass rate in grade 12, which is the last schooling grade, does not match the economic development of the country. Only 70.2% of learners passed grade 12, and 30% failed. Less than half of that 70% passed grade 12 with exemption, i.e, with university entrance. This is the only cohort than can proceed to university (Motshekga, 2012).

In a personal interview, a student teacher doing her service learning in an English home language school with children from an African background reported that learners who did not speak English at all found it difficult to follow the lessons in English. There was very little learning taking place in the classroom, and this created a feeling of dejection among the teachers. Written assignments were never done, simply because of the language barrier. Learners came from an African background and teachers from an English-as-a-first-language background. The student teacher decided to allow learners to discuss work in their mother tongue. Those who were able to express themselves in English were grouped with those who could not. This helped the non-English speakers to fall back on their knowledge of their mother tongue to get around the task. More work was done and comprehension improved. Ability to express an opinion also improved. In a study on the reading comprehension of children in Tshivenda, one of the nine indigenous languages in South Africa, Mudzielwana (2012) observed that learners were able to decode the words but not the meaning. When asked questions based on the text, they were unable to respond. She found further that teachers seemed oblivious to the fact that they should encourage learners to make associations or connections with the text and "evaluate their initial predictions about the text" (2012, p. 134). If teachers are unfamiliar with methods of teaching, particularly reading, their students will be poor readers and suffer negative consequences because of their academic performance.

The importance of teachers as role models in their home language and the additional language(s) cannot be overemphasized. Teachers need to be proficient in the language *and* be well trained in understanding how to teach the mother tongue and an additional language and why particular approaches to teaching are more beneficial than others.

Grappling with the Language for Education: Where to Go?

This is a difficult question, as the language issue is central to positive educational outcomes. This section reflects on some of the recommendations from the literature review and the previous research conducted by us, and from the teachers interviewed by the authors.

Teachers in this study showed a generally positive outlook about the future. They unanimously indicated that they needed more training to help them cope with the changing face of the communities they teach. They commended the use of the mother tongue as important but insisted that more can be achieved in homogeneous communities.

The face of South Africa has changed radically over the 19 years since the advent of democracy. From the homeland system, which kept different ethnic groups separate, it has progressed to a free society wherein people can settle anywhere, irrespective of language differences. According to the teachers interviewed, "this has made the teaching of African languages difficult, as children at schools speak different home languages."

Despite the fact that there are predominant languages within this multilingualism, teachers feel that English is the answer to the language problem. However, the teaching of English has always been problematic, as teachers themselves are not proficient in speaking the language (Nel & Müller, 2010). Language is learned in a mediocre way, with no room provided for excellence, and this naturally leads to learners who are mediocre language users. However, there are a number of ways to ensure that proper learning is developed and enhanced (Skutnabb-Kangas, 2009), and these are explained below.

The mother tongue should be the main teaching language for the first 6 years of a child's life. All children speaking one of the indigenous languages should have their first language or mother tongue (or one of them, in the case of multilingual children) as their main medium of education during at least the first 6 years of life (or, in extreme cases, at least the first 3 years). This was explained previously in Figure 8.1.

The effective teaching of a dominant local or national language as a subject should take place. Children whose language is an indigenous one should have good teaching of a dominant local or national language as a second language, which is English in South Africa. Competent bilingual teachers should teach it beginning in first or second grade—or possibly later, if they are surrounded by speakers of the dominant language. It should be studied as a subject throughout the entire education process. It should be studied as a second language, using second-language pedagogy/methods. Teacher B, in spite of the challenges of using Setswana as a medium of instruction, insinuated that children learn better in Setswana. She further suggested that good Setswana readers tend to become good English readers.

In South Africa, English instruction takes place in the majority of schools where there are no first-language speakers of English. Children depend on the teacher to learn the language. The language is absent outside the classroom, where learning of the language would normally take place informally. This compounds the already-complex state of language teaching.

Well-trained bilingual or multilingual teachers are recommended. A monolingual teacher, especially one who does not know the children's language, will be unable to compare the languages and explore with children what is common to the languages and what needs to be learned separately for each language. Such a teacher will not be able to help children develop metalinguistic awareness. Therefore, children who are to become bilingual need a teacher who speaks at least one other language. PRAESA is also of the opinion that bilingual education is an option in a multicultural and multilingual context.

Parents, communities, and educational authorities need sufficient research-based knowledge about educational choices. For parents to be able to choose the best form of education for their children, they need research-based information about the processes and methods of multilingual education and the long-term consequences of the alternatives.

Since systematic inequality in societies is reflected and reproduced in schools, changes in both school and society are needed to increase access to quality education. Educational authorities and those in power need more information about how the present system harms humanity and the global society through economic, educational, and creativity-related waste. Schools are one of the causes of diminishing linguistic diversity.

Conclusion

Equipping children with languages that will open doors for them while grounding them in their own indigenous languages should be the priority of any educational system. An educational system that encourages children to sever ties with their cultural background by denying them the right to learn in a familiar language is taking away their rights as citizens of a country. As Neville Alexander (2007) comments on the role of the mother tongue:

> We have to persuade our communities about the potential of African languages as languages of power and languages of high status. It is our task as language activists and professionals to do this, it is the task of the political, educational and cultural leadership of the continent to do this and to create the conditions that will make it possible to realize this proposition. (p. 20)

References

Alexander, N. (2003). *Language Education Policy, National and Sub-saharan identities in South Africa*. University of Cape Town, Cape Town. Council of Europe.

Alexander, N. (2007). Linguistic diversity in Africa in a global perspective. In N. Alexander & B. Busch (Eds.), *Literacy and linguistic diversity in a global perspective: An intercultural exchange with African countries* (pp. 13–22). Strasbourg: European Centre for Modern Languages/Council of Europe Publishing. Retrieved April 30, 2013, from http://archive.ecml.at/documents/A3_LDL_E_web.pdf

Alexander, N., & Busch, B. (Eds.). (2007). *Literacy and linguistic diversity in a global perspective: An intercultural exchange with African countries*. Strasbourg: European Centre for Modern Languages/Council of Europe Publishing. Retrieved April 30, 2013, from http://archive.ecml.at/documents/A3_LDL_E_web.pdf

Ball, J. 2010. *Enhancing learning of children from diverse language backgrounds: Mother tongue–based bilingual or multilingual education in early childhood and early primary school years*. UNESCO. Retrieved May 1, 2013, from http://unesdoc.unesco.org/images/0021/002122/212270e.pdf

Bangbose, A. (2007). *Language and literacy issues in Africa*. In N. Alexander & B. Busch (Eds.), *Literacy and linguistic diversity in a global perspective: An intercultural exchange with African countries*. Strasbourg: European Centre for Modern Languages/Council of Europe Publishing. Retrieved April 30, 2013, from http://archive.ecml.at/documents/A3_LDL_E_web.pdf

Bullard, J. (2010). *Creating environments for learning*. Upper Saddle River, NJ: Pearson Education.

Cummins, J. (1996). *Negotiating identities: Education for empowerment in a diverse society*. Los Angeles: California Association for Bilingual Learners.

Cummins, J. (2000). *Language, power and pedagogy*. Clevedon, UK: Multilingual Matters.

Department of Education (DoE). (2001). *Education white paper 6—Special needs education: Building an inclusive education and training system*. Pretoria, RSA: DoE.

Department of Education (DoE). (2010). *The status of learning and teaching in South African public schools*. Pretoria, RSA: DBE.

Donald, D., Lazarus, S., & Lolwana, P. (2000). *Educational psychology in social context* (2nd ed.). Cape Town, RSA: Oxford University Press.

Donald, D., Lazarus, S., & Lolwana, P. (2009). *Educational psychology in social context*. (3rd ed.). Cape Town, RSA: Oxford University Press.

Henning, E., & Dampier, G.A. (2012). Linguistic liminality in the early years of school: Urban South African children "betwixt and between" languages of learning. *South African Journal of Childhood Education, 2*(2), 100–119.

Heugh, K. (2005). Teacher education issues: Implementation of a new curriculum and language in education policy. In Alexander, N. (Ed.) *Mother tongue-based bilingual education in South Africa: the dynamics of implementation.* Series: Multilingualism, Subalternity and Hegemony of English, 4: 137-158. Frankfurt am Main: Multilingualism Network & Cape Town: PRAESA.

Hoadley, U., Murray, S., Drew, S., & Setati, M. (2010). *Comparing the learning bases: An evaluation of Foundation Phase curricula in South Africa, Canada (British Columbia), Singapore and Kenya.* Pretoria, RSA: Umalusi.

Howie, S., Venter, E., van Staden, S., Zimmerman, L., Long, C., du Toit, C., Scherman, V., and Archer, E. (2008). *PIRLS 2006: Progress in international reading literacy study 2006. Summary Report.South African children's reading literacy achievement.* University of Pretoria. Pretoria: Centre for Evaluation and Assessment.

James, A., & James, L. (2004). *Constructing childhood: Theory, policy and social practice.* New York: Palgrave Macmillan.

Mashiya, N. (2010). Mother tongue teaching at the University of KwaZulu-Natal: Opportunities and threats. *South African Journal of Childhood Education, 1*(1), 109–122.

Motshekga, A. (2012, January 4). *Statement during the announcement of the 2011 National Senior Certificate Grade 12 examination results by Mrs Angie Motshekga, Minister of Basic Education.* National Library Auditorium, Pretoria.

Mudzielwana, N.P. (2012). *Teaching reading comprehension to grade 3 Tshivenda-speaking learners.* Unpublished doctoral dissertation, University of Pretoria, RSA.

Nel, N., & Müller, H. (2010). The impact of teachers' limited English proficiency on English second language learners in South African schools. *South African Journal of Education, 30,* 635–650.

Phatudi, N.C. (2012, 5 January). Mother tongue teaching in South Africa. Presentation on Radio Metro FM, Johannesburg, RSA.

Phatudi, N.C. (2013). Introducing EFAL as LOLT in South Africa. In N. Phatudi (Ed.), *Introducing English as first additional language.* Cape Town, RSA: Pearson Publishers.

Phatudi, N., & Moletsane, M. (2013, accepted for publication). Foundation Phase teachers' experiences in mother tongue teaching, *Journal of Educational Studies.*

PRAESA (Project for the Study of Alternative Education in South Africa). (2012). Why is mother tongue based education so significant? *African Leader, 41.* Posted on July 2, 2012, on http://www.praesa.org.za/why-is-mother-tongue-based-education-so-significant/

Ramphele, M. (2009, 8 March) Mother tongue. *Sunday Times.*

Republic of South Africa. (1996). South African Constitution. Pretoria, Republic of South Africa.

Senosi, S. (2004). *The support for learning provided by the parents of Foundation Phase learners in a township school.* Unpublished doctoral dissertation, University of Pretoria, RSA.

Skutnabb-Kangas, T. (2004). *The right to mother tongue medium education: The hot potato in human rights instruments.* Paper presented at the 11 Meteor International Symposium, Europe 2004: A New Framework for All Languages. Tarragona, Catalunya, Spain.

Skutnabb-Kangas, T. (2009). *The stakes: Linguistic diversity, linguistic human rights and mother-tongue–based multilingual education or linguistic genocide, crimes against humanity and an even faster destruction of biodiversity and our planet.* Keynote presentation at Bamako International Forum on Multilingualism, Bamako, Mali, January 19–21, 2009.

United Nations. (1989). *United Nations Convention on the Rights of the Child.* Geneva: United Nations.

Education Rights Issues in Diverse Contexts

CHAPTER NINE

Pursuing Democracy Through Education Rights

Perspectives from South Africa

Bekisizwe S. Ndimande & Beth Blue Swadener

This chapter discusses children's rights issues as they relate to education and daily life in post-apartheid South Africa. We draw from two related studies conducted with township parents regarding the extent to which children's rights have been understood and achieved in this new democracy, both in terms of equity of access to education and broader understandings of children's rights—beyond education rights. Our work seeks to understand ways in which Black communities view education and other children's rights. The first study was a collaborative qualitative study connecting a broader discussion of children's rights, particularly as they are formulated in the UN Convention on the Rights of the Child (UNCRC, 1989), the African Charter on the Rights and Welfare of the Child (1990), and the Children's Act of 2007, to the perspectives of Black parents (meaning indigenous in South Africa) and professionals. Drawing from these interviews, we analyze ways in which children's rights and the Children's Act are understood, contested, and interpreted. The second study utilized focus groups with Black parents in townships and concentrated on educational options, choice, and access for their children after apartheid education was repealed. The democratic Constitution of 1996 and the South African Schools Act (SASA) of 1996 both provided space for equity of access to education, especially to marginalized students who were denied quality education under apartheid. Both studies had at their core an examination of children's rights—particularly education rights—and we share highlights from our findings in this chapter.

In South Africa, colonialism and apartheid brought gross violations of human and children's rights for many years. It was not until the demise of apartheid in 1994 that South Africa began to legally institute human rights issues for all, including the rights of the child. The democratic Constitution (Constitution of the Republic of South Africa, 1996) played a major role in the recognition of human rights. It provides for rights necessary for the child to develop in a socially conducive environment and be supported in meeting social and physical needs. Specifically, Section 28 (clause 1a) of the Bill of Rights states that every child has the right to basic nutrition, shelter, health care, and social services. And, according to Section 29(1), everyone has a right to a basic education.

While there has been legislation in South Africa focused on children since the 1920s, the Children's Act (2005, amended in 2007) was the first act in South Africa other than the South African Schools Act (SASA, 1996) to speak directly to the rights of *all* children. Some of the broad areas it covers include the care and protection of children, early childhood development prevention and early intervention, provision of child and youth care centers, child welfare services, early childhood development programs, protection of children from abusive treatment, the provision of health care to children, caring for children with disabilities, advocating for parental responsibilities and rights, children's rights to education, and all other important social aspects necessary for raising children in a democratic environment. As evident in its preamble, this act embodies strong democratic principles of raising and protecting children.

The defeat of apartheid also brought important sociopolitical and educational changes. With the goal of transforming the nation, the democratically elected government legislated a series of progressive changes to redress the previous inequalities in its social institutions. Since education was crucial in this change (Nkomo, 1990; Samoff, 2001), the South African Schools Act (SASA) of 1996 repealed all forms of apartheid schooling, including school segregation. The goal was to create a uniform and democratic school system. As Samoff (2001) also notes, "Education had been at the center of the anti-apartheid struggle. Its task, everyone agreed, was social transformation" (p. 25).

We frame our analysis within anti-colonial theories (Biko, 2002; Cary, 2004; Dei, 2011; Fanon, 1963; McLeod, 2000; Myers, 2001; Ngugi wa Thiong'o, 1993; Skutnabb-Kangas & Dunbar, 2010). Further, we engage a neoliberal critique in sub-Saharan Africa (Bond, 2005; Brock-Utne, 2000; Desai, 2002; Pillay, 2002; Swadener, Wachira, Kabiru, & Njenga, 2007) to show the limitations of policies constructed within Western perspectives and implemented in an African country with less attention to the local cultural values as they relate to children. Taken together, these perspectives help us underscore the importance of contradictions as well as colonial tendencies present in these initiatives and ways in which they are interpreted in everyday life and professional practice in the conceptualization and implementation of children's rights.

Our chapter reveals that the changes and recommendations made for equity education were also faced with real challenges in practice. It reflects a range of opinion from the participants about what constitutes children's rights, especially among marginalized communities. Parents tended to better understand and embrace protection and provision rights than children's participation rights, or giving children's views due weight. The findings also show some positive aspects of children's rights in terms of access to better education, while raising issues related to challenges of equity in education, given the persistent savage distributions of resources and racial discrimination in post-apartheid South Africa.

Design and Methods

This chapter draws from qualitative research conducted in two related studies, focusing on the perspectives of parents and professionals in the Gauteng province, one of the nine provinces of South Africa. Recent statistics show that South Africa has a population of approximately 51.8 million and that Gauteng is the most populated province, with 12.3 million people (Statistics South Africa, 2011). We chose Gauteng province because it is one of South Africa's most racially, ethnically, and linguistically diverse provinces. Most parents who participated were Black[1] with different ethnic backgrounds—for example, Zulu, Sotho, or Tswana. Most of the parents were also mothers, and all the voices in this chapter are voices of female participants and mothers. It is not uncommon to have more mothers participate in the education of their children; see, for example, Griffin and Smith (2005), who show that mothers tend to participate more in the education of their children.

One of the studies conducted focus groups with 122 parents. These interviews had more than five participants, but fewer than eight. The other related study conducted focus group interviews with five Black parents and individual interviews with two professionals. One of the professionals was White, and the other was Black. The interviews lasted 1–2 hours and were conducted in the homes of the participants and in other community-based settings. In both focus groups and individual semi-structured interviews, we asked about a range of issues, including the following broad topics: (1) what participants knew and thought about children's rights, (2) how they viewed the Children's Act of 2007 and its implications for education and other rights, (3) Black or indigenous parents' views of the benefits and costs of desegregated education in post-apartheid South Africa. In particular, we focused on an array of quality issues as well as the persistence of racism and lack of adequate resources.

We translated some of the interviews into English in cases where indigenous languages such as IsiZulu and SeSotho were used. The use of these indigenous languages was important for several reasons. Parents were able to respond in IsiZulu and SeSotho, the most frequently spoken indigenous languages in Gauteng province. This allowed for expression of their thoughts without the barriers of using a second language. We do not suggest, however, that participants who use indigenous languages in the interviews were unable to speak or communicate in English. These parents grew up in a state that forced them to learn and speak colonial languages, including in its schools (Ndimande, 2013). Part of this approach is meant to affirm a decolonizing framework in research by positioning marginalized people at the center of research.[2] All interviews were transcribed, and data were analyzed using qualitative narrative analysis. This included the use of open coding based on the research questions, and noting particular phrases, discourse patterns, issues raised, and identities of our participants.

Our overall methodology was framed on decolonizing research (Denzin, Lincoln, & Smith, 2008; McCarty, 2009; Mutua & Swadener, 2004; Ndimande, 2012b; Skutnabb-Kangas & Dunbar, 2010; Smith, 1999; Swadener & Mutua, 2008) and utilized a critical analysis of discourse and constructs employed on behalf of children and their rights and voices, particularly those in indigenous communities. According to Smith (1999), decolonizing research challenges underlying colonizing practices in research, which involve "discovery," exploration, and appropriation in research. Therefore, Smith (1999) asserts that research needs to be decolonized in order to challenge colonizing methods that do not include the cultures and knowledge of indigenous peoples when research is conducted about/on them.

Themes and Issues

This section presents several of the themes and issues raised by participants, organized in part to address the larger questions framing this volume. We highlight narratives of parents in Black townships and professionals regarding three broad themes: (1) views on children's rights and the Children's Act of 2007, particularly from indigenous perspectives; (2) children's rights to education and changes under the post-apartheid Constitution, reflected in education laws that desegregated the schools; and (3) challenges in gaining equal access to educational opportunities for children.

Broader Views on Children's Rights and the Children's Act
We begin this discussion with the views of Black parents and professionals discussing the broader issue of children's rights and, more specifically, the Children's Act of 2007. Parents and professionals raised a number of concerns, many of which were cultural. We discussed the three categories of rights: provision, protection, and participation. Provision and protection rights were more widely understood and accepted, while child participation rights were less understood and

sometimes viewed as a threat to cultural norms such as respecting elders and roles and rights of parents and teachers. We will focus primarily on ways in which their discussions of children's rights related to education rights in the following section.

Parents in this study did not question their role in providing for children's needs and considered this an important children's right. Provision rights, in their view, included access to education and health care, especially for children with disabilities. Seipati, a parent and an educational administrator, stated that there were "huge gaps for children with disabilities—from resources for physical needs to preventing and dealing with abuse, especially in hostels." Other issues included lack of provision for basic care and nutrition.

Parents also stated that they were happy that public schools were now in a position to provide a safer space for their children. Some parents felt that children's rights were also connected to the education of poor children. For instance, she told us that children on welfare grants are provided with tuition waivers at school and are put on lunch programs. Children of low-income families can now receive free school uniforms and books through grade 12.

Some parents said that schools were best situated to provide for and exemplify children's rights because most parents in the township were not familiar with the concept of rights as promulgated by the Children's Act. They viewed schools as conduits to provide these rights to children. As Ntombi stated, "Parents look to teachers to raise their children. Some parents did not finish school themselves or never received proper education, such as the 15-year-old mothers in the townships—parental responsibility is also important for children's rights." One of the important provisions in which schools were involved focused on the rights of girls. Seipati said that teen pregnancy is something unavoidable. In the past, schools would not allow pregnant teenagers to attend school. However, the Children's Act reversed this practice. Pregnant teenagers can now attend school—that is, they are treated the same as teenage fathers.

Participation rights are often the least understood and most controversial category of child rights (Una, 2010). As previously discussed, these include a range of ways in which children can access and share information, be consulted about issues affecting them, and express their citizenship rights. Professionals in this study appeared to appreciate the role of children's more active engagement, voice, and participation rights. Some of the parents, however, felt that children were becoming overly "empowered" in ways that showed disrespect for elders and cultural traditions.

One of the positive views on child participation rights came from Seipati, who spoke to the importance of children finding a voice, engaging with democratic decision making, and having greater participation in their school community. She stated:

We now have RCLs [Representation Councils of Learners], whose focus is to build leaders.... [These] are part of school governance; two student members sit on the governing body of the school. [In] case of expulsions, this body can "hear" these cases and represent the students involved.

While parents both commented on the importance of children knowing their rights and participating more fully as young members of a democratic society, they tended to be critical and cautious of some of the unintended consequences of children having a greater voice. As Nunu, one of the parents (and also a teacher), put it:

In schools, according to new laws, discipline guidelines, etc., you cannot reprimand; you can, up to a point, but children know their rights and will say, "Don't shout at me" and then the teacher may need to write a letter to parents or explain their actions.

This view was echoed by others who felt that there might even be an unintended hierarchy of rights, with children increasingly at the top.

Contested Children's Rights

Our findings from both interviews and focus groups pointed to the complexities and contradictions in the ways in which children's rights and the Children's Act were understood or "read" by participants. None of the participants opposed the introduction and strengthening of children's rights. In the media coverage we analyzed (for example, "Act Fast-Tracks Kids," 2007; Ngobese, 2007), the concept of children's rights was welcomed, embraced, and discussed as something that was necessary for the children of the new South Africa. However, some parents were concerned about the way some rights were defined and/or implemented, many involving cultural tensions and the way in which children's rights discourse was shaping family and community patterns of interaction. Because of these concerns, we argue that although the Children's Act was a desirable endeavor, it came with contradictions and complexities in terms of understanding children's rights within the cultural context of local communities.

Our data revealed that parents and community leaders were concerned about issues related to cultural and religious values. For instance, one of the major concerns for parents regarding a provision of the Children's Act was that they did not agree that teenage girls should have a right to abortion without parental knowledge and consent. They were also concerned about the act's provision of contraception to children age 12 and above without the consent of parents. For them, such laws threaten to erode indigenous cultural values that dictate that children cannot engage in birth control or abortion without their parents' knowledge. Many parents and community leaders perceived such rights as antithetical to their cultural values and practices, which emphasize the need for children to be guided by the parent, rather than children making decisions—especially decisions of that magnitude—without their parents' or guardian's knowledge.

Even those who supported the act were still conflicted about certain sections of it. For instance, some parents expressed views that the Children's Act gives more power to children, causing many children to disrespect adults. This is something that is not acceptable in several local communities, including but not limited to indigenous ones. The notions of rights at school and need for respect of elders and others at home created tensions. NomaSonto, one of the parents who is also a teacher, articulated what she called the "disconnect of rights"—that is, those modeled through the school and those that should be linked to cultural practice.

> [T]here has been a strong reaction to the Children's Act—many have freaked out regarding introducing children to contraception and abortion issues! There are cultural arguments against it—parents and teachers will say, "This is not in our culture!"

Some other comments embodied an implicit critique of child rights documents and policies as reflecting Western values that were often misunderstood by children and even their teachers. Ntombi, a mother and a teacher, states: "I had a chance to teach Life Orientation.... [I]t is difficult to teach this—the language of these concepts is English and these are very difficult for children to understand [and many misunderstand]!" Her interpretation of rights discourse as "English"— read Western and dominant—raises issues of whether child rights concepts should be communicated and interpreted in indigenous languages, knowledges, and practices.

The following section connects broader issues to a specific discussion of education rights through the voices of Black parents living in townships.

Education as a Right in Post-Apartheid South Africa

Black parents, the focus of both studies, felt that education was a right and discussed specific aspects of their attempts to provide a better education for their children. These specifics offer a window onto how education for all and education rights are complex and contradictory, particularly in contexts in which apartheid, which favors White supremacy, has been the official policy. Sharing some parallels with school desegregation and children's rights discourse, these excerpts from the data/studies are intended to shed light on some of the issues that must be confronted in order to fully address children's rights to an equitable and inclusive education. Most parents said that the official desegregation of White-only schools and access to schools with better resources gave Black communities more choices and made progress in addressing children's rights to equal education.[3] Several themes within the broad topic of children's education rights emerged, and they are illustrated with quotes from parents in the following sections. While they didn't focus on child participation rights *per se*, they focused on provision rights as a means of accessing a better education in terms of quality and resources. In linking these narratives to the themes of this book, we would argue that parents were taking both a national policy and a localized view of education rights. In other words, they were keenly aware of the significance of the end of official apartheid and the new Constitution, but were dealing with the contradictory issues of life in the townships and were making sacrifices to assure their children's right to a better education. Many were choosing to send their children to formerly White-only schools. Some quotes illustrating these tensions, contradictions, and commitments to education follow.

Some parents sent their children to formerly White-only schools because they said they were entitled to send them to any schools they wished. They believed that there shouldn't be segregation anymore and, more importantly, that education is a right for all people in the Republic of South Africa. Therefore, it seemed reasonable for them to send their children to any school that could provide decent education, as expressed by Jabulile, one of the mothers who sent her children to a formerly White school.

> Look, I like Ekuthuleni secondary school. They have trained teachers, yet I feel I need to take my child to a formerly White-only school in suburban areas. I have my own reasons for this and I have also checked my pockets. Everybody has the right to send their kids wherever they want as long as they can afford it.

Jabulile's view is in agreement with that of most parents, who believed that because they pay taxes for these schools, they should be entitled to schools with better facilities. They expressed the view that their children should reap the benefits of their tax money as well.

Better educational facilities and resources. Most parents stated that they chose to send their children to formerly White-only schools in suburban areas because these schools had better educational facilities and resources than the Black schools in the township. This right to equal access to educational resources was raised by many parents in the townships. The concern about school resources related to five broad issues: teaching resources, teacher discipline, English proficiency, smaller class sizes, and good academic results. Nompumelelo expressed her views on resources in the following statement.

> There are no facilities in our Black schools. I discovered that [formerly] White [-only] schools have all the resources, for example, natural science experiment materials. In our [Black] schools, when you speak of a glass beaker, you have to draw it on the board because there aren't any materials for experiments. Children won't be able to see the real one. But in [former] White schools, they do have those materials. In short, I took my children there for better facilities.

Most parents agreed with Nompumelelo. They stated that in formerly White-only schools, their children get introduced to the Internet because these schools have access to computers. They can go to computer centers to do research on projects using the Internet. They claimed that these schools' media center is also well equipped, unlike township schools.

Nomagugu, one of the mothers who transferred her children to a wealthy school in the suburbs, added her view regarding resources.

> [A]nother thing is that those schools have libraries—a very good thing. That is the reason all children there are able to read the language. Another thing about the facilities—I think our government has to prioritize efforts to provide facilities in the township too. The government has to build libraries in township schools too. The government has to build science labs as well. Science is not only theoretical; it has to be learned practically as well. For me, these are some of the reasons that I send my children to a formerly White-only school.

Class size. Smaller class size in formerly White-only schools was another factor that influenced parents' decision to take their children there. Parents mentioned a range of issues related to smaller class size, including better management in teaching a small class, easier access to remedial education, and access to psychologists, all things that do not happen in a crowded township classroom. Speaking about children gaining attention more from teachers in these schools, Mapule said the following:

> I like the fact that classrooms…are not overcrowded. Children there are able to get full attention. Teachers in those schools make certain all students understand the work and whether they are completing their homework. If there is any problem, they are quick to contact you.

Thembekile made a similar comment regarding how much more attention students appeared to receive from teachers in formerly White-only schools.

> I think there is enough attention [to students] in those schools. The teacher-student ratio is good. They have approximately 20 to 25 students in a classroom compared to 60 students in township schools. You can also notice that children in formerly White-only schools come home with "constructive" homework and they know what they are doing because they receive full attention from teachers. In our [township] schools, a teacher only begins to know students' names by September,[4] when the year is almost over. We [teachers] have a lot of children in our classrooms.

English learning and academic success. Almost all parents who send their children to formerly White-only schools believe that one of the best things about these schools is the teaching of the English language. Nandi, who earns her salary by cleaning the houses of White families in the suburban areas, says the learning of English is important for her children.

The main thing we want is to have our children be able to speak English fluently. They get to learn English in formerly White-only schools. Here in township schools you find educated teachers who speak broken English. These teachers here in the township like to translate everything into native languages, instead of using English only. You also find teachers here in the township "mixing" [switching back and forth] languages. That is the reason we take our children to formerly White-only schools because they will learn proper English there.

Most parents stated that they were attracted to formerly White-only schools because of what they perceived as their high standards and the educational climate that facilitates better academic results in those schools. Khuwa, a working-class parent who works on a part-time basis for a company in the city, shared her views about academic results.

When you check the statistics, in most cases suburban schools are in the lead. You do not get a 100% pass rate in township schools, yet you can get a 100% pass rate in formerly White-only schools.... [I] was attracted by the results of the school; they [formerly White-only schools] are capable of producing better results than schools here [in the township].

Although all the parents interviewed were clear about wanting their children to access better schools, they were also aware of the challenges their children faced in formerly White-only schools. In the next section we will discuss these challenges and share the parents' voices on these issues.

Challenges in Gaining Equal Access to Educational Opportunities for Children

All parents concurred that it was important to reform the former apartheid system that segregated education along racial lines, which they agreed had caused grave inequalities in education and adversely affected the older Black generation. Parents asserted that all children of South Africa have the *right*, not the privilege, to access any school their parents wished them to attend, as stipulated in the country's education policy and the Constitution. However, they were concerned that only White schools were desegregated, not the Black schools. They expressed concern that this one-way process of desegregation has resulted in the mistreatment of Black children in these schools.

While the post-apartheid state had legislated equal educational opportunities through the South African Schools Act of 1996, parents thought that township schools had not received the kind of support needed to overcome the legacy of inferior education imposed during apartheid. They were of the opinion that desegregated schools had not embraced the presence of Black students. Most Black parents who sent their children to these schools expressed concern about the racism their children still faced. The other theme related to parent choices was the extra costs of sending their children to the formerly White schools.

Racism and discrimination in desegregated schools

The majority of parents were concerned about racism and discrimination in the desegregated schools. While they were aware of the racial and cultural prejudices in desegregated schools, they nonetheless chose them as a means to a better future for their children. We have categorized the issues they mentioned concerning racism into four common themes: (1) discrimination based on Afrikaans language, (2) differential treatment, (3) segregated classrooms, and (4) denial of access. Finally, we include a brief discussion of the cost of education as another barrier.

Black parents stated that they were not treated equally with White parents in these schools. They said that, for example, school principals, who are usually White males, can act in a racist manner when arranging and conducting school meetings, especially when it comes to language and communication. Thokozile, a working-class mother of three who lives in one of the townships surrounding the capital city, Pretoria, complained about the use of Afrikaans as an exclusionary practice.

> If you want to see that they want to drive us away, just check the parents' meetings. The principal would start addressing the meeting in Afrikaans and when you ask him to switch to English, he would say: "Wait, I will get to English later." However, when he finished talking in Afrikaans, he wouldn't switch to English. He would just say (in Afrikaans): "Die vergaardering is klaar en hy sal nie meer praat nie" ["the meeting is over" and he "is done talking"]. That is why I say they are trying to drive us away from these schools.

In addition, some White school principals have not been open to holding meetings with Black and White parents together. Buyi, a working-class mother who lives in one of the townships close to the capital city, Pretoria, said Black parents are not treated the same as White parents when it comes to meetings and discussions of school programs. Buyi said:

> Let me cite an example of racism in these schools. There is this school…that used to call parents' meetings. However, the parent meetings were called on different days for different parents. The principal would call a meeting for Black parents today and the next day another meeting for White parents. So it was segregated. There was not even a single complaint from the School Governing Body…. You know, even if you went to the principal and talked to him about this, he would just tell you that it has been like this from the beginning.

One of the parents' complaints was about segregated classrooms in some schools. They said that some teachers and principals have created strategies to segregate White and Black students, using the Afrikaans language as a proxy for this segregation and by seating Afrikaans-speaking students on one side of the classroom. Thandeka, a working-class mother of four who is currently unemployed, reflected:

I am worried about segregation in these schools. For example, they would do an Afrikaans class and an English class knowing very well that Black children will go to the English class while White children will go to the Afrikaans class. In my daughter's school, they never have White children in English classes or Black children in Afrikaans classes. It is strictly White in Afrikaans and Black in English. This is where segregation troubles me.

Another problem Black parents encountered when they enrolled their children in formerly White-only schools was access. Most parents who send their children to such schools complained that, while the Constitution allows them to send their children to desegregated schools, it is not easy because of the schools' gate-keeping policies. Noluthando, an upper-middle-class parent and former township school teacher who now works for the provincial department of education as an administrator, said:

Admission is another problem. They admit [Black students] for the sake of post-establishment, i.e., you have to have one teacher per forty learners. For them to keep the teaching positions open, they are compelled to admit Black children. Now, as soon as the [Black] students have been admitted, they begin all this racist nativism and they now and then suspend Black students. I have seen [Black] students who get suspended for 5 days. This is how it works: If a Black student gets a 5-day suspension, she or he has to go home. However, if a White student gets the same suspension (5 days), she or he stays at school and receives private instruction. She or he won't be sent home.

Cost of Education

In the South African public school system, especially in wealthy schools, school expenses include tuition fees, transportation—especially if children commute from townships to suburban areas—and miscellaneous fees such as small donations for school events, field trips, and so forth (Ndimande, 2006). All parents believed that formerly White-only schools are expensive. Most of them stated that they could barely afford to pay for their children to attend integrated, suburban schools. Some schools send children back home if school fees are not paid in full, disrupting learning and causing a hardship for families.

Some parents said that these high expenses were not simply about finances but about keeping Black students out of White schools. Ncane, a mother of four who works at a grocery store in the city, said she finds that it is difficult even to get information about financial support.

If you are an unemployed parent, and you cannot afford the school fees, you don't get all the information about how to apply for partial exemption from paying fees. There is no access to information for Black parents, but White parents have that information. Unfortunately, it is also the White parents who can afford to pay school fees.

In summary, one lens of viewing children's rights to education in post-apartheid South Africa is through the voices of Black parents. The preceding sections have foregrounded parents and professionals' opinions about children's rights in regard to the Children's Act of 2007, as well as the cultural tensions related to these rights within the indigenous contexts. In addition, parents have identified strategies for addressing their children's education rights, as well as negotiating the barriers they encountered in these efforts.

Discussion

These are challenging times for children's rights and access to education, not just in South Africa but in other nations as well. Education is no longer perceived as a public good to strengthen democracy in communities, but rather as an individual commodity. Put simply, neoliberalism has converted education into measurable outcomes—standardized test scores—despite debates about what counts as knowledge and whose knowledge is taught in schools (Apple, 1995; Giroux, 1983). While there have been progressive efforts to transform schools—for example, desegregation, diversity in curriculum, and equal access to quality education—there has also been increasing opposition to these efforts. Conservative modernization (Apple, 1993) has steered school reforms in retrogressive directions in order to maintain the status quo. Take, for instance, the call for a return to core knowledge and to Western values (Hirsch, 1996) and support for private markets in education and for school "choice" policies (Chubb & Moe, 1990). These are but a few examples of conservative modernization and resistance to reforms that provide equity of access and opportunities in the United States. However, these trends are international and affect marginalized parents in many nations, including South Africa. In this context, it is not at all puzzling that township schools lack adequate resources and face discrimination despite a new Constitution that declares a strong commitment to the rights of all children (Motala, 2006; Ndimande, 2006, 2012a; Vally & Dalamba, 1999).

Our findings also reveal the complexities and challenges of enacting policies that reflect universal assumptions about children and their place in society, particularly in the already-complicated set of relations found in a postcolonial, post-apartheid setting such as South Africa. The "global politics of educational borrowing and lending" (Steiner-Khamsi, 2004) and the circulation of neoliberal Western policies through international agreements and funding-related requirements, are part of the landscape in which child rights legislation is adopted in the Global South. While we do not argue against the Children's Act and the CRC, data from this study underscore the importance of taking a culturally nuanced view of the ways in which the CRC and national legislation such as the South African Children's Act are understood, enacted, critiqued, resisted, and adapted.

Policy-Practice Gap

In the participants' discourse, as well as in national media accounts, our data provided evidence of gaps between policy on paper and policy in practice, as related to children's education rights, including desegregation, and the Children's Act. This policy-practice gap reflected divides between formal/legal structures versus more informal/traditional values and practices. Parents tended to convey the sense that the policies they were aware of in the Children's Act often did not reflect their cultural values or childrearing views. Some expressed the concern that parents and communities were not sufficiently consulted in establishing children's rights policies and that some of the ideas represented more Western views and were inconsistent with traditions of respect for elders and local community structures.

In making sense of participants' views of children's rights and the Children's Act as they relate to the policy-practice gap, it is important to situate the findings in the post-apartheid context of South Africa. Post-apartheid policy changes cannot be understood outside the broader policy framework and the influence of Western institutions such as the World Bank and the International Monetary Fund (IMF) in sub-Saharan Africa (Brock-Utne, 2000; Swadener et al., 2007). Put simply, social policies in the post-apartheid government are associated with and influenced by the Western discourse of economy, race, culture, gender, class, and politics. This policy-practice gap is exemplified by South Africa's adoption of neoliberal policies that devalue a bottom-up approach in planning and implementing policies, in this case the Children's Act. Bond (2005), Desai (2002), Pillay (2002), and others argue that post-apartheid social policy is influenced by neoliberal politics, which reflects Western perspectives on social issues. Since neoliberalism is mostly concerned with the individual, it does not consider collective participation or communal values in which the individual lives. This is problematic in a nation like South Africa, which has a long tradition of local community participation and respect for local values.

This, together with the increasing role of Western consultants in national policy formulation, has come to reveal how international "specialists" come to inform local policies. Such policies do not necessarily reflect the views and aspirations of the poor and marginalized peoples, but only those who are privileged and more attracted to Western than African values. The issue of cultural difference and racial privilege becomes critical in creating the disconnect between those who propose these policies and the majority of the people who are culturally different and of less privileged socioeconomic status, and thus less likely to be asked to participate in the formulation of these proposals.

We argue that the policy-practice gap that has led to the lack of consultation among diverse South African communities can turn an otherwise strong document with good intentions into a more controversial one. The input of local communities should be reflected in such policies in order to affirm democratic processes in human and children's rights issues. In the next section, we further analyze the Children's Act within the discourse of anticolonial theories. We use this literature to illuminate implications for the post-apartheid South African context and children's rights.

Children's Rights and Local Communities

Issues of children's rights in post-apartheid South Africa cannot be discussed outside the historical context of colonialism, apartheid, and decades of marginalization of the subaltern groups in this nation. Colonialism and apartheid were not simply about economic dominance and separation of communities by race, but more importantly about the denial of human rights to the oppressed. While the post-apartheid democratic Constitution made it possible for human rights to be restored to those who were marginalized, this transformation posed other challenges. Put differently, while the discourse of freedom, democracy, and human rights is invoked, this discourse takes place within the neocolonial field of power, that is, the laws and the definition of rights as constructed within the Western discourse.

Given the context of South Africa, we use the anti-colonial discourse, which problematizes the neocolonial knowledge production and cultural assumptions still present in nations that were once colonized. Anti-colonial literature is part of the decolonizing agenda that forces both the colonized and the colonizers to break away from the colonial frames of reference with a renewed subjectivity (Dei, 2011). Anti-colonial scholars (Biko, 2002; Cary, 2004; Dei, 2011; Fanon, 1963; McLeod, 2000; Myers, 2001; Ngugi wa Thiong'o, 1993) remind us that more authentic decolonization of African countries involves actively challenging colonial ways of knowing and interpretation of the social policies in postcolonial nations. Unless colonial discourse is challenged, postcolonial states will continue to be undermined and excluded in terms of cultural, socioeconomic, and political decision making. This literature reveals the power perpetuated by the enlightenment project of colonization and territorialization socially and politically. Cary (2004), for instance, argues that the former colonized are embedded in a messy terrain left behind by their colonizers and manifested institutionally, culturally, socially, and spiritually.

This literature explicitly argues that ideas of social reform, no matter how progressive they may appear, are typically formulated and informed by the unequal ideological relations of power between former colonies and their colonizers, in which the ideas of the latter become the yardstick for distinguishing between good and bad values and social norms. For instance, this chapter shows that although the Children's Act of 2007 was a progressive effort to bring safety and well-being to children, including access to a better life, these rights were largely articulated in the language of the West. And although schools were desegregated in South Africa after the defeat of apartheid in 1994, indigenous communities in this nation are still marginalized and discriminated against in most schools that serve both Black and White communities. The voices of these parents have clearly enunciated this lingering colonial legacy of social and ideological marginalization. And the fact that Black schools do not have adequate resources is also indicative of the neocolonial and neoliberal policies in this nation, whose social policy encourages individual success while ignoring the importance of the success of all schools, regardless of the community they serve.

Closing Reflections

We return to one of the key questions raised in this book—"What would education look like if children's rights truly mattered?"—and conclude the chapter by discussing how education in South Africa could more fully honor the rights of all children to a quality and accessible education.

This chapter has offered evidence that post-apartheid South Africa is committed to human rights, including children's education rights, as stipulated in the 1996 Constitution. The Children's Act of 2007 generally embodies good intentions and includes important policies intended to protect and empower the children of South Africa to fulfill the goals of democracy. Not only does it encourage adults' responsibilities in caring for children; it also provides legal protection for children so that they are respected as full human beings. Stated simply, the Children's Act brings attention to the importance of children and the idea that they should be cared for and raised in appropriate ways and should have access to opportunities that include a decent education, health care, and the general provisions for a child in a still-growing democracy. The notion of the village raising a child (Swadener, Kabiru, & Njenga, 2000), including provision and protection of that child, was echoed in many of the interviews.

The tensions and contradictions that emerged in our findings mirror the complexities and challenges of enacting laws and policies that reflect universal assumptions about children without a careful consideration of the contexts in which these will operate. While post-apartheid South Africa is part of the global society, it has a unique and complicated history of colonialism and oppression that has not yet been expunged. This is also exacerbated by the neoliberal influence on policies, which denies bottom-up participation from communities. This policy-practice gap becomes crucial in the relationship between the people who have been included or excluded in the formulation and implementation of this act.

We need a broader conversation, outreach, and explanation of the intent and the larger context of the provision of children's rights policies to be brought to communities. This could take place through education of children and communities. The dissemination of this information should be available in all languages, not just in English, as most communities in South Africa do not speak English as their first language. Through forums and debates, these policies can be discussed and modified to fit the context and the goal as defined by the communities. Most importantly, children and youth should be involved directly in these discussions. Their views deserve a fair hearing.

It is in the context of such complexities and contradictions that policymakers and administrators should consider a more grassroots and inclusionary approach to both policymaking and educating the public on the importance of children's rights. We have provided examples of ways in which parents and teachers interpret the discourse and policies associated with children's rights and can serve as an example of the importance of listening carefully to community members, especially those in marginalized communities, so as to truly advocate for human rights for all communities, including children. Further, our chapter has revealed that issues of access to education in post-apartheid South Africa are complex and contradictory. Whereas the democratic Constitution and the South African Schools Act allow access to better education for all children, schools in Black neighborhoods continue to have inadequate resources, a phenomenon that has compelled parents of these children to make decisions about sending their children to fully resourced schools in suburban areas. Yet the schools with adequate resources, as revealed in interviews with parents, also discriminate against Black children.

Education for all and the rights of children remain challenging and often elusive principles when nations and local communities attempt to put them into practice—particularly in contested spaces with racist legacies and persistent issues of social and education exclusion, as found in South Africa. We believe that research undertaken in partnership with members of marginalized communities, including parents and children, shows promise for more effective implementation of education rights for all.

Notes

1. We use the words *Black* and *indigenous* interchangeably. We draw from Smith (1999), who uses the word *indigenous* to connect all marginalized peoples around the world.
2. See, for instance, Ndimande (2012b), who argues for the importance of decolonizing research and indigenous languages and knowledge in qualitative research in post-apartheid South Africa.
3. It is true that these choices are also complex and contradictory in that Black parents who send their children to formerly all-White schools can face the challenges of racism and discrimination in these schools; see, for example, Ndimande (2012a).
4. In South Africa, the academic year begins in late summer (mid-January) and ends at the beginning of the next summer (late November or early December).

References

Act fast-tracks kids to adulthood. (2007, July 5). *Sowetan*, p. 18. Retrieved May 1, 2013, from http://www.sowetanlive.co.za/sowetan/archive/2007/07/05/act-fast-tracks-kids-to-adulthood

African Charter on the Rights and Welfare of the Child. (1990). Adopted by the Twenty-Sixth Ordinary Session of the Assembly of Heads of States and Government of the OAU, Addis Ababa, Ethiopia, July 1990. OAU Doc. CAB/LEG/24.9/49.

Apple, M.W. (1993). *Official knowledge: Democratic education in a conservative age*. New York: Routledge.

Apple, M.W. (1995). *Education and power* (2nd ed.). New York: Routledge.

Biko, S. (2002). *I write what I like: Selected writings*. Chicago: The University of Chicago Press.

Bond, P. (2005). *Elite transition: From apartheid to neoliberalism in South Africa*. Pietermaritzburg: University of KwaZulu-Natal Press.

Brock-Utne, B. (2000). *Whose education for all? The recolonization of the African mind*. New York: Falmer Press.

Cary, L.J. (2004). Always already colonizer/colonized: White Australian wanderings. In K. Mutua & B.B. Swadener (Eds.), *Decolonizing research in cross-cultural contexts: Critical personal narratives* (pp. 69–83). Albany: State University of New York Press.

Children's Act. (2010). Act No. 38 of 2005; amended by Children's Amendment Act, Act No. 41 of 2007; Gazette no. 33076, Notice no. 261, 01 April 2010.

Chubb, J., & Moe, T. (1990). *Politics, markets, and America's schools*. Washington, DC: The Brookings Institute.

Constitution of the Republic of South Africa. (1996). As adopted on May 8, 1996, and amended on October 11, 1996.

Dei, G.J.S. (Ed.). (2011). Introduction. In *Indigenous philosophies and critical education: A reader* (pp. 1–13). New York: Peter Lang.

Denzin, N.K., Lincoln, Y.S., & Smith, L.T. (Eds.). (2008). *Handbook of critical and indigenous methodologies*. Thousand Oaks, CA: Sage.

Desai, A. (2002). *We are the poor: Community struggles in post-apartheid South Africa*. New York: Monthly Review Press.

Fanon, F. (1963). *The wretched of the earth*. New York: Grove Press.

Giroux, H.A. (1983). *Theory and resistance in education: A pedagogy for the opposition*. South Hadley, MA: Bergin & Garvey.

Griffin, A.I., & Smith, D.E. (2005). *Mothering for schooling*. New York: RoutledgeFalmer.

Hirsch, E.D., Jr. (1996). *The schools we need and why we don't have them*. New York: Doubleday.

McCarty, T.L. (2009). Empowering indigenous languages—What can be learned from Native American experiences? In T. Skutnabb-Kangas, R. Phillipson, A.K. Mohanty, & M. Panda (Eds.), *Social justice through multilingual education* (pp. 125–139). Buffalo, NY: Multilingual Matters.

McLeod, J. (2000). *Beginning post-colonialism*. New York: St. Martin's Press.

Motala, S. (2006). Education resourcing in post-apartheid South Africa: The impact of finance equity reforms in public schooling. *Perspectives in Education, 24*(2), 79–93.

Mutua, K., & Swadener, B.B. (Eds.). (2004). *Decolonizing research in cross-cultural contexts: Critical personal narratives*. Albany: State University of New York Press.

Myers, W.E. (2001). The right rights? Child labor in a globalizing world. In W.H. Alan, A.W. Neil, & L.F. Jude (Eds.), *The analysis of the American Academy of Political and Social Science. Children rights* (pp. 36–55). London: Sage.

Ndimande, B. S. (2006). Parental "choice": The liberty principle in education finance. *Perspectives in Education, 24*(2), 143–156.

Ndimande, B. S. (2012a). Race and resources: Black parents' perspectives on post-apartheid South African schools. *Race Ethnicity and Education, 15*(4), 525–544.

Ndimande, B. S. (2012b). Decolonizing research in post-apartheid South Africa: The politics of methodology. *Qualitative Inquiry, 18*(3), 215–226.

Ndimande, B. S. (2013). From Bantu education to the fight for socially just education. *Equity & Excellence in Education, 46*(1), 20–35.

Ngobese, N. (2007, August 30). Parents speak on the Child Act. *Witness*, p. 11.

Ngugi wa Thiong'o. (1993). *Moving the centre: The struggle for cultural freedoms.* Portsmouth, NH: Heinemann.

Nkomo, M. (1990). Introduction. In M. Nkomo (Ed.), *Pedagogy of domination: Toward a democratic education in South Africa* (pp. 1–15). Trenton, NJ: Africa World Press.

Pillay, D. (2002, October 6). Between the market and a hard place. *Sunday Times,* p. 24.

Samoff, J. (2001). "Education for all" in Africa but education systems that serve few well. *Perspectives in Education, 19*(1), 5–28.

Skutnabb-Kangas, T., & Dunbar, R. (2010). *Indigenous children's education as linguistic genocide and a crime against humanity? A global view. GálduČála: Journal of Indigenous Peoples' Rights, 1.* Retrieved May 1, 2013, from http://www.e-pages.dk/grusweb/55/

Smith, L.T. (1999). *Decolonizing methodologies: Research and indigenous peoples.* Dunedin, New Zealand: University of Otago Press.

South African Schools Act. (1996, November 15). *Government Gazette of the Republic of South Africa, 377.*

Statistics South Africa. (2011). *Census 2011—census in brief.* Pretoria, RSA.

Steiner-Khamsi, G. (2004). *The global politics of educational borrowing and lending.* New York: Teachers College Press.

Swadener, B.B., with Kabiru, M., & Njenga, A. (2000). *Does the village still raise the child? A collaborative study of changing child-rearing and early education in Kenya.* Albany: State University of New York Press.

Swadener, B.B., & Mutua, K. (2008). Decolonizing performances: Deconstructing the global postcolonial. In N.K. Denzin, Y.S. Lincoln, & L.T. Smith (Eds.), *Handbook of critical and indigenous methodologies* (pp. 31–43). Thousand Oaks, CA: Sage.

Swadener, B.B., Wachira, P., Kabiru, M., & Njenga, A. (2007). Linking policy discourse to everyday life in Kenya: Impacts of neoliberal policies on early education and childrearing. In A. Pence (Ed.), *Africa's future/Africa's challenge: Early childhood care and development in sub-Saharan Africa* (pp. 407–426). New York: The World Bank.

Una Children's Rights Learning Group. (2010). *Children's rights in Una and beyond: Transnational perspectives.* Una Working Paper 7. Belfast: Una (http://www.unaglobal.org).

United Nations. (1989). *United Nations Convention on the Rights of the Child.* Geneva: United Nations.

Vally, S., & Dalamba, Y. (1999). *Racism, "racial integration" and desegregation in South African public secondary schools.* Johannesburg: South African Human Rights Commission.

CHAPTER TEN

Claiming the Right to Quality Education in Nicaragua

Harry Shier, Martha Lidia Padilla, Nohemí Molina

Torres, Leonilda Barrera López, Moisés Molina Torres,

Zorayda Castillo, & Karen Alicia Ortiz Alvarado

Education rights can be thought of as comprising rights *to*, *in*, and *through* education. The idea of quality in education is bound up with all three. On returning to power in 2007, the Nicaraguan Sandinista government outlawed all charges for public schools. This made education free of charge (though not free of costs) and represented significant progress toward fulfilling the right *to* education. However, with no corresponding budget increase, this move failed to address the issue of quality, so that rights *in* and *through* education were still major issues.

This chapter describes the project "Safe, Quality Schools," run by local NGO CESESMA (Centre for Education in Health and Environment) in rural communities in the remote coffee-growing region of northern Nicaragua. This project tackled rights *in* education by recognizing children not only as consumers of education, but as researchers, advocates, and change agents organizing to influence the educational system in which they are the central actors.

In the pages that follow, this chapter will examine three key project documents in order to reconsider the project's outcomes and achievements as they relate to this education rights framework. The analysis supports the conclusion that a human rights-based approach to education, policy, and programming that also promotes the empowerment of children and young people as key stakeholders, can stimulate significant change in adverse circumstances, provided it goes beyond simple notions of the child's right to attend school and incorporates the ideas of respect for human rights in education and quality of education.

Analyzing this experience helps us understand the interdependence of rights to, in, and through education. Families make decisions about their children's schooling based on many factors. Poverty and the pressure for children to work play a part, but also important are perceptions about the safety of the school, how children are treated, the quality of teaching, and the relevance of what is taught. If rights in education are not attended to, the result is that many children will not enjoy their right to education, nor will they go on to enjoy other rights through education.

Human Rights–Based Approaches in Education

In poorer countries it is an everyday reality that not all children go to school, and in these circumstances governments and civil society organizations have often interpreted the right to education simply as the right to go to school. Development goals have been orientated toward getting more children—especially girls and children who work—into schools, thus leaving fewer children outside the school system. Millennium Development Goal (MDG) No. 2, "Achieve universal primary education by 2015," is a well-known example of this development thrust.

More recently, however, it has been recognized that school outcomes depend on a complex interrelationship between attendance rates and a variety of other factors, including school safety and the quality of the educational experience from both the children's and their parents' points of view (see, for example, UNESCO, 2005). If the ultimate goal is to improve educational outcomes, this will require attention to the issues of school safety and the quality of education, alongside the problems that limit access and availability.

At a global level, the coming to the fore of human rights–based approaches in development in the past decade has led to a refocusing of education policy and strategies (see Theis, 2004; Save the Children, 2005; United Nations, 2003; United Nations Development Programme [UNDP], 2006) that has enabled both governments and NGOs to start moving beyond the MDG-inspired "get more kids into school" approach. While there exists today "a vast and bewildering assortment of international human rights conventions, covenants, and treaties" (Tomaševski, 2004, p. ii) in the children and youth field, the UN Convention on the Rights of the Child (UNCRC) provides the basic framework in relation to education.

Implementing the UNCRC in the context of schools and schooling involves at least three essential components (drawing on Tomaševski, 2001; and Verhellen, 2000):

1. The right *to* education: making education available and accessible to all children everywhere.

2. Rights *in* education: ensuring that children's rights in general are respected and complied with in education systems.

3. Rights *through* education. This has two linked meanings. First, it refers to human rights education (Verhellen, 2000, p. 110). This implies more than just informing children that they have rights. It also needs to develop children's self-concept as rights-holders and the skills and confidence they require to claim and defend rights and to call failing duty-bearers to account. Second, as Coomans (2007) points out, it draws our attention to the fact that education is a foundation for the enjoyment of many other rights throughout one's lifetime. With education, a person has more opportunities to secure employment and thereby avoid poverty and the rights violations that poverty brings. Educated people have more opportunities to express their views publicly and have them listened to, or to put forward rights claims and demand a response. Tomaševski (2001) insists, however, that the fulfillment of rights *to* and *in* education is a necessary prerequisite for fulfilling this third element.

In 2007, a global framework for the application of these new ideas was offered by UNESCO and UNICEF with their joint framework document, *A Human Rights–Based Approach to Education for All* (UNESCO/UNICEF, 2007), based largely on the UNCRC. This framework supports the model of rights *to*, *in*, and *through* education and adds a new emphasis on the right to quality education. While UNICEF (2000), among others, has provided a definition of quality education,[1] the project described in this chapter (as will be explained later) eschewed such prefabricated concepts and enabled local stakeholders, principally children and young people, to develop their own ideas of what quality education meant for them.

The Right to Education in Nicaragua

International NGO Save the Children has been an important promoter of rights-based approaches in work with children throughout the world. Since 2004, Save the Children[2] in Nicaragua has been concerned about the ineffectiveness of the country's education policies and programs and has sought to demonstrate how a rights-based approach could serve to improve this situation.

In Nicaragua, from 1990 until 2006, a succession of inefficient neoliberal, pro-free market governments not only failed to invest in education, but encouraged a culture of illegal charging to develop in public schools, flouting Nicaragua's constitutional guarantee of free public education for all and making school attendance a financial burden for parents. As a result, many poorer families simply abandoned their local schools and put their children to work. In larger families, hard choices were made about which children could go to school and which would have to work. In these choices, boys were often favored by being sent to school while girls were kept at home for domestic work.

When the Sandinista National Liberation Front (FSLN in Spanish) won the 2006 presidential elections and returned to power after 16 years in opposition, the new education minister's first act upon entering office was to issue a decree outlawing all charging of fees and other "contributions" in public schools, thus once again making Nicaraguan children's constitutional right to free education a reality, as it had been in the revolutionary 1980s (Jacobs, 2009). This led to an immediate increase in school enrolment and attendance, but, without a corresponding increase in national education spending (exacerbated by the loss of the illegal income schools had been generating locally by charging parents), there were no new teachers, classrooms, desks, books, or other resources. While the basic right *to* education had been guaranteed for the majority of Nicaraguan children, the *quality* of education and respect for rights in education now became the most important concerns.

The "Safe, Quality Schools" Project

Against this background, Save the Children identified the northern coffee-growing zone as one of the worst-affected areas (Shier, 2009), and with local partners CESESMA (based in San Ramón) and La Cuculmeca (based in Jinotega), they started to develop a plan focusing on five of the poorest and educationally least well-served of the coffee-growing districts. Gradually, the proposal for the project known as "Safe, Quality Schools" took shape with the overall aim to "contribute to the realization of children and young people's rights with emphasis on the rights to quality education, to live without violence, and to participate" (Save the Children, Nicaragua, 2008). The specific objectives were:

1. to improve the quality of education by promoting the active role of children and young people in school, improving access and retention of students;

2. to promote relationships based on positive effect, equality, and respect toward children and young people in school;

3. to promote the participation of children and young people and other stakeholders in the community, in order to generate capacity and encourage collective action in defense of children's rights; and

4. to develop capacity in local organizations for promotion of social change.

The project identified just over 4,000 children as directly involved, with an additional 35,000 as indirect beneficiaries, and—as a long-term goal—the potential to influence national education policies. A notable aspect of this project is that it recognizes children not only as consumers of education (or, in NGO language, "beneficiaries"), but as researchers, advocates, and change agents, organizing to influence the educational system in which they are the central actors. This marked a significant challenge to prevailing approaches to educational development in this region.

Methodology of This Study

The discussion of the project's work is based on an analysis of three key documents, each one the result of a participatory process involving different stakeholders, created at a distinct stage of the project's development. The first is an unpublished report of a participatory appraisal of the quality of education in the districts to be covered by the project carried out by CESESMA and La Cuculmeca in 2006–2007 with the involvement of multiple stakeholders, including children and young people. The second is a booklet called *Safe, Quality Schools—A View from the Children and Young People*, published by CESESMA in 2010, 3 years into the project, in which children and young people express in their own words what the ideas of a safe school and quality education mean for them. Finally, in 2012, a team of education workers, most of whom had worked on the project since the beginning, met to reconstruct the process and review the principal achievements. They were facilitated in this over two sessions using an adapted focus group methodology, and the written report of these sessions (also unpublished) forms the third key document to be considered here.

The documents will be reviewed one by one, followed by an analysis drawing on all three to develop a number of conclusions about the effective application of rights-based approaches in education in this particular context.

Initial Multi-Stakeholder Participatory Appraisal of the Quality of Education

CESESMA and La Cuculmeca began by carrying out a participatory appraisal of the quality of education in the five districts in which the Safe, Quality Schools project was to be implemented, involving children and young people (both school students and children outside the formal education system), parents, teachers, community leaders, local officials, and NGO workers. The following brief summary of the key points from their unpublished 2007 report shows the complex reality of education in children's lives in these communities and makes it clear that the elimination of school fees and charges discussed above, while clearly a step in the right direction, was in no way an adequate policy response for guaranteeing children's education rights.

The appraisal report found that the typical primary classroom offered little or nothing to interest or motivate the learner. Most teachers were using old-fashioned teaching methods relying on rote learning and repetition without active involvement of the learner. Children were sent to school when parents could afford it and sent to work when they couldn't, leading to irregular attendance. A further consequence was that it was common to find teenagers in primary classrooms side by side with 6- and 7-year-olds. Children were tested at the end of each school year, and those who failed had to repeat the year instead of advancing a class. This contributed to the wide age range and diversity of learning needs in each class, and also led to boredom and frustration for many students. There was a serious lack of books and other educational materials, with the few that existed often inappropriate or irrelevant to the lives and interests of rural children. There were no resources to encourage active or participatory learning. School buildings were generally in poor condition with insufficient space for the children attending. The more remote coffee plantations did not have purpose built schools, so communities had to improvise classrooms in whatever space was available, often failing to meet even the most basic quality or hygiene standards.

Teacher training was considered to be of poor quality, with teachers ill prepared and rarely able to develop their skills through reflective practice. In particular, teachers had no knowledge of or experience with participatory learning, or how to manage a crowded classroom without the threat of physical punishment. To add to teachers' problems, in more remote communities a single teacher generally had to teach two or three grades at the same time. The Ministry of Education found it almost impossible to recruit and retain qualified teachers for isolated rural schools, and many primary teachers were therefore untrained and unqualified. Moreover, many children lacked a stable home where their schooling was supported and encouraged. When putting food on the table was the family's main concern, and children's work contributed to their family's survival, the potential of schooling to produce long-term benefits was often disregarded. These children had to combine school attendance with farm work or coffee plantation work. This caused particular problems, as the coffee harvest overlapped with the first and last months of the school year, so the children were more likely to be made to repeat grades or to drop out altogether after repeated failures. Few of these children made it beyond grade 3, let alone grade 6. Many coffee-picking families adopted a nomadic lifestyle during the harvest, creating additional barriers to education for their children.

Finally, in this region, children became accustomed to violence as a way of life. Verbal and physical violence were seen as normal childrearing practice, and this approach continued in school, where physical and humiliating punishments were considered essential to maintaining discipline. Sexual abuse was widespread, and in Nicaragua's *machista* (sexist) culture, the abuse often went unreported and unpunished. Sexual abuse of students by teachers has been reported to be endemic (see Amnesty International, 2010, for a thoroughly researched report on the nature and extent of this problem).

Safe, Quality Schools Booklet of Children and Young People's Perceptions, 2010

The second document to be considered is the booklet *Safe, Quality Schools—A View from the Children and Young People*, published by CESESMA in 2010 and available online. In a gathering facilitated by CESESMA, 134 children (girls and boys) from different schools in the three districts covered by the project met and talked about what a safe school meant to them and shared their ideas about what quality education would be like. Instead of a summary of the document, which would entail paraphrasing the content in adults' words, the following is a representative sample of how the children themselves defined what makes a safe, quality school (translated from Spanish by Harry Shier). While there is certainly a lot more that could be said about these comments, the authors prefer to invite the reader to engage with the children's words as they were spoken:

- "A safe school is a nice big school, painted, with plenty of desks, a good floor, windows, toilets for everyone."

- "Choose a good place to build it. It shouldn't be close to steep slopes, rivers or cantinas where they sell liquor, and the pupils shouldn't have to walk long distances because something might happen to them."

- "The school should have a big library with all kinds of books: story books, history books, dictionaries, Spanish books, English books."

- "A safe school is where there's a teacher who respects the pupils. We don't want shameless teachers who think they're smart and are too busy flirting with their female pupils to teach the lesson properly."

- "Teachers and school heads should be well prepared so the pupils can learn well. They should have been to university, should be professional teachers."

- "It should be according to the rules, without corruption. When a pupil has money, this shouldn't guarantee them good marks, or that they automatically go up to the next grade."

- "We should have space to play. The school yard should be bigger."

- "It's when your parents attend the parents' meetings and support school activities. Even if they can't read they help us do our homework."

Project Team Focus Group on Challenges and Achievements[3]

In 2012, about 5 years into the project (now in a second phase of funding from Save the Children), the team that worked on the project met to discuss it over two sessions. The first of these was used mainly to construct a visual time line of the project from 2007 to the present, identifying milestones, changes, setbacks, and developments. The second session was used to ask and answer a number of questions about what had been achieved, how, and why. The following are the main achievements that the project team identified.[4]

Children's reading network. Children became volunteer reading promoters organizing storytelling sessions and sharing storybooks to encourage reading for pleasure, in contrast to the way reading was treated as no more than a taxing chore in the typical classroom.

Parents' groups undertaking school mapping. School mapping is an established method of identifying those features that affect access to education in a community or neighborhood, and in this case it was found to be useful in identifying why some children were not attending school and involving the community in looking for ways to overcome the barriers.

Alternative crafts, media, and vocational workshops. These included carpentry, dressmaking, organic food-growing courses, arts and crafts workshops, children's theater groups, and a children's radio project.

Work with student councils. Nicaragua's 2004 Law of Educational Participation provides for every school—primary and secondary—to have an elected student council with the right to be consulted on decisions affecting the students. However, many of these were said to be ineffective, as they were dominated and manipulated by school heads and thus were relegated to token status. Workshops were conducted for student council members to help them assert themselves in decision making, particularly in relation to claiming rights on behalf of the students they represented. A complex issue the project had to deal with in this context was that the existing, legally mandated autonomous student councils had been sidelined by a new student-union model imposed by the ruling FSLN party. While this new model offered children and young people greater access to power and influence in important decisions, there were concerns that this, too, was open to manipulation, since it was under the control of a centralized, adult-run party political machine. However, a rights-based approach, if coherently applied, can render this a non-issue. Children and young people have the right to authentic, non-manipulated participation, and helping them to empower and assert themselves to achieve this is a legitimate objective that does not change, whether the would-be manipulators are teachers and school authorities or political parties.

Girls groups and "reconstructing masculinity" groups with boys and young men. Working with girls was a well-established area in CESESMA, seen as vital in working toward gender equality in a male-dominated society and realizing girls' and young women's right to live without violence or discrimination. The parallel work with boys and young men was a more recent initiative, helping them to recognize that being a real man does not need to involve subjugation of or violence toward women and girls.

Children and young people's participation in local and national policy initiatives. This included lobbying for increased investment in children and youth in local council budgets, a national campaign for investment in education, a national youth campaign against sexism, and participation in the National Movement Against Sexual Abuse.

Children as researchers and consultants. Children researched the state of environmental education in their schools and communities and made recommendations to improve this. Another group was involved in writing and designing a child-friendly version of the UN Committee on the Rights of the Child's recommendations to the government of Nicaragua (CODENI, 2012). In 2012, three children's advisory groups were elected to advise CESESMA on program and policy development, with a special emphasis on monitoring and evaluation. Also in 2012, teams of young researchers were formed to investigate perceptions of, and attitudes toward, child workers in their communities, as part of an international Save the Children program aimed at reducing economic exploitation of child workers.

Child protection policies. One area in which children have had significant policy influence has been the development of child protection policies in local schools. Though it seems astonishing from a Global North perspective, child protection had not previously been recognized as an issue in Nicaraguan schools, and some of the consequences of this failing can be seen in the children's comments quoted above. In this project, instead of the usual top-down process, child protection policies were developed in a participatory way from the bottom up. Children worked in teams to identify the risks to which they felt they were exposed—both at school and traveling to and from school—and to propose changes in conditions, practices, attitudes, and abilities that would help safeguard them from these risks. Groups of parents and teachers carried out similar analyses. Next, smaller working groups involving students, parents, and teachers met to synthesize their findings and develop draft policy documents. Finally, there were meetings among teachers, parents, and students to review and adopt the policies. At the time of this writing (December 2012), the implementation stage is under-way, with children and young people also taking a leading role in monitoring and evaluation.

Based on this reconstruction and review, the project team identified what it saw as the main lessons learned from the experience so far. One of these was the importance of an intervention strategy that involves all the key stakeholders: first and foremost the children and young people (both in and out of school), but also their parents, teachers, community leaders, school heads, education ministry officials, local politicians, and coffee farmers. The strategy requires that all these actors be seen as capable of taking on a positive and active role in helping to achieve safe, quality schools, and seeking to get them sharing and collaborating rather than quarreling. This does require, however, that adult actors be willing to accept and respect children and young people as protagonists in the collective struggle for the right to education.

The project team also believed it was important that the policy objective—in this case the creation of safe, quality schools for all children—was a shared vision, that is, something the different stakeholders had come together to define and therefore could believe in. The concept of a safe, quality school they were striving to realize was not one that had been presented to them by Save the Children or the Ministry of Education, but one that they themselves had generated through a shared process of appraisal, reflection, and analysis.

It was recognized that the main duty-bearer in relation to the right to education was the state. Children could not—and should not—seek to take on the responsibilities that the government shirked. This meant that the relationship between the community, the NGOs, and the Ministry of Education was a complex one that needed to be handled carefully. In order to play their own role in bringing about changes in education, the children, the parents, and the NGOs that support them needed a positive collaborative relationship with the Ministry of Education. Their challenge to the ministry, though forceful, could not be hostile or aggressive. However, the maintenance of this positive relationship, and the commitment of local actors to playing their part in improving education, helped ensure greater openness on the part of ministers and officials to the serious demands being put forward. Having said this, however, the strategy of positive collaboration with the Ministry of Education was a cause of constant frustration for local actors, since it was obvious to everyone that unless central government increased the national education budget, many of the necessary changes simply could not be achieved.

Rights To, In, and Through Education: Complementary and Interdependent

To return to the analysis of education rights begun at the beginning of this chapter, the Safe, Quality Schools project has helped all those involved develop a more realistic conception of the significance of the right to education. Nicaraguan government policy now provides that almost all the country's children can attend school without the obstacles previously posed by the charging of illegal fees. In other words, they have made great strides in guaranteeing the right *to* education. However, this does not mean they have fulfilled their obligations in relation to this right. There remains a small but significant child population that never attends school (there are no reliable statistics, but it could be as high as 5% in rural areas), and in addition to these children, half of those who start primary school drop out before completing it. As a result, there are over 48,000 primary school–age children—about 8% of the total—who are not attending school (UNESCO, 2012). Therefore, making schooling free of charge, though important, is not enough to guarantee the right to education.

The reasons why children do not go to school are complex, and there are nearly always multiple factors at play. The following analysis draws on published work by teams of Nicaraguan child researchers (CESESMA, 2012) who identified and listed what they perceived as the main factors preventing access to education in their communities.

Some of the factors that prevent children from going to school are related to infrastructure problems. For example, there may be no school close to the child's home and no viable or affordable means of transportation to get to the nearest school. Many factors are clearly related to poverty, because even when the school does not charge, there are costs involved in attending, such as transport, uniforms, shoes, and school materials. While Nicaraguan law clearly states that school uniforms are not obligatory, there is shame and stigma attached to having to go to school without one. There is also the opportunity cost of lost earnings or unpaid domestic or farm labor if children who would otherwise be working are sent to school. In northern Nicaragua, the opportunity for children to make a substantial contribution to the family income occurs during the months of the coffee harvest (November to January), which coincide with the beginning and end of the school year. However, missing these months of schooling increases the likelihood of failing a grade and having to repeat it, and thus puts at risk the benefit of attending school the rest of the year, with early dropout the most likely outcome. One of the teams of child researchers made a specific study of the effects of alcohol in its community and found that fathers' alcoholism was an additional factor contributing to problems at school and non-attendance in many families.

In short, whether poor, rural children get to enjoy their right to education depends on difficult decisions to be made by themselves and their parents. It is too easy to say that poor families have no choice in the matter. Along with the stories of children who had to sacrifice their education in order to work and help support their family, the Safe, Quality Schools project has documented testimonies from desperately poor parents who chose to make extraordinary sacrifices to ensure that their children attended school. Despite their poverty, these parents did feel that they had a choice to make, however difficult. It is important to note, however, that these are not simple choices of whether to send children to school or to work. Most primary school-age children in the areas covered by the project do both, so the decisions that families have to make are about how best to combine school and work. For example, the money earned on the coffee plantation may be necessary to buy school uniforms and shoes, or to pay bus fare to the nearest secondary school.

It is when families have to make these difficult decisions that the interdependence of the right *to* education, rights *in* education (particularly in relation to the quality of education), and rights *through* education becomes sharply focused. When sending their children to school, and keeping them in school, presents so many challenges to poor families, it does not take much to tip the balance, so the family decides that schooling is not worth the sacrifice. If we look at the quality factors identified by the children themselves in the extracts from the *Safe, Quality Schools* booklet cited above, these negative factors are all too clear. If the school has no proper toilets or clean water, and if it has no playground, a dirt floor, and not enough desks for its students, it is hard to maintain enthusiasm for learning. If the lessons are dull and repetitive and seem to have no relevance to pressing, real-life needs, and if there is no protection from sexual harassment or the risk of abuse by teachers—along with additional risks on the long and difficult journey to and from school—the temptation to abandon school and find an alternative in paid work is in many cases overwhelming.

With regard to many of these problems, responsibility lies with the main duty-bearer, the state, and its failure to recognize education as a spending priority. The Safe, Quality Schools project did include a token contribution from Save the Children of materials for mending leaky school roofs. However, while this was seen as a useful tactic for maintaining good relations with the Ministry of Education, it was also perceived as a dangerous precedent, as fixing school roofs must be clearly demarcated as the duty of the state. The other approach used was strenuous participation in an ongoing national campaign to encourage increased government investment in children and youth (which the government has ignored equally strenuously for the past 6 years).

Other problems, however, are susceptible to being addressed by the combined efforts of local stakeholders. While this does not absolve the state of its responsibility as duty-bearer, it can be an empowering experience for local communities and provide a model for the state to replicate. The Safe, Quality Schools project's effort to get all local stakeholders involved in developing, implementing, and monitoring child protection policies is one example. This makes schools safer places for children and thus contributes directly to the fulfillment of their rights *in* education. If there is a difficult decision to be made about whether to stay in school or to leave, or, for parents, a decision on whether to send children to school or send them out to work, then feeling that the school is safe, that the children are protected, that real efforts are being made to reduce the risks of physical violence and sexual abuse are all positive factors that will help tip the balance in favor of staying in school. Attention to children's rights *in* education can thus be seen as an integral component of their right *to* education.

The connection with rights *through* education can also be demonstrated through the work of the Safe, Quality Schools project. Examples include these:

- vocational training workshops (carpentry, dressmaking, etc.) gave young people new options for earning a decent living in their own community, thereby reducing the need for emigration and family breakup;

- the children's radio project provided a platform for raising awareness of rights issues (though aimed at children and young people, surveys showed that teachers and council officials often listened to the weekly program to keep abreast of children and young people's concerns);

- the youth theater groups, as well as young women's and young men's groups, empowered young people to tackle discrimination and violence, thus defending their fundamental human rights;

- the children's reading network opened up access to a whole range of rights by tackling illiteracy.

In conclusion, the right *to* education requires education to be available and accessible to all. However, in the case of poor working children like those in northern Nicaragua, if school is not safe, if the curriculum is not relevant, if the students are not treated with respect, if the teaching is unprofessional and the resources are inadequate—in other words, if children's rights *in* education are not fulfilled—then the decision will be made either by parents or by young people themselves to stay away, and so the right *to* education is also violated. As Tomaševski (2001) explained, rights *to* and *in* education are both essential prerequisites for the eventual enjoyment of rights *through* education, thus completing the linkage or interdependence of all three elements.

While the principal duty-bearer in respect of education rights is, and will remain, the state, one thing the Safe, Quality Schools project has demonstrated is how active, empowered citizens—particularly children and young people themselves—can play a positive role in identifying rights violations and voluntarily taking on the responsibilities that correspond to them as stakeholders in promoting rights awareness, defending their rights (and other people's), and holding the state to account for its failings.

Notes

1. UNICEF's definition of "quality education" (UNICEF, 2000, p. 4):
   Learners who are healthy, well-nourished, and ready to participate and learn, and supported in learning by their families and communities.
   Environments that are healthy, safe, protective and gender-sensitive, and provide adequate resources and facilities.

Content that is reflected in relevant curricula and materials for the acquisition of basic skills, especially in the areas of literacy, numeracy and skills for life, and knowledge in such areas as gender, health, nutrition, HIV/AIDS prevention, and peace. Processes through which trained teachers use child-centered teaching approaches in well-managed classrooms and schools and skillful assessment to facilitate learning and reduce disparities. Outcomes that encompass knowledge, skills and attitudes, and are linked to national goals for education and positive participation in society.

2. Before Save the Children adopted a unified presence in 2009, several national Save the Children agencies operated side by side in Nicaragua. The project described here was initiated by Save the Children, Norway, before being passed to the merged Save the Children, Nicaragua.

3. Unpublished report, 2012.

4. Methodologically speaking, it should be stressed that these are what the project team (the people closest to the work on the ground) *perceived* as the achievements of the project on the day of the focus group, and not necessarily the results of independent evaluation.

References

Amnesty International. (2010). *Listen to their voices and act: Stop the rape and sexual abuse of girls in Nicaragua.* London: Amnesty International Publications.

CESESMA. (2010). *Escuelas seguras y de calidad: Una mirada desde las niñas, niños y adolescentes.* San Ramón, Nicaragua: CESESMA. Retrieved December 4, 2012, from http://www.cesesma.org/documentos/CESESMA-escuelas_seguras.pdf [Spanish only]

CESESMA. (2012). *Learn to live without violence.* San Ramón, Nicaragua: CESESMA; and Preston, England: The Centre for Children and Young People's Participation (University of Central Lancashire).

CODENI. (2012). *Niñas, niños y adolescentes contribuyendo para que se cumplan nuestros derechos en Nicaragua.* Managua, Nicaragua: CODENI.

Coomans, F. (2007). Content and scope of the right to education as a human right. In Y. Donders & V. Volodin (Eds.), *Human rights in education, science and culture* (pp. 183–230). Paris and Aldershot: UNESCO Publishing and Ashgate.

Jacobs, K. (2009). *The new education, a giant and inspiring task: Interview with Miguel de Castilla, Minister of Education.* Managua, Nicaragua: Tortilla con Sal. Retrieved December 3, 2012, from http://www.tortillaconsal.com/decastilla_en.html

Save the Children. (2005). *Child rights programming: How to apply rights-based approaches to programming* (2nd ed.). Stockholm, Sweden: Save the Children.

Save the Children, Nicaragua. (2008). *Fundamentos de escuelas seguras y de calidad.* Managua, Nicaragua: Save the Children. Retrieved December 4, 2012, from http://www.savethechildren.org.ni/index.php?option=com_docman&task=doc_download&gid=20&Itemid=27 [Spanish only]

Shier, H. (2009). Pathways to participation revisited: Learning from Nicaragua's child coffee-workers. In B. Percy-Smith & N. Thomas (Eds.), *A handbook of children and young people's participation* (pp. 215–229). Oxford: Routledge.

Theis, J. (2004). *Promoting rights-based approaches: Experiences and ideas from Asia and the Pacific.* Stockholm, Sweden: Save the Children.

Tomaševski, K. (2001). *Human rights in education as a prerequisite for human rights education.* Right to Education Primers No. 4. Stockholm, Sweden: Raoul Wallenberg Institute/Swedish International Development Agency.

Tomaševski, K. (2004). *Manual on rights-based education: Global human rights requirements made simple.* Bangkok, Thailand: UNESCO.

UNESCO. (2005). *Education for all global monitoring report 2005*. Paris: UNESCO.

UNESCO. (2012). *Education for all global monitoring report 2012*. Paris: UNESCO.

UNICEF. (2000). *Defining quality in education*. New York: UNICEF.

UNICEF/UNESCO. (2007). *A human rights–based approach to education for all*. New York: UNICEF.

United Nations. (2003). *Statement of common understanding on a human rights–based approach to development co-operation*. Geneva: United Nations.

United Nations Development Programme (UNDP). (2006). *Applying a human rights–based approach to development cooperation and programming*. New York: UNDP.

Verhellen, E. (2000). *Convention on the Rights of the Child* (also 4th ed., 2006). Antwerp, Belgium: Garant.

CHAPTER ELEVEN

Getting an Education

How Travellers' Knowledge and Experience Shape
Their Engagement with the System

Colette Murray

In 2005, following years of lobbying by Traveller organizations for appropriate provision in education for Travellers, the Republic of Ireland engaged in a consultative partnership with Traveller organizations—Pavee Point, the Irish Traveller Movement, and the National Traveller Women's Forum—to develop and produce a comprehensive strategy for Traveller education. In 2011 Traveller supports in education were cut in an unprecedented and draconian manner. The state's stance on Traveller education has consistently fallen short in its recognition of the specific needs and rights of Travellers in education. This chapter discusses the situation of Travellers in Ireland linked to recent European policy developments regarding Roma and Traveller integration and the EU Agenda for the Rights of the Child (European Commission [COM], 2011b). It is well documented that Travellers and Roma experience marginalization across Europe (European Union Agency for Fundamental Rights [FRA], 2010a; UNICEF, 2011). They face prejudice, discrimination, and racism, and ongoing disrespect is widespread. In his report on Roma and Travellers' human rights, Council of Europe Commissioner for Human Rights Tomas Hammarberg stated that "efforts to secure the fundamental human rights of Roma in practice can and must be Europe's present and future" (Hammarberg, 2012, p. 224).

The divide between the education sector and the early childhood education and care (ECEC) sector cannot be ignored when it comes to planning for appropriate Traveller education. Education, and in particular ECEC pre-service education, have not made the connection across key human rights commitments or agencies such as the European Union Agency for Fundamental Rights, or Fundamental Rights Agency[1] (FRA). Making these links is crucial for informing an education and ECEC sector in addressing diversity, equality, and inclusion, as I have argued elsewhere (Murray & Urban, 2012, p. 61). The nature of the Roma and Traveller situation generally and specifically in education and ECEC requires recognition and respect across all national and local strategies, the will to lead at the political level, and the appropriate engagement of long-standing Roma and Traveller NGOs and Roma and Traveller communities. A fundamental joining of forces at all levels is required to move from sectoral to more systemic solutions nationally and locally. Travellers, and more recently Roma, are intensely marginalized in Irish society.

Who Are the Travellers?

Irish Travellers are a small, indigenous ethnic group (30,000) with a nomadic tradition whose presence in Irish society was first officially recorded in the 12th century. Recent genome research has shown that, biologically, Travellers have been a separate population from the general Irish population for at least a thousand years (Kenny, 2011). There are large communities of Travellers globally in England, the United States, and Australia. The community has a long-shared history, with common cultural characteristics and traditions evident in the organization of family, values, language, and social and economic life (Murray, 1997, 2002). The extended family, not a particular geographical location, is the embodiment of community for Travellers. While family is also considered important to the dominant population, their notion of community is generally associated with a geographical location.

In the past decade the Travellers' nomadic lifestyle has been constrained by Irish legislation, specifically the Housing Miscellaneous Act (Trespass Law) of 2002. The legislation makes it a criminal offence to trespass on and occupy public or private property. This offence is punishable by immediate eviction, a month in jail and/or a €3,000 fine, and the confiscation of property. When the legislation became effective, the state promised it would not be used against Travellers living on the roadside and awaiting accommodation. Instead, it was to be used in instances of large-scale illegal encampments. This turned out not to be the case.[2]

The legislation has resulted in considerable hardship for Traveller families. With their lifestyle undervalued and many families forced into substandard housing, their practice of living with extended family has been inhibited. This has led to isolation and loneliness for many Travellers, which in turn has had an effect on their well-being and has led, in some cases, to serious mental health concerns (Kelleher et al., 2010). While not the only factor affecting mental health in the Traveller community, forced assimilation by means of state policy does have its ramifications. The 2010 Traveller All Ireland Health Study shows, for example, that the suicide rate among young Travellers is six times that of the general population and that suicide accounts for approximately 11% of all Traveller deaths.

The criminalization of nomadic practice means that many Travellers are living in settled-type[3] accommodation. This is not necessarily freely chosen (Kenny & Binchy, 2009). This is similar to the Roma history of nomadism and settlement. Of all Travellers, 42% are under 15 years of age, compared with 21% of the general population, and 63% of Travellers are under 25 years of age, compared with 35% of the general population.

Inclusion: The Blind Spot

In 2008, Conor Lenihan T.D.,[4] then Minister of State with special responsibility for integration policy, highlighted in an opening address at a conference for the development of an intercultural education strategy (IES) the need for positive cultural integration of new communities. Genuine commitment to cultural integration would have included Travellers. Instead, Traveller children and their community were absent from this discourse. The origins of the development of an IES lie in a government commitment at the 2001 World Conference Against Racism in Durban to develop and implement the National Action Plan Against Racism (NPAR). One of NPAR's ten outcomes for the education sector included the development of an intercultural education strategy (IES) (Department of Education and Science, 2010). This development was primarily driven by Traveller NGOs in Durban. It was alarming to see Travellers ignored in the IES and the focus placed only on the integration of migrants and English "language acquisition and education continuance" (Department of Education and Skills, 2008, p. 7). It confirms the view that Travellers continue to be seen as a subculture of poverty and not as a cultural entity. This is underlined by the fact that responsibility for Traveller education sits under social inclusion in the Department of Education and Skills.

The lack of recognition of Travellers as an ethnic minority group in Ireland also continues to reinforce this position, despite the fact that key policy documents now recognize the cultural context of the Traveller community (see, for example, Department of Justice, Equality and Law Reform, 1995; Kelleher, 2010; DES, 2006; and Department of Health and Children, 2002). Key European documents have criticized the state for non-engagement with the Traveller ethnic identifier question. The decision was reversed only through continued lobbying by the Traveller NGO sector and, as a result, Travellers were included in the *Intercultural Education Strategy 2010–2015* (Department of Education and Skills, 2010). This also has implications for marginalized immigrants, especially the Roma.

Who Are the Roma?

Roma are the largest minority ethnic group in Europe. Their global population is estimated to be 10–12 million, and 8 million are domiciled in the EU. Like

Travellers, Roma are not a homogeneous group, and their nomadic traditions have been constrained. Under communist law in Eastern Europe, nomadism was not permitted; as a result, Roma are largely sedentary. Some operate as peripatetic nomads, which means that they travel in order to practice their trades and skills where they can (Pavee Point, 2009). In common with the Traveller community, the extended family is central to Roma values and culture. With the enlargement of the EU and an upsurge in anti-Roma violence and discrimination (European Network Against Racism [ENAR], 2012), many Roma have been forced to move and, in essence, have become nomadic. Many Roma families are also migrating to Western Europe, including Ireland, seeking a better life. Roma do not share a particular homeland, but, akin to Travellers, they are a minority ethnic group and share a common ancestry, history, culture, and language, as well as a tradition of nomadism.

Travellers and Roma also share the same experience of collective negative stereotyping and stigmatization. However, the extermination of Roma during World War II has left a deep scar in the Roma psyche. Many Roma continue to see the dominant group and authority as a threat. In this time of economic crisis, scapegoating has increased, and Roma (ENAR, 2012) and Travellers (Pavee Point, 2011a) have become easy targets for extremists and the far right. There are an estimated 5,000–7,000 Roma who are legally resident in Ireland and who have come from EU countries such as Romania, Slovakia, the Czech Republic, Poland, and Bulgaria (Pavee Point, 2009). The Roma population is young: 35.7% are under 15, compared to 15.7% of the EU population overall. The average age is 25 among Roma, compared with 40 across the EU (European Commission [COM], 2010b, sec. 1.3.3, p. 5).

Roma and Travellers: The Connection

Irish Travellers and Roma are not linked by origin. Roma originate in northwestern India and speak a language called Romani. Travellers originate in Ireland and have their own distinctive languages (Shelta and Cant). However, the importance of extended family, beliefs, and values associated with family culture and traditions are shared. Nomadism has shaped the Traveller and Roma mind-set and can be seen most strongly in their economic relations with the settled community, "whether travel is still a current reality for any group or individual or whether it has become a deferred dream" (Liégeois, 2008; cited in Kenny & Binchy, 2009, p. 128).

In recent European policy discourse, Roma and Travellers are intrinsically linked. Roma is being used as the umbrella term to describe a number of groups, including people who identify as Roma, Travellers, Sinti, Ashkali, Manouche, Dom, and Lom (COM, 2011a; FRA, 2010b, 2012). The use of the word *Roma* as an umbrella term for all groups, while not intended to marginalize, can have unintended consequences internally (within communities) and externally (in European or state discourse)—for example, Roma-only organizations or Travellers-only organizations invited to policy meetings at European or national levels.

A European Focus

In May 2011 the European Commission announced a European Framework for National Roma Integration Strategies up to 2020 (COM, 2011a). The same year the communications *An EU Agenda for the Rights of the Child* (COM, 2011b) and *Early Childhood Education and Care: Providing All Our Children with the Best Start for the World of Tomorrow* (COM, 2011c) were published and endorsed at the EU level. The focus on a Roma/Traveller integration strategy is long awaited and very welcome.

Despite the plethora of strong policy documents and EU Commission communications, concrete links across areas of concern are still lacking. Currently the response by EU member states to the development of their individual Roma strategies has been limited and half-hearted. Their efforts have been criticized by the European Commission and by the European Roma Policy Coalition with these words: "Such complacency is neither acceptable nor sustainable" (ERPC, 2012).

National Traveller/Roma Integration Strategy

The Irish response is an excellent example of the lack of will to address convincingly Travellers' and Roma's marginalized position in the state. The strategy is incongruous, as it cites examples of initiatives that have already had their funding cut. These include the mediation service in Pavee Point (2010) and the internship program "Not Like Us" for young Travellers in the state offices led by the Taoiseach's (Prime Minister's) Office in 2006 which, though successful, was never mainstreamed. Despite the explicit remit of the document (National Roma Integration Strategy), the Roma community is relatively invisible in the document. There is a brief reference to education linked to gaining proficiency in the English language, but Roma are not mentioned in the area of health, despite the Health Service Executive (HSE) child protection concerns (Pavee Point/HSE, 2012). These concerns emanate from the abject poverty that Roma families from Romania and Bulgaria are living in as a consequence of immigration policies—for instance, the Irish Naturalization and Immigration Service (INIS, 2007) Exemption Order and the Habitual Residence Condition Act (HRC, 2009). Habitual residence is a condition that applicants must satisfy in order to qualify for certain social welfare assistance payments, including child benefits. HSE professionals working with Roma families reveal that "if it wasn't for the poverty, there wouldn't be a child protection issue at all for Roma" (Pavee Point, 2012, p. 21).

The Irish strategy outlines the importance of two key strategies: the *Intercultural Education Strategy 2010–2015* (Department of Education and Skills, 2010) and the *Report and Recommendations for a Traveller Education Strategy* (DES, 2006). Both strategies could be regarded as significant for Traveller and Roma inclusion in education. The latter is based on the core "principle of inclusion with emphases on equality and diversity and the adoption of an intercultural approach"

(Department of Justice and Equality, 2011, p. 7). To date, neither of these strategies has had a significant outcome for Traveller children or young people in education. Any advances that have been made have recently been undermined by the severe cuts to all Traveller supports by the department in 2011.

Traveller organizations consider it disingenuous that the state has produced a national Traveller/Roma strategy that ignores the failure of the current strategies. It cites successful programs that were not mainstreamed and in particular gives limited focus to racism, discrimination, and social and cultural oppression of the Traveller and Roma communities in Ireland. This is more than a missed opportunity (Pavee Point, 2012); it is a flagrant disregard for the rights of Travellers and Roma in education. The document makes reference to an entitlement to preschool (one free pre-school year since 2010). Despite the EU Commission communication on ECEC, early childhood education and care is not given any prominence in the document.

The European Roma Policy Coalition has strongly criticized member states' strategies, revealing that "many of them [are] so deeply flawed that they cannot even be regarded as a first step forward." The Irish national integration strategy for Travellers and Roma (DJE, 2011) is an example of such a flawed strategy (Pavee Point, 2012).

Education Strategy

Developed in partnership with Traveller NGOs on the Advisory Committee for Traveller Education (ACTE) over a 2-year period from 2004 to 2005, the Traveller education strategy was published by the Department of Education and Science (now Skills) as *The Report and Recommendations for a Traveller Education Strategy* (DES, 2006). This title has led to some confusion and, over a period of 6 years, has led to considerable frustration for Traveller organizations pursuing the education agenda. The ambiguous title of the document has effectively created ambivalence for the implementation of the "Education Strategy" or, indeed, Traveller progress in education.

Following the publication of the report, the state disbanded the Advisory Committee for Traveller Education (which included Traveller NGOs), despite an explicit recommendation on the structures for implementing the strategy: "the ACTE should continue to advise the Minister and evaluate the progress of Traveller education as the strategy is being implemented" (DES, 2006, p. 98). For the next 4 years it proved impossible for Traveller organizations to get accurate information, or in fact any implementation plan from the Department of Education and Skills to monitor, assess, and advise on the developments in Traveller education. Following intensive lobbying for the reinstatement of the ACTE in 2009, the DES established a Traveller Education Strategy Advisory and Consultative Forum with limited power—in other words, no direct line to the

Minister for Education. No implementation plan[5] has been forthcoming, despite numerous requests for a plan, targets, and monitoring of the strategy by Traveller NGOs. Prior to the budget of 2011, the Department of Education and Skills moved only on recommendations that cut resources to Traveller families, justifying them on the basis of this statement in the Traveller education strategy: "In implementing the policy of inclusion, all support services should be provided in a way that is based on identified *need* rather than on Traveller *identity* (emphasis added, p. 33).

Cuts included transport for Traveller children to school and the closure of Traveller segregated pre-schools. Shortly thereafter, in 2011, all resources for Traveller children and young people were withdrawn under the National Budget of 2011 (Department of Finance, 2011), including the Visiting Teacher Service, Resource Teachers for Travellers, and Traveller Training Centres for young people and adults.

This decision was based on the demands of the International Monetary Fund (IMF),[6] along with cuts to English-as-a-second-language supports. These were easy targets, since these cuts to marginalized and discriminated sectors in society would not elicit cries of concern from the general population.

The Irish National Traveller/Roma Integration Strategy (DJE, 2011) reiterates this principle of "individual educational need" rather than "Traveller identity" and states that it will "underpin future actions including allocation of resources. The Department's aim is to prioritise available resources to maximum effect across the education sector to enhance educational outcomes for all children and adults including Travellers" (p. 7). There is a convenience in focusing on a principle that supports the action you wish to carry out within the current economic climate. The now-overused statement by the State Department—"no cost action"—for example, supports a climate of inaction. However, there are explicit underpinning values and principles in the "Education Strategy" that should be informing the implementation of the strategy:

> It is clear that [the] best practice requires that due regard be given to the *rights of the child*, both as an individual and as a member of their community [emphasis added]. The UN Convention on the Rights of the Child (1989) compels us to take account of the child's needs and the child's culture in all aspects of education. It further requires us to ensure that the rights of the child are upheld without discrimination of any kind. This report reflects the voice of the child principle as enshrined in the UN Convention on the Rights of the Child (1989) and in the National Children's Office Publication *Young Voices* (2005, p. 9). (DES, 2006, p. 9)

Further:

> All education services should be provided in a way that is equitable and fair and that addresses the *danger of racism and discrimination*. This report considers equity in the

provision of education service. This requires an acceptance that equity is based not just on equality of access but on *equality of participation* and outcome and that the particular needs and culture of Travellers requires an *innovative* approach to planning. (p. 9; emphasis added)

Traveller organizations are not opposed to a focus on the specific "needs" of Traveller children. Indeed, Traveller organizations have lobbied for Traveller children to be included in mainstream classes, to be assessed on their need rather than their identity for specific provision such as additional support for literacy, and so forth. The *Report and Recommendations for a Traveller Education Strategy* (DES, 2006) is a very comprehensive document. Under the section on early childhood education there are, for example, 7 recommendations with 22 specific actions outlined to meet those outcomes. The recommendation to remove segregated Traveller preschools has been implemented (and welcomed); however, the lead-up actions to this recommendation have been ignored. This would appear to be the department's general approach to the implementation of the education strategy. The neglect of the prerequisites for the specific outcomes of integrated services has led Traveller organizations to chronicle their concerns.

The Equality and Diversity Early Childhood National Network (EDENN), along with Traveller NGOs, continues to lobby for the mainstreaming of an appropriate diversity and equality approach in pre-service education, in keeping with the education and intercultural strategies. There remains, however, a lacuna in thinking at departmental and teacher/ECEC training college levels. While Travellers are placed under social inclusion in the department, the focus is on their "gaps" or their deficient educational attainment, with no emphasis placed on their cultural inclusion or the ongoing issues of anti-Traveller/Roma racism and discrimination.

Those charged with delivering interculturalism in training colleges have been funded under the Department of Foreign Affairs and Aid Action. The remit of Aid Action is to focus on development and global educational issues. Travellers and Traveller issues are marginalized in this framework and are dependent on interested individuals leading, for example, the intercultural agenda. The current coordinator of the Development and Intercultural Education Project (DICE) has a background and interest in Traveller issues, but Traveller issues remain on the periphery and are not mainstreamed.

Teaching Council guidelines also promote ethical values of respect, trust, care, and integrity as underpinning standards for teachers.

Respect

Teachers uphold human dignity and promote equality and emotional and cognitive development. In their professional practice, teachers demonstrate respect for spiritual and cultural values, diversity, social justice, freedom, democracy, and the environment.

Trust

Teachers' relationships with pupils/students, colleagues, parents, school management and the public are based on trust. Trust embodies fairness, openness and honesty (2012, p. 5). Inclusion as a national priority informs the Teaching Council's *Code of Professional Conduct for Teachers* (2012) and *Initial Teacher Education: Criteria and Guidelines for Programme Providers* (2011). The absence of a focus on rights beyond children's right to a voice and the lack of an anti-discriminatory, anti-racist focus is a major concern. While the concepts of equality and diversity are present, they are not defined. Traveller lifestyle remains deficient in the minds of Irish society and in teacher training, guidelines, pre-service training, and so forth. The "head-in-the-sand" mind-set is endemic to the system, and it will require a major shift in thinking to support changes in the system.

Attitudes Toward Travellers and, More Recently, Roma

Mac Greil (2011), in his comprehensive work on prejudice in Ireland, raised concerns about the level of negative attitudes toward the "Romanians" (Roma) in Ireland today and warned of "the seeds of discrimination against this ethnic category" identified in his research findings (p. 144). In a report on his mission to assess the human rights situation in Ireland, Tomas Hammarberg (2007) stated that "Travellers have been subjected to discrimination and racism in the fields of education employment, housing, health care, media reporting and participation in decision-making." He further stated that he considers it "essential that Travellers are effectively protected against discrimination and racism under national and international law" (Council of Europe, 2007). The European Commission acknowledges that "Roma in Europe face prejudice, intolerance, discrimination and social exclusion in their daily lives. They are marginalised and live in very poor socio-economic conditions" (COM 173–174, 2011a). The EU Fundamental Rights Agency (2011) has catalogued the discrimination and disadvantage experienced by Roma, including difficulties when they migrate to another EU member state. Roma experience problems with border/visa officials, including demands for bribes by corrupt officials, when leaving and/or returning to their countries of origin. Traveller marginalization and oppression have been documented in Ireland by many scholars, including Mac Greil (1997, 2010, 2011), and in Europe through the UNICERD, UNCRC, and the Fundamental Rights Agency (Murray & Urban, 2012). The EU Commissioner for Human Rights recommends that member states "take proactive measures so that Roma and Travellers are given a real chance to overcome a long history of exclusion" (Hammarberg, 2012, p. 223).

An At-Risk Category

The state's relationship with Travellers continues to be ambivalent. The flawed implementation of the Traveller education strategy and intercultural education strategy exemplify this. But where does it come from? The examples below, while partly historical, show the prevalent attitude toward the Traveller community.

Traveller as Deficit

> If you cannot make citizens of [the Travellers], put them into homes. It would be better than [having] them going around rearing their children without education and giving them no chances. You may not succeed in one generation but you might succeed with the second generation. (Dáil; cited in Helleiner, 2000, p. 71)

Blame the Traveller

The Minister for Education described Traveller children as "similar in any respect to other educationally retarded children," a situation aggravated, he said, by "social disabilities and other consequences of their unsettled way of life" (1985).

Contemporary Comment: What Has Changed?

"The biggest issue facing Travellers, aside from school transport and from the disadvantage associated with the community, is the general antipathy that resides within the community towards education" as stated by Jim Mulkerrins, Principal Officer, Social Inclusion Unit (Department of Education and Skills in the House of the Oireachtas Discussion, 2011). In this speech he makes a direct link to Traveller culture.

Mac Greil's recent research (2011) reminds the state of the need for, and consequences of, not providing appropriately for the inclusion of the Traveller community in Irish society. "The overall position of [the] Traveller is very serious and will not improve without a new initiative from the State at the national and local levels" (p. 541).

Traveller Experiences of Education: A Historical Perspective

The voices below come from interviews carried out with Traveller adults and young people to record the experiences of Travellers in education. The Travellers interviewed have young children in the school system now or are about to start families. The aim was to explore how Traveller experiences inform their relationship with the education system and their wishes for their children. Interviews were conducted by the author between 2008 and 2011 in response to the ongoing state critique of Travellers' perceived lack of engagement with the education system. Examples recorded include Travellers' experiences at school from the 1980s to 2011. The decision to carry out the interviews stemmed largely from the ongoing critique of Traveller parents' "lack of responsibility" regarding their children's school attendance. With the anecdotal knowledge of the ambivalent relationship Travellers have with the system, these interviews were carried out to formally record Traveller experiences and their understanding of the education system in their own words. We relate their experiences here.

One day the school inspector turned up in class, to apply a history test. The prize for the highest score was a star and a pen. As J [Age: 36] loved history he scored 100% and was duly congratulated by the visiting inspector, who handed over the prize and departed the classroom. The joy was short lived, for Mrs… [teacher], his class teacher, quickly took the prize back off him. "I don't know how you did it," she said, "but I know you cheated."

KJ [30] suffered a year of total invisibility at the hands of a teacher who actively excluded her from class activities. In one memorable incident, her "key moment," K and a group in her class were invited to Aras an Uchtarain [President's residence] to receive a prize. "In an unfortunate turn of events," explained the teacher, there wasn't enough room for four children at the award ceremony, and so K was told she couldn't attend.

TC [19] put the vicious circle of invisibility and low expectations in perspective. There is no point in going on with school when you cannot read or write, "cos it would just get harder as you went along; you have no confidence in yourself." The best-case scenario was a "let up" in the system, thanks to the kindness of a sympathetic individual. This reinforced the concept that progress was a matter of generosity dispensed by a settled person rather than a fundamental right to fulfill your potential.

The older Travellers were far better equipped to analyze their experiences than their younger counterparts. This may be the result of their developed understanding of discrimination and oppression as part of their work in Traveller organizations, or simply their age and life experience. They were able to place their experience in a broad context of institutional discrimination. The younger interviewees blamed themselves for their poor academic output. "I didn't understand all the things that happened until I grew up and looked back because it was the norm," said H [36]—a comment replicated by every interviewee. "It's only when you get to a certain point in your life that you start seeing things for what they were," said P [30].

T [19] blamed the Travellers for their own misfortune. "Bad school, too many Traveller in the class," he concluded, even though settled children outnumbered Traveller children by about five to one. The statement reveals the chronic low self-esteem prevalent among young Travellers, trapped within an education system that has utterly failed their needs.

The older Travellers could pinpoint discrimination, isolation, and the pattern of marginalization, but younger Travellers often viewed such injustices as the norm. One young boy, P [15], told me he was in a special class "just to catch up with all the rest." In hindsight, M [38] recognized the "special Traveller classes as a policy of containment." It is challenging to construct a fair and equitable education system for Traveller children while the world outside the school gate remains resolutely opposed to their very existence (Mac Greil, 2010, 2011). Recent improvements and modifications within the system have weakened certain apartheid-style practices, notably the compulsory shower for Traveller children attending school in the 1980s, and special classes are now also abandoned. The younger interviewees recognized that the education system, likened to the broader economic caste, leaves no room for Travellers. "It's all the same to Travellers, how good they are, they'll never get a job," concluded T [19].

While the broad pattern of exclusion is repeated, each Traveller experience has its own flavor. It must be noted that the Traveller community's negative experience of the school system has left deep wounds. The promise of employment has also not come to fruition for those who have remained in school until 18. This combined knowledge leaves little will within the community to fight the reactionary culture of early departure from school. And while the 2011 comments of Jim Mulkerrins (DES, 2011), Oireachtas Committee (2011), are more tame in the language used, the state continues to undermine Traveller culture, and the rhetoric of "blame the parents" has a long history. State responsibility is absent in the discourse. Traveller children, like their parents, continue to be framed as having *needs* rather than *rights*; their culture remains defined as a problem, and anti-Traveller racism legitimizes policies of assimilation.

The state seems limited in its ability to work out why Traveller children have fared so poorly in education. It continues to describe Travellers as an "at-risk" category by the mere fact of being born Travellers. The solution to the problem continues to be linked to permanent accommodation in local authority housing (supported by the Housing Miscellaneous Act), a possible prior step to the eventual disappearance of Traveller culture. However, we now have an additional "problem": the arrival of a substantial population of Roma. The message directed at Travellers and Roma is that they are responsible for their situation. It is widely accepted (dominant knowledge) that we benefit from education. If educated you will get a job; you will have a future. But in the current recession nothing is certain. However, Traveller and Roma experience tells them that regardless of the recession, "there is no or very little employment" for them. Children recently interviewed show that this knowledge is embedded. M [12] stated: "Settled people get work and settled people get more money." At the same time, these children also recognized that "Travellers have the right to be treated equally," according to R [13].

In response to these circumstances, Travellers and Roma have developed alternative economies. These are often restricted or eventually regulated by the state, which makes them difficult but necessary for survival. Traveller and Roma knowledge tells the community that education has not been provided. The experience of Travellers and Roma in education and their love for their children tells the community that their children may be discriminated against and hurt in the state education system. "I get in trouble when I talk, but the country people don't get into trouble for the same thing," said M [12]. J [12] added: "in school we get called 'knackers'[7] by the settled children."

So why go there? How do we bridge state knowledge and Traveller/Roma knowledge and love to move toward a rights-based approach within the education system where we actually recognize the identity and rights of Traveller and Roma children to develop to their full potential?

Possible Way Forward

Equality of Condition (Baker, Lynch, Cantillon, & Walsh, 2004) linked to an Anti-bias Approach (Derman-Sparks, 1989) offers an alternative way to look at Traveller and Roma exclusion. At the same time it offers a way to meet the expectations of the state and Travellers by engaging in the education system, including early childhood education. Equality of condition, argue Baker et al. (2004), "recognizes that inequality is rooted in oppression, and in social structures that can be changed" (p. 33).

> Those who espouse equality of condition seek to focus on root causes and to identify how inequalities are generated and passed on from generation to generation by structures and systems. They promote the need to review the structures in society...so that people can realise a sense of belonging and ownership in society. Equality of condition is about "enabling an empowering people to make real choices among real options." (Baker et al., 2004 in Crowley, 2006, p. 17 cited in Murray & Urban, 2012, p. 23)

It focuses on five key dimensions: equality of respect and recognition, resources, love, care and solidarity, equality of power, and working and learning (Baker et al., 2004, p. 43).

Oppression and Discrimination

The anti-bias approach developed specifically for early childhood pro-actively addresses issues of oppression and discrimination by working from four specific goals for adults and children.

Anti-Bias Goals for Children:

1. To support children's identity (individual and group) and their sense of belonging;

2. To foster children's empathy and support them to be comfortable with difference;

3. To encourage each child to critically think about diversity and bias; and

4. To empower children to stand up for themselves and others in difficult situations. (Derman-Sparks, 1989)

One initiative is making a difference. It is funded under Dormant Accounts by the Department of Education and Skills Education Unit, situated in the Offices of the Department of Children and Youth Affairs, and is titled Preschool Education Initiative for Children from Minority Communities. The initiative is rolling out diversity and equality training, "Ar an mBealach" (Murray, Cooke, & O'Doherty, 2004/2011) developed by the "éist" project in Pavee Point and the Equality and Diversity Early Childhood National Network (EDENN) (www. edenn.org). The project focuses on attitudinal change and the competencies of the adult in addressing social justice, equality, and diversity for both majority and minority children and adults. This work is linked to the anti-bias goals that have been adapted to the Irish sector by the éist project.

The *éist* project has systematically linked its early childhood training to Irish equality legislation, the work of FRA, UNICERD, UNCRC, the EU Commission, and the Council of Europe (Murray & O'Doherty, 2001) and the Diversity in Early Childhood Education and Training (DECET, www.decet.org; European Network, 2011) principles. The national project is working with 32 county and city child care committees and 450 practitioners. The evaluation has recently been published. Results show that attitudinal change is being achieved and contributes to high-quality practice. This program supports mainstream training and practice to address social justice and equality issues in ECEC. The approach could potentially be a way forward for the education system, Travellers, and Roma.

These questions are paramount: Can we be bold, brave, and open enough to initiate solidarity in action among the state, voluntary organizations, and the Traveller community? Can we create conditions where it is possible to have an open discourse on anti-Traveller/Roma racism and the oppressive constraints internalized (Freire, 2000) by many Travellers and Roma? Can we replace the lens that sees Traveller- and Roma-related initiatives as beyond settlement, assimilation, and second-language acquisition? In order to legitimately offer Travellers and Roma a better experience in education, we require ongoing critical interrogation of the unequal power relations in systems as well as hearing and engaging with the diverse experiences of Traveller and Roma.

Final Word

When asked what she would like to say to the Minister of Education and Skill, a young Traveller girl, S, age 7, said:

> I'd like to tell him that there is nothing wrong with being a Traveller and there is nothing to be ashamed of. When you are a Traveller you are a Traveller, you can't change it and

you might as well tell anyone you know that you are a Traveller. People in your class, that are not Travellers, they would probably understand and they would listen to you and still be your friend, people who are good and sensible.

Notes

1. The European Union Agency for Fundamental Rights (FRA) is an advisory body of the European Union established in 2007. The FRA helps to ensure that fundamental rights of people living in the EU are protected. It does this by collecting evidence about the status of fundamental rights across the European Union and providing advice, based on evidence, about how to improve the situation (fra.europa.eu/).
2. See *www.irishstatutebook.ie/2002/en/act/pub/0009/index.html.*
3. Travellers refer to members of the dominant population as Settled people or Country people.
4. A TD (Teachta Dála) is a member of Dáil Éirann, the lower house of the Oireachtas (the Irish Parliament).
5. At the time of writing this article, the Department of Jobs, Enterprise and Innovation lifted the restrictions on work for Romanians and Bulgarians. This means that from now on Roma from these countries will not need a work permit to work in Ireland. It also means that immigrants will be in a position to partake in Community Employment Schemes. This is a welcome development. Monitoring of the benefits to Roma will be necessary (www.djei.ie/press/2012/20120720a.htm).
6. As a consequence of the financial crisis and the collapse of the banking system, the Irish government in 2010 requested support from the EU and the International Monetary Fund (IMF). The request was approved under condition of severe "austerity" measures affecting all areas of public service.
7. "Knacker" comes from the association with the "knacker's yard" as a place where old horses were slaughtered. The association has led to the labelling of Travellers as "knackers," meaning beyond use. It is used as a slur against the Traveller community. The term, thus, is very offensive to Travellers.

References

Baker, J., Lynch, K., Cantillon, S., & Walsh, J. (2004). *Equality from theory to action.* Basingstoke, UK: Palgrave Macmillan.

Children's Rights Alliance/The National Youth Council of Ireland. (2005). *Young voices: Guidelines on how to involve children and young people in your work.* Dublin: The Stationery Office.

Council of Europe. (2007). *Report by the Commissioner for Human Rights, Mr. Thomas Hammarberg on his visit to Ireland, November 2007.* Retrieved from www.dfa.ie/uploads/documents/Political%20Division/final%20report%20ireland.Pdf

Crowley, N. (2006). *An ambition for equality.* Dublin: Irish Academic Press.

Department of Education and Science (DES). (2006). *Report and recommendations for a Traveller education strategy.* Dublin: The Stationery Office.

Department of Education and Skills/Office of the Minister for Integration. (2010). *Intercultural education strategy 2010–2015.* Dublin: The Stationery Office.

Department of Finance. (2011). *Budget 2011.* Dublin: The Stationery Office. Retrieved from www.budget.gov.ie/budgets/2011/2011.aspx

Department of Health and Children. (2002). *Traveller health. A national strategy 2002–2005.* Dublin: The Stationery Office.

Department of Justice and Equality. (2011). *Ireland's national Traveller/Roma integration strategy.* Dublin: The Stationery Office.

Department of Justice, Equality and Law Reform. (1995). *Report of the Task Force on the Travelling Community.* Dublin: The Stationery Office.

Derman-Sparks, L. (1989). *Anti-bias curriculum: Tools for empowering young children.* Washington, DC: National Association for the Education of Young Children.

Diversity in Early Childhood Education and Training (DECET). (2011). *Diversity and social inclusion. Exploring competences for professional practice in early childhood education and care.* Brussels: DECET.

European Commission (COM). (2010a). *The European Economic and Social Committee and the Committee of the Regions: The social and economic integration of the Roma in Europe.* Communication 133. Brussels: European Commission.

European Commission (COM). (2010b). *Roma in Europe. The implementation of European Union instruments and policies for Roma inclusion—Progress report 2008–2010.* Brussels: European Commission.

European Commission (COM). (2011a). *An EU framework for national Roma integration strategies up to 2020.* Communication 173/4. Brussels: European Commission.

European Commission (COM). (2011b). *An EU agenda for the rights of the child.* Communication 60. Brussels: European Commission. Retrieved from http://ec.europa.eu/justice/policies/children/docs/com_2011_60_en.pdf

European Commission (COM). (2011c). *Early childhood education and care: Providing all our children with the best start for the world of tomorrow.* Communication 66. Brussels: European Commission.

European Network Against Racism (ENAR)/European Roma Information Office. (2011 [cited as 2012 throughout the document]). *Debunking myths and revealing myths about Roma.* Brussels: ENAR & ERIO.

European Network Against Racism (ENAR). (2012). *Racism in Europe—ENAR shadow report 2010/11.* Brussels: ENAR.

European Roma Policy Coalition (ERPC). (2012). Press statement. Retrieved from http://roma-policy.eu/erpc-welcomes-european-commissions-negative-assessment-of-the-national-roma-integration-strategies/

European Union Agency for Fundamental Rights (FRA). (2009). *Data in focus report: The Roma.* Retrieved from http://fra.europa.eu/sites/default/files/fra_uploads/413-EU-MIDIS_ROMA_EN.pdf

European Union Agency for Fundamental Rights (FRA). (2010a). EU-MIDIS: *European Union minorities and discrimination survey.* Retrieved from http://fra.europa.eu/en/project/2011/eu-midis-european-union-minorities-and-discrimination-survey

European Union Agency for Fundamental Rights (FRA). (2010b). *The fundamental rights position of Roma and Travellers in the European Union.* Retrieved from http://fra.europa.eu/sites/default/files/fra_uploads/1012-roma-travellers-factsheet_en.pdf

European Union Agency for Fundamental Rights (FRA). (2012). *The FRA's work for the Roma.* http://fra.europa.eu/fraWebsite/roma/roma_en.htm

European Union Agency for Fundamental Rights (FRA)/United Nations Development Programme. (2012). *The situation of Roma in EU member states: Survey results at a glance.* Retrieved from http://fra.europa.eu/sites/default/files/fra_uploads/2099-FRA-2012-Roma-at-a-glance_EN.pdf

Freire, P. (2000). *Pedagogy of the oppressed* (30th anniversary ed.). New York: Continuum.

Habitual-Residence-Condition Act. 2009. Retrieved May 22, 3013, from www.welfare.ie/.../

Hammarberg, T. (2007, November). [On his visit to Ireland.] Retrieved from http://www.dfa.ie/uploads/documents/Political%20Division/final%20report%20irelan d.pdf

Hammarberg, T. (2012). *Human rights of Roma and Travellers in Europe*. Brussels: Council of Europe. Retrieved from http://www.coe.int/t/commissioner/source/prems/prems79611_ GBR_CouvHumanRig htsOfRoma_WEB.pdf

Helleiner, J. (2000). *Irish Travellers: Racism and the politics of culture*. Toronto: University of Toronto Press.

Housing Miscellaneous Act (Trespass Law) of 2002. Retrieved May 20, 2013, from *www.irishstatutebook.ie/2002/en/act/pub/0009/sec0024.htm*

Irish Naturalisation Immigration Service Retrieved May 18, 2013 from *www.inis.gov.ie/*

Kelleher, C. (Ed.). (2010). *All Ireland Traveller health study: Our Geels*. Dublin: University College Dublin, School of Public Health, Physiotherapy and Population Science. Retrieved May 10, 2013, from http://www.dohc.ie/publications/aiths2010/ExecutiveSummary/AITHS2010_ SUMMARY_LR_All.pdf?direct=1

Kenny, M. (2011). *An integrated approach to conflict among Travellers, at family, community and structural context levels*. Dublin: Pavee Point.

Kenny, M., & Binchy, A. (2009). Irish Travellers, identity and the education system. In P.A. Danaher, M. Kenny, & J. Remy Leder (Eds.), *Traveller, nomadic and migrant education* (pp. 117-131). London: Routledge.

Lenihan, C. (2008). *Towards an intercultural education strategy—National consultation*. Retrieved from www.nccri.ie/pdf/Minister%20Lenihans%20Speech.doc

Mac Greil, M. (1997). *Prejudice in Ireland revisited*. Kildare: The Survey and Research Unit, Department of Social Studies, NUI Maynooth.

Mac Greil, M. (2010). *Emancipation of the Travelling people*. Kildare: The Survey and Research Unit, Department of Social Studies, NUI Maynooth.

Mac Greil, M. (2011). *Pluralism and diversity in Ireland*. Dublin: Columba Press.

Murray, C. (1997). *Pavee children: A study on childcare issues for Travellers*. Dublin: Pavee Point.

Murray, C. (2002). The Traveller child: A holistic perspective. In *Diversity in early childhood: A collection of essays* (pp. 44–63). Dublin: Barnardos. Retrieved May 10, 2013, from http://www. barnardos.ie/assets/files/publications/free/Diversity.pdf

Murray, C. (2006). *The conceptualisation of diversity and equality in early childhood care and education*. Unpublished MSc thesis, University College Dublin.

Murray, C., Cooke, M., & O'Doherty, A. (2011). *Ar an mBealach/On the way*. Dublin: Pavee Point. (Original work published 2004)

Murray, C., & O'Doherty, A. (2001). *"éist": Respecting diversity in early childhood care, education and training*. Dublin: Pavee Point.

Murray, C., & Urban, M. (2012). *Diversity and equality in early childhood: An Irish perspective*. Dublin: Gill and Macmillan.

National Children's Office. (2005). *Young voices: Guidelines on how to involve children and young people in your work*. Dublin: The Stationery Office. Retrieved May 10, 2013, from http://www. dcya.gov.ie/documents/publications/31267_Young_Voices_.pdf

Oireachtas Report. (2011). *Special educational needs: Discussion*. Dublin: Joint Committee on Jobs, Social Protection and Education Debate. Retrieved May 10, 2013, from http://debates. oireachtas.ie/FAJ/2011/10/18/00004.asp

Pavee Point. (2009). *Barriers to Roma accessing health services*. Dublin: Pavee Point.

Pavee Point. (2011a, April 20). Man faces court over incitement to hatred through Facebook. Retrieved May 10, 2013, from http://paveepoint.ie/?s=Man+Faces+Court

Pavee Point. (2011b). *Towards a national Traveller and Roma integration strategy 2020*. Dublin: Pavee Point.

Pavee Point. (2012). *Pavee Point response to Ireland's national Traveller/Roma integrations strategy*. Dublin: Pavee Point.

Pavee Point/Health Service Executive (HSE). (2012). *Roma communities in Ireland and child protection consideration*. Dublin: Pavee Point & HSE.

Rorke, B. (2012). *Killing time: The lethal force of anti-Roma racism*. Retrieved from http://www.opensocietyfoundations.org/voices/killing-time-lethal-force-anti-roma-racism

Teaching Council. (2011). *Initial teacher education: Criteria and guidelines for programme providers*. Dublin: The Teaching Council.

Teaching Council. (2012). *Code of professional conduct for teachers*. Dublin: The Teaching Council.

UNICEF/European Social Observatory in collaboration with the Belgian Federal Planning Service (Ministry) for Social Integration. (2011). *Preventing social exclusion through the Europe 2020 strategy: Early childhood development and the inclusion of Roma Families*. Retrieved from http://www.ecdgroup.com/pdfs/Preventing-Social-Exclusion.pdf

Urban, M., Vandenbroeck, M., Van Laere, K., Lazzari, A., & Peeters, J. (2011). *Competence requirements in early childhood education and care*. Brussels: European Commission.

CHAPTER TWELVE

When Boys Are Pushed-Pulled Out of School

Rights to Education in the Philippines

Leodinito Y. Cañete

Bound by Convention and Poverty

In putting forward its international development agenda, the United Nations Educational, Scientific and Cultural Organization (UNESCO) acknowledges that education is a fundamental human right in the exercise of all other human rights because it promotes individual freedom and empowerment and yields important development benefits. Further, it recognizes that education is a powerful tool by which economically and socially marginalized adults and children can lift themselves out of poverty and participate fully as citizens. UNESCO also reports that millions of children and adults remain deprived of educational opportunities, many as a result of poverty (UNESCO, n.d.).

The United Nations has laid down international legal requirements to ensure the right to education. These instruments promote and develop the right of every person to enjoy access to education of good quality, without discrimination or exclusion, by requiring governments to fulfill their legal and political obligations. The primary global instrument for realizing the right to education that nations are bound to implement is the Convention on the Rights of the Child (UNCRC). The convention sets standards and obligations, both interdependent and indivisible, for the dignity and worth of every child everywhere. Thus, in ensuring the right to education, one cannot provide it in the absence of other rights, nor can it be claimed at the expense of other rights.

By agreeing to undertake the obligations of the convention, the Philippine government committed to protecting and ensuring children's rights and agreed to be held accountable before the international community. While the Philippines has signed and ratified the UNCRC, many government policies and practices do not include or recognize children's rights. The combined third and fourth periodic reports of the Philippines to the UNCRC (2008a) expressed concern over the increasing number of children who are not able to go to school. The report noted that for those who are in school, boys are twice as likely as girls to repeat a grade or dropout. Furthermore, the school readiness scores of grade 1 entrants indicated that boys performed generally worse than girls. Thus, teachers need to be better informed on what their students' lives are like, what competencies and understandings they might bring to school if school were ready to receive them, and what social and cultural contexts have a bearing on their interactions in the classroom.

In September 2009, a UN press release detailed the UNCRC's report of an increase in dropout rates in schools and a decreasing government budget for education over the years. In addition, it reported that the highest school dropout rate occurred in grades 1 and 2, a finding that revealed children's inadequate preparedness for school. In that press release, the top five causes for the dropout rates were identified as poverty, distance from school, and parents' attitude toward school, peer influence, and fear of teachers. With respect to education, the Philippine delegation said that there had been a reduction in outlays for education, but the government was doing its best to provide an adequate education budget.

It has long been recognized that education plays a key role in national development (United Nations, Department of Economic and Social Affairs, Population Division, 2003). There is evidence that government education spending improves the well-being of an individual and enhances his or her ability to earn income in the future. Thus, channeling education expenditures to the poor holds promise for breaking the intergenerational cycle of poverty (Manasan, 2007; Manasan, Cuenca, & Villanueva-Ruiz, 2007). Education is also a major determinant of an individual's well-being because it empowers him or her in the choice of work, place of residence, family size, health, lifestyle, and personal development. In the aggregate, all these individual choices and decisions have dramatic consequences for the country's development, particularly when they are supported by responsive demographic policy that promotes managing population quality and migration, and not just reducing fertility. It has been found that large family size can be an important contributor to poverty in the Philippines, since there is a link between the number of children and school attendance (Orbeta, 2005).

Tabunda and Albert (2002; cited in Maligalig & Albert, 2008) found that poverty issues stemming from basic education are complicated by emerging gender issues. The logistic regression model that both authors ran using the best explanatory variables for not attending school showed that those who belong to the bottom 30% of the income deciles are 2.8 times more likely to be out of school than those in the upper 70% income group. In addition, the results indicate that boys are more likely than girls not to attend schools, all other factors being equal. More specifically, boys are 1.4 times more likely not to attend schools than girls.

In the Philippines, while education may be a mechanism for the poor to be freed from the shackles of poverty, studies have shown that the poor are less likely to obtain a basic education (Maligalig & Albert, 2008). Children from poor families are forced to stay out of school not only because they cannot afford the costs but also because, given the poor quality of education, it makes more sense for them to work rather than stay in school. Both cost and quality factors are inherently tied to poverty because poor families have to sacrifice sending their children to school, especially during periods of crisis. This condition limits the opportunities for poor families to send their children to schools that provide quality education (Maligalig & Albert, 2008).

Studies have supported the World Bank's claims about the importance of female education (Knowles, Lorgelly, & Owen, 2002; Lorgelly & Owen, 1999). Results of those studies suggest that educational gender gaps are an impediment to economic development, thus lending credence to the World Bank's emphasis on the importance of female education in raising labor productivity. However, there is good reason to believe that female and male education affect society in different ways.

What happens when opportunities to earn income lure a boy away from his studies, and he experiences the freedom brought about by the income that he earns? Under what circumstances will a boy give up schooling in favor of work? A commissioned study cites compelling economic and sociocultural reasons for the apparent progress of girls in school and pressing expectations of boys to augment income for their families (Labajo et al., 2006).

The emerging school dropout patterns of boys growing up in poverty represent a growing area of concern not only in the Philippines but also in the United States and the rest of the world (Martino & Pallota-Chiarolli, 2003; Pollack, 1999; Tyre, 2008). It should be emphasized that this problem has been glossed over for years, perhaps because the recognized global problem is that boys outperform girls in many other countries. It needs to be pointed out that in the Philippines boys are being outperformed by girls, and this has been going on for quite some time. However, reliable regional data is needed to draw an accurate picture of the domestic scenario in the Philippines. The regional data will also point to the areas in which boys are at risk of indirect discrimination due to denied access to an effective education. Furthermore, data gathered will provide evidence of male disadvantage in education outcomes such as early departure from school.

Tyre (2008) revealed that by every measure, boys in the United States are failing: they like school less, do less well, and get expelled more often than girls. If they do finish high school, they are unlikely to attend college and even more unlikely to graduate from college. From the moment they step into the classroom, boys begin to struggle. They get expelled from preschool nearly five times as often as girls; in elementary school they are diagnosed with learning disorders four times as often. By the eighth grade, huge numbers are reading below basic level. By high school, they are heavily outnumbered in advanced placement classes and, except in the realm of athletics, show indifference to most extracurricular activities. Boys now account for less than 43% of those enrolled in college, and the gap widens every semester. The growing gender imbalance in education portends massive shifts for the next generation in terms of how much they earn and whom they marry.

UNICEF Philippines (2009) estimates that 2 million children who ought to be in school are not. There are roughly 13 million school-age children, but participation rates in public elementary schools have decreased since 2000. Out of ten first-grade students, only seven will likely reach the fifth grade. Worse, only 67% will eventually complete basic elementary education. Although public education in the Philippines is free, the ability of schools to retain students has been poor.

Recent survey data revealed dwindling personal interest as the predominant reason why more poor rather than non-poor boys leave school. This particular reason is difficult to dissect, because it may be due to several interconnected and underlying factors such as limited information on the value of education. In many instances, poor boys or their parents do not see the return on education. They believe that the education system is not producing relevant results for their boys and their families. Boys become frustrated in school because they are not able to cope with lessons because of a challenging school or household environment.

For whatever reason, it is evident that Filipino boys have been outperformed by their Filipina counterparts for a long time. This shifting gender parity has repercussions for the state's accountability in fulfilling children's rights to, in, and through education. Confronted by this evidence, we ask the broad question: What would change in boys' education in the Philippines if children's rights really mattered?

Given that poverty issues that are complicated by emerging gender issues are also rights issues, this study aims to answer the following two questions:

- What factors push-pull boys away from schools in the Philippines?
- Are poor rather than non-poor boys at greater risk for not attending school?

Emerging School Dropout Patterns Among Males

This investigation hinges on an earlier study by the author using data from the 2000 Philippine Census of Population and Housing. That study revealed that in Cebu (one of the most developed provinces in the Philippines) there was no significant difference between males and females — regardless of whether they were in urban or rural areas — in terms of their participation in pre-school sessions and for those who had not completed any grade from urban areas. For both levels of the compulsory basic education program, it was only in the elementary level that there were significantly more boys than girls attending schools in all the cities and municipalities of Metro Cebu and the rest of the province. At the secondary level, there was a complete reversal of the picture, because it was the girls who were attending and completing high school instead of the boys (Cañete, 2011).

Another paper (Nava, 2009) examined the effect of poverty on dropping out of school for various gender groups, school levels, and school locations. Its findings were based on interview data from dropouts, parents of dropouts, teachers, and school administrators of four purposely selected elementary and secondary schools in urban and rural locations. The study revealed that employment activities were common among older male dropouts, while domestic duties such as caring for younger siblings were most common with females in rural areas. Low motivation was also evident among male and younger school dropouts (Nava, 2009).

A Philippine Institute for Development Studies (PIDS) policy brief concluded that the primary reason for dropping out in the country is lack of personal interest. This reason is quite difficult to analyze because of demand-side issues such as poor information on the value of education. The study determined that the poor may be "very impatient" and do not see the returns in education (which may only be felt a few years down the road) as an attractive proposition. The reason can also be a supply-side issue wherein the education system is not producing relevant results for school-age children and their families. Finally, lack of personal interest can be a result of the interaction of demand and supply-side issues — for example, the accumulation of frustrations in school that occur when students are not able to cope with lessons because of a poor school environment and/or poor household environment (Orbeta, 2010).

Knowles, Lorgelly, and Owen (2002), in their analysis of a re-parameterized model wherein education enters the model as a gender gap, suggested that the interpretation of the coefficient on educational gender gaps depends crucially on what other education variables are included in the equation. Their empirical results suggest that female education has a positive and significant impact on labor productivity across countries. But the role of male education is less clear.

Lorgelly and Owen (1999) studied the effect of female and male schooling on economic growth in the Barro-Lee model, which provided evidence that growth is positively related to schooling. They validated Stokey's observations that the findings of Barro-Lee's model were largely due to the influence of four Asian countries (Hong Kong, Singapore, Taiwan, and South Korea) that have very high levels of growth but very low levels of female schooling, and that deleting the female education variable would cast doubt on the statistical significance of the male education variable. Using deletion diagnostics and partial scatter plots to identify influential observations, the results obtained point to the fragile nature of both the significant negative effect of female education and the significant positive effect of male education in the Barro-Lee model.

In 2005, the Philippine Center for Investigative Journalism (PCIJ), an independent, nonprofit media agency that specializes in investigative reporting, released a two-part investigation on why boys are dropping out of school. The report found that more girls finish high school and end up in college because boys have to work at a time when more families find it increasingly hard to scrape out a living. Moreover, the boys tend to be diverted from school by all sorts of distractions, including computer gaming. Large class sizes and the generally deteriorating quality of education also add to the male dropout rate, as these conditions make it harder to keep the boys' attention on school work (Chua, 2005a).

Meanwhile, at home, parents are busier and are less able to supervise teenage children and encourage them to remain in school. The result is that there are now more illiterate boys than girls. Women account for 70% of overseas Filipino workers and increasingly dominate local employment as well. This gender imbalance has consequences for families and for society as a whole. It means that men will also be dropping out of the labor force, adding to the strain on marriages and family harmony. Marriages break up because of the education and employment gap, resulting in rising numbers of female-headed households. Society, meanwhile, has to deal with the social consequences of large-scale male unemployment. Educators expect joblessness among Filipino males to worsen as more and more boys dropout of high school and join the ranks of the unemployed. The impact of boys not getting enough education is already being felt in the country's literacy rates and more so in university enrollment, which means wasted human potential. In the Philippines, with mostly male-headed households and with most of the men unemployed or underemployed, this situation may pose a challenge to many marriages, which are often frayed by arguments that arise because wives earn more than their husbands (Chua, 2005b).

Research Methods

This study used data from the *2008 Annual Poverty Indicators Survey* (APIS), a nationally representative survey conducted by the National Statistics Office from January to June 2008. The APIS provided non-income indicators related to poverty at the national and regional levels. The APIS has a summarized version of income and expenditure items that provides some comparison of social indicators across regions, albeit roughly on the prevalence of poverty, the depth of poverty, and the severity of poverty.

The 2008 APIS covered approximately 40,000 housing units drawn from the 2,835 *barangays*[1] that served as enumeration areas (EA) spread across the 17 administrative regions. An EA is an area with discernible boundaries consisting of approximately 350 contiguous households. For operational considerations, a maximum of 30 housing units were selected per sample EA.

The primary source of information for the APIS is the household head, if available at the time of the survey. All household heads in the housing units were interviewed except for housing units with more than three households. In such a housing unit, three households were randomly selected with equal probability. The lowest 30% income stratum refers to the bottom 30% of the total families in the income distribution. This grouping of families was used as a proxy for those falling below the poverty line. In descending order of family income, the highest 70% refers to the upper 70% of the total families in the income distribution. It is the complement of the bottom 30%. The income strata provided the economic feature of the data necessary for statistical analysis.[2]

The 2008 APIS determined the educational attainment of family members 5 years of age and older. It also determined whether a family member age 6–24 was currently attending formal school, and if so, his or her current level. If not, the reason for not attending school is asked.

Boys in the Philippines Still Lack Interest in School

Table 12.1 shows the number of males ages 6–24 who did not attend school during SY2008–2009 in all regions. Of the total 6.3 million, 2.8 million were from the lowest 30% income stratum (poor) and 3.5 million from the highest 70% income stratum (non-poor).

For Tables 12.1 and 12.2, the reasons for not attending school during SY2008–2009 are ordered as follows: (1) schools are very far; (2) no school within the *barangay*; (3) no regular transportation; (4) high cost of education; (5) illness/disability; (6) housekeeping; (7) marriage; (8) employment/looking for work; (9) lack of personal interest; (10) cannot cope with school work; (11) finished schooling; (12) problem with school records; (13) problem with birth certificate; (14) too young to go to school; and (15) unspecified others.

From Table 12.2, it can be gleaned that nationwide, the most popular reason for not attending school was a lack of personal interest (reason 1) among males in the lowest 30% income stratum. The same is true in 14 other regions —Cagayan Valley, CALABARZON, MIMAROPA, Bicol, Western, Eastern, and Central Visayas, Zamboanga Peninsula, Northern Mindanao, Davao, SOCCKSARGEN, Caraga, ARMM, and Ilocos, where at the same time the high cost of education also topped the list of reasons. Poor males in NCR and Central Luzon likewise reasoned that the high cost of education was their primary reason for not being in school during the survey period. The next two most commonly stated reasons, perhaps expectedly, are economic in nature: specifically, high cost of education and employment or looking for work. High cost of education must be highlighted

Table 12.1 *Percent of male population 6–24 years of age who were not attending school during SY 2008–2009, listed by reason for not attending school, by region, and income stratum*

Location	Income Stratum	Percent of male population 6–24 years old who were not attending school during SY2008–2009 by reason for not attending school															Total	Pop. ('000)
		1	2	3	4	5	6	7	8	9	10	11	12	13	14	15		
Philippines	Lowest30%	2.2	0.5	0.3	26.0	2.7	0.8	5.3	18.6	36.7	1.4	1.2	0.4	0.5	2.4	0.9	100	2,833
	Highest70%	0.4	0.0	0.2	20.1	2.6	0.6	6.3	23.0	23.0	0.7	10.0	0.5	0.2	0.7	0.7	100	3,469
National Capital Region	Lowest30%	0.0	0.0	0.8	34.8	10.0	2.3	4.5	22.0	18.9	1.0	0.9	0.0	0.9	2.2	1.5	100	55
	Highest70%	0.0	0.0	0.2	17.9	2.9	0.4	6.8	38.9	17.3	0.5	11.8	0.7	0.3	0.7	1.4	100	512
Cordillera Administrative Region	Lowest30%	1.8	0.4	0.8	18.5	3.6	0.9	6.1	8.7	53.0	4.0	1.3	0.4	0.0	0.0	0.4	100	46
	Highest70%	1.1	0.0	0.0	15.6	3.9	1.0	6.3	21.3	31.3	1.8	15.7	0.4	0.0	0.0	1.4	100	57
Region I Ilocos	Lowest30%	0.0	0.0	0.0	33.9	3.0	0.0	9.1	14.5	33.9	1.6	1.9	0.0	0.0	1.3	0.6	100	145
	Highest70%	0.0	0.0	0.0	31.0	2.7	0.5	5.1	22.9	23.4	0.7	13.7	0.0	0.0	0.0	0.0	100	200
Region II Cagayan Valley	Lowest30%	1.4	0.0	0.7	36.8	2.8	0.4	8.9	6.0	37.9	1.4	1.5	0.0	0.0	1.4	0.8	100	109
	Highest70%	1.2	0.0	0.0	28.5	2.0	0.3	9.5	10.8	33.8	3.0	9.1	0.3	0.0	0.8	0.8	100	139
Region III Central Luzon	Lowest30%	1.6	1.9	0.4	39.2	1.7	0.4	5.9	28.9	16.8	0.0	1.6	0.0	0.0	0.8	0.7	100	151
	Highest70%	0.1	0.0	0.1	21.1	2.7	0.7	7.2	40.4	18.5	0.2	8.0	0.2	0.4	0.0	0.3	100	505
Region IVA CALABARZON	Lowest30%	0.6	0.0	0.3	26.1	2.2	1.2	5.5	25.6	34.3	0.5	0.3	0.0	1.3	1.4	0.7	100	196
	Highest70%	0.4	0.0	0.2	15.1	2.0	1.0	6.4	47.0	18.2	0.3	7.7	0.5	0.1	0.9	0.3	100	558
Region IVB MIMAROPA	Lowest30%	3.5	0.0	0.0	25.4	1.8	0.0	6.9	12.6	43.6	1.3	1.3	0.8	0.0	1.8	1.2	100	137
	Highest70%	0.5	0.0	0.0	20.3	1.6	0.0	5.4	23.1	29.8	0.0	16.5	1.6	0.0	0.0	1.1	100	65
Region V Bicol	Lowest30%	2.7	0.6	0.2	29.2	4.2	0.6	4.4	19.0	31.8	2.8	0.6	0.2	0.3	2.4	1.1	100	268
	Highest70%	1.1	0.0	0.4	29.1	5.4	0.7	6.0	20.3	23.2	1.3	11.3	0.7	0.0	0.3	0.4	100	150
Region VI Western Visayas	Lowest30%	1.9	0.2	0.2	22.0	4.3	0.4	4.5	23.2	34.4	0.8	2.1	1.1	0.6	2.6	1.9	100	302
	Highest70%	1.0	0.0	0.0	21.6	2.9	0.3	3.7	30.2	23.0	0.3	12.9	1.3	0.8	0.3	1.6	100	216
Region VII Central Visayas	Lowest30%	1.2	1.3	0.8	19.1	1.2	1.9	3.8	28.5	34.4	3.0	1.2	0.5	0.6	2.3	0.2	100	214
	Highest70%	0.2	0.0	0.8	15.7	2.7	1.3	4.8	39.6	24.2	0.9	8.5	0.4	0.4	0.0	0.0	100	270
Region VIII Eastern Visayas	Lowest30%	0.4	0.6	0.2	21.9	2.2	0.6	5.3	10.2	52.3	1.6	1.0	1.2	1.4	0.6	0.6	100	223
	Highest70%	0.7	0.0	0.0	27.3	2.3	0.4	5.4	10.7	41.6	2.2	8.2	0.4	0.0	0.0	0.8	100	116
Region IX Zamboanga Peninsula	Lowest30%	5.7	0.8	0.3	22.3	2.5	1.4	4.4	8.4	46.3	1.4	0.9	0.3	0.3	3.4	1.7	100	157
	Highest70%	0.0	0.0	0.0	20.0	0.8	0.9	4.9	25.5	33.2	0.9	11.7	0.4	0.0	0.4	1.2	100	107
Region X Northern Mindanao	Lowest30%	2.7	0.8	0.0	23.3	4.5	0.8	4.1	24.8	35.5	0.8	1.1	0.0	0.0	1.5	0.0	100	171
	Highest70%	0.7	0.0	0.0	16.3	1.8	0.4	8.7	29.1	25.5	1.1	13.3	0.0	0.0	0.4	2.7	100	127
Region XI Davao	Lowest30%	2.6	0.3	0.6	26.2	1.4	0.3	5.7	16.0	41.4	0.8	1.2	0.0	0.5	2.7	0.5	100	151
	Highest70%	0.5	0.0	0.7	17.3	2.6	0.3	6.9	34.4	27.2	0.5	7.4	0.2	0.0	1.4	0.4	100	175
Region XII SOCCKSARGEN	Lowest30%	3.2	0.2	0.7	24.3	2.2	1.0	6.8	18.2	37.1	0.4	1.4	0.4	1.0	1.9	1.3	100	195
	Highest70%	0.3	0.0	0.7	22.3	3.8	0.0	8.2	24.1	26.3	0.6	12.3	0.7	0.0	0.4	0.3	100	114
Region XIII Caraga	Lowest30%	1.7	0.5	0.9	23.0	2.9	0.3	3.4	21.8	41.5	0.7	1.5	0.0	0.0	0.5	1.2	100	124
	Highest70%	0.5	0.0	0.0	19.2	2.3	0.5	3.9	35.9	29.2	0.5	6.9	0.0	0.0	0.5	0.5	100	63
Autonomous Region in Muslim Mindanao	Lowest30%	4.9	0.5	0.9	25.4	0.3	2.1	3.7	12.7	34.2	2.7	1.0	0.2	0.0	10.8	0.6	100	188
	Highest70%	1.3	0.0	0.0	16.8	0.8	1.2	4.8	35.9	23.6	1.3	4.9	0.8	0.4	8.3	0.0	100	94

Source: National Statistics Office

because, despite the fact that elementary school attendance is mostly in public schools where there are virtually no school fees, there are other costs besides school fees that have prevented school-age boys from attending school, a fact that is often forgotten or unaccounted for. Marriage accounts for the fourth-most-popular reason among the poor males nationwide and in CAR, Ilocos, Central Luzon, CALABARZON, MIMAROPA, Bicol, theVisayas, Davao, SOCCKSARGEN, and Caraga, while being too young to be in school is the fourth-most-popular reason given among boys in ARMM. Administrative concerns about school records and problems with birth certificates figured very low in the reasons given for not attending school. The survey results also revealed that unavailability of schools and lack of regular transportation to school are not very common reasons for dropping out of schools among poor males.

Among non-poor males nationwide, employment or looking for work was the most often cited reason. The same trend was observed in nine other regions —NCR, Central Luzon, CALABARZON, Western Visayas, Central Visayas, Northern Mindanao, Davao, Caraga, and ARMM. Non-poor males from CAR,

Table 12.2 *Ranks of reason given by male population 6–24 years old for not attending school, by region and income stratum*

Location	Income Stratum	Rank of reason given by male population 6–24 years old for not attending school during SY2008–2009 by reason for not attending school														
		1	2	3	4	5	6	7	8	9	10	11	12	13	14	15
Philippines	Lowest30%	7	12	15	2	5	11	4	3	1	8	9	14	12	6	10
	Highest70%	12	15	13	3	6	10	5	1	2	7	4	11	13	7	7
National Capital Region	Lowest30%	13	13	12	1	4	6	5	2	3	9	10	13	10	7	8
	Highest70%	14	14	13	2	6	11	5	1	3	10	4	8	12	8	7
Cordillera Administrative Region	Lowest30%	7	11	10	2	6	9	4	3	1	5	8	11	14	14	11
	Highest70%	9	12	12	4	6	10	5	2	1	7	3	11	12	12	8
Region I Ilocos	Lowest30%	10	10	10	1	5	10	4	3	1	7	6	10	10	8	9
	Highest70%	9	9	9	1	6	8	5	3	2	7	4	9	9	9	9
Region II Cagayan Valley	Lowest30%	7	13	11	2	5	12	3	4	1	7	6	13	13	7	10
	Highest70%	8	13	13	2	7	11	4	3	1	6	5	11	13	9	9
Region III Central Luzon	Lowest30%	7	5	11	1	6	11	4	2	3	13	7	13	13	9	10
	Highest70%	12	14	12	2	6	7	5	1	3	10	4	10	8	14	9
Region IVA CALABARZON	Lowest30%	10	14	12	2	5	8	4	3	1	11	12	14	7	6	9
	Highest70%	10	15	13	3	6	7	5	1	2	11	4	9	14	8	11
Region IVB MIMAROPA	Lowest30%	5	12	12	2	6	12	4	3	1	8	8	11	12	6	10
	Highest70%	9	10	10	3	6	10	5	2	1	10	4	6	10	10	8
Region V Bicol	Lowest30%	7	10	14	2	5	10	4	3	1	6	10	14	13	8	9
	Highest70%	8	14	11	1	6	9	5	3	2	7	4	9	14	13	11
Region VI Western Visayas	Lowest30%	8	14	14	3	5	13	4	2	1	11	7	10	12	6	8
	Highest70%	9	14	14	3	6	11	5	1	2	11	8	8	10	11	7
Region VII Central Visayas	Lowest30%	9	8	12	3	9	7	4	2	1	5	9	14	13	6	15
	Highest70%	13	14	9	3	6	7	5	1	2	8	4	10	10	10	14
Region VIII Eastern Visayas	Lowest30%	14	10	15	2	5	10	4	3	1	6	9	8	7	10	10
	Highest70%	9	12	12	2	6	10	5	3	1	7	4	10	12	12	8
Region IX Zamboanga Peninsula	Lowest30%	4	12	13	2	7	9	5	3	1	9	11	13	13	6	8
	Highest70%	12	12	13	3	9	7	5	2	1	7	4	10	12	10	6
Region X Northern Mindanao	Lowest30%	6	9	12	3	4	9	5	2	1	9	8	12	12	7	12
	Highest70%	9	12	12	3	7	10	5	1	2	8	4	12	12	10	6
Region XI Davao	Lowest30%	6	13	10	2	7	13	4	3	1	9	8	15	11	5	11
	Highest70%	9	14	8	3	6	12	5	1	2	9	4	13	14	7	11
Region XII SOCCKSARGEN	Lowest30%	5	15	12	2	6	10	4	3	1	13	8	13	10	7	9
	Highest70%	11	13	7	3	6	13	5	2	1	9	4	7	13	10	11
Region XIII Caraga	Lowest30%	6	11	9	2	5	13	4	3	1	10	7	14	14	11	8
	Highest70%	7	12	12	3	6	7	5	1	2	7	4	12	12	7	7
Autonomous Region in Muslim Mindanao	Lowest30%	5	12	10	2	13	8	6	3	1	7	9	14	15	4	11
	Highest70%	7	13	13	3	10	9	6	1	2	7	5	10	12	4	13

Source : National Statistics Office

Cagayan Valley, MIMAROPA, Zamboanga Peninsula, and SOCCKSARGEN, like their poorer counterparts, also cited lack of personal interest as the most compelling reason not to attend school. High cost of education also figured prominently among the reasons why non-poor Filipino males were not attending school during the survey period.

Among most of the poor males and many non-poor males nationwide, the primary reason for not attending school is lack of personal interest. Understanding this particular reason is quite complex, because it is shared by boys who came from families belonging to the highest 70% and the lowest 30% income strata and who may have their own compelling explanations for their choice.

The non-poor boys may find their home and school environments too comfortable and end up becoming complacent or indifferent about their motivation to finish school. Non-poor boys may also tend to be diverted from school by

Table 12.3 One-way ANOVA: Reason for not attending school versus income stratum and location

Income Stratum
(Lowest 30% and Highest 70%)
Location (Administrative regions in the Philippines)

Reason	DF	SS	MS	F-Value	p-Value	DF	SS	MS	F-value	p-Value
1 Schools are very far	1	20.340	20.340	16.560	0.001	16.000	24.250	1.520	1.230	0.340
2 No school within the barangay	1	1.930	1.930	14.460	0.002	16.000	2.135	0.133	1.000	0.500
3 No regular transportation	1	0.650	0.650	9.760	0.007	16.000	2.001	0.1250	1.880	0.109
4 High cost of education	1	272.800	272.800	15.390	0.001	16.000	745.700	46.600	2.630	0.031
5 Illness/disability	1	1.700	1.700	0.780	0.389	16.000	58.640	3.660	1.690	0.152
6 Housekeeping	1	0.650	0.650	3.860	0.067	16.000	7.711	0.482	2.860	0.021
7 Marriage	1	3.560	3.560	2.290	0.150	16.000	63.380	3.960	2.550	0.035
8 Employment/looking for work	1	1050.600	1050.600	45.890	0.000	16.000	2179.900	136.200	5.950	0.000
9 Lack of personal interest	1	931.900	931.900	64.090	0.000	16.000	1863.800	116.500	8.010	0.000
10 Cannot cope with school work	1	2.226	2.226	4.590	0.048	16.000	20.605	1.288	2.660	0.030
11 Finished schooling	1	744.490	744.490	145.000	0.000	16.000	94.020	5.880	1.140	0.395
12 Problem with school record	1	0.360	0.3603	5.170	0.037	16.000	4.4547	0.278	4.000	0.004
13 Problem with birth certificate	1	0.596	0.596	4.330	0.054	16.000	2.491	0.156	1.130	0.403
14 Too young to go to school	1	15.289	15.289	41.040	0.000	16.000	145.952	9.122	24.490	0.000
15 Others	1	0.095	0.095	0.260	0.615	16.000	6.951	0.434	1.200	0.359

things such as computer gaming. External community factors like these interact with internal school factors such as large class sizes and deteriorating quality of education to push and pull boys out of school.

The other popular reason for not attending school among both poor and non-poor boys is employment or looking for work. For poor boys it becomes more sensible for them to work rather than stay in school. However, non-poor males may have cited their contribution to the household income as a compelling reason for not going to school. The high cost of education as the main reason for both poor and non-poor males to leave school is very intriguing. While basic education is freely available, the poor may still opt to leave school because of its hidden costs. Maligalig and Albert (2008) confirmed the relationship between non-attendance in school and household income, namely, the percentage of children who are not attending school decreases as income (of the household to which the children belong) increases. Citing the high cost of education as the reason to stop schooling among non-poor boys, however, is difficult to comprehend but may be explained by their families' lack of support of their efforts to finish school.

Table 12.3 combines the one-way ANOVA for reason for not attending school versus income stratum that combines the lowest 30% and highest 70% income strata and reasons versus location, covering the 17 administrative regions of the Philippines. This table reflects the following reasons that were not significantly different according to income stratum: (5) illness/disability; (6) housekeeping; (7) marriage; (13) problem with birth certificate; and (15) unspecified others. This means that among the poor and the non poor, the 10 remaining reasons showed significant correlation to household income levels.

The following reasons were very popular among poor males: distance of home from schools; no school within the *barangay*; lack of regular transportation; high cost of education; illness/disability; domestic chores; marriage; lack of personal interest; inability to cope with school work; problem with birth certificate; too young to go to school; and unspecified others. Non-poor males reported that the primary reasons for their not attending school were that many of them were employed or at least looking for work, that they encountered a problem with school records, or that they have finished schooling.

The following reasons for not attending school showed no significant correlation to the various administrative regions of the Philippines: (1) schools are very far; (2) no school within the *barangay*; (3) no regular transportation; (5) illness/disability; (11) finished schooling; (13) problem with birth certificate; and (15) unspecified others.

The following reasons for not attending school showed significant difference by location: high cost of education and marriage among males in Cagayan Valley; housekeeping chores and too young for school among boys in ARMM; marriage; employment or looking for work in industry-rich CALABARZON; lack of personal interest in poverty-stricken Eastern Visayas; inability to cope with school work among males on the Cordilleras; and problem with school records for both MIMAROPA and Western Visayas.

When Push Comes to Shove

With the exception of having finished school (reason 11), all reasons are expected to negatively impact society. As implied in Chua (2005b), boys who do not finish school will most likely join the ranks of the illiterate. Boys not getting enough education are deemed to affect the country's literacy rates, which will in turn lessen enrolment in institutions of higher education and lead to wasted human potential.

With women gaining more autonomy due to educational attainment and job placement—factors that reduce a woman's propensity to marry—a change in marriage and fertility decisions is expected. Furthermore, since women tend to marry men richer or more educated than themselves, any problem of non marriage is not dispersed throughout society but is concentrated in two groups with dim wedding prospects: men with no education and women with a lot. This situation may produce cross border brides, a growing phenomenon observed in vital civil registration data. Almost 90% of intermarriages involve Filipino brides.

In the Philippines, lack of personal interest is clearly the predominant factor for poor and non poor males that, independently or simultaneously with other factors, acts to push pull them from school. There is also the prevalence of economic reasons for leaving school —high cost of education and employment or looking for work. Poor rather than non poor boys have a preponderance for not attending school in terms of magnitude and coverage of their reasons. Clearly, boys not attending school will have an impact on society.

The generally held assumption that gender equality can be expected to promote economic growth may take on a fresh perspective. Empirical evidence points to different societal manifestations of shifting gender parity conditions that may affect poor males. Thus, the African proverb about educated girls educating a family and the whole nation remains intuitively appealing.

Poverty issues stemming from basic education are complicated by associated gender and rights issues. The widespread incidence of poor boys not attending school suggests a failure in the Philippines' commitment to the welfare and protection of its children (boys most especially) through their equal right to a progressive education. Since education remains a strategic investment in better performance, the Philippines could do well to respond to the recommendations raised by the United Nations in 2009, as President Benigno S. Aquino III also embarks on education reforms. The flagship of these reforms is the expansion of basic education from a 10-year cycle to a globally comparable 12-year cycle and includes, among other goals, universal preschool; full basic education for Muslims in the Philippines adaptive to their culture and grounded on a solid curriculum in communication, science, and math; and rationalized media of instruction that promotes trilingualism (English, Filipino, and mother tongue).

These reforms, when viewed through the "right to education" lens, tend to magnify the problem that has been sidestepped for years that boys who are being pushed pulled out of school in alarming numbers and in widespread areas are actually denied access to an effective education and are at risk for indirect discrimination. By legitimizing the issue of why fewer boys now attend and finish basic education, appropriate and timely investments from both the public and private sectors of the Philippines can be made to ensure that all children, with special attention to the excluded boys, enjoy their right to education.

In an era that demands scientifically based teaching, educators should have an accurate, evidence based picture of what their students' lives are like, what competencies and understandings they might bring to school if school were ready to receive them, and what social and cultural contexts have a bearing upon the interactions that occur in the classrooms. Teachers have to be familiar with their students' lives, or they may be accused of deficit thinking. Bomer and colleagues (2008) warn educators about an in-service teacher education program in the United States that makes claims that lack supporting evidence and, even worse, are contradicted by anthropological, sociological, and other research on poverty. In its comprehensive analysis of the truth claims of that program, Bomer's group concludes that its characterizations of people living in poverty leaves more teachers misinformed, leading to a situation in which poor students are more likely to be placed in lower tracks or lower ability groups.

The Philippines, too, needs a transformational framework for understanding the lives of poor boys to ensure that they can fully claim their right to education. The education community can benefit from research and review of social psychological approaches to community empowerment programs such as that of Efren Peñaflorida's pushcart classrooms for urban street children in Metro Manila (CNN, 2009). Peñaflorida's advocacy, which began as a youth project aimed at diverting students' attention from street gangs and toward community activism and personal development, is very relevant to the growing challenge of boys being pushed-pulled out of school, because it provides an outside-the-box solution to a perennial problem. Given the magnitude of the educational challenge, both the public and private sectors need to develop a transformational education framework that tackles individuals' sense of mastery of their lives that preserves their dignity and self-respect.

Notes

1. The Local Government Code of the Philippines defines a *barangay* — a contiguous territory with at least 2,000 inhabitants—as the country's basic political unit.

2. In the 2008 APIS, MIMAROPA, Region IV B, and CALABARZON, Region IV A, were reported as two separate regions. The province of Lanao del Norte and Iligan City, which were formerly under Region XII, were reported under Region X. The province of South Cotabato and the new province of Sarangani, General Santos City, and Koronadal City, which were formerly under Region XI, were transferred to Region XII.

References

Bomer, R., Dworin, J.E., May, L., & Semingson, P. (2008). Miseducating teachers about the poor: A critical analysis of Ruby Payne's claims about poverty. *Teachers College Record, 110* (12), 2497–2531.

Cañete, L.Y. (2011). Reviewing the effects of population growth on basic education development. *CNU* [Cebu Normal University] *Journal of Higher Education, 5*, 138–147.

Chua, Y.T. (2005a). *When classes open today, many boys won't be in school.* Philippine Center for Investigative Journalism. Our Latest Report. Retrieved from http://pcij.org/stories/2005/boys.html

Chua, Y.T. (2005b). *The boys aren't in school and they can't find jobs either.* Philippine Center for Investigative Journalism. Our Latest Report. Retrieved from http://pcij.org/stories/2005/boys2.html

CNN. (2009). Pushcart educator named CNN Hero of the Year. Retrieved from http://www.cnn.com.ph/2009/LIVING/11/16/cnnheroes.tribute.show/index.html

The Economist. (2011, August 20). The flight from marriage. pp.17–20.

Knowles, S., Lorgelly, P.K., & Owen, P.D. (2002). Are educational gender gaps a brake on economic development? Some cross-country empirical evidence. *Oxford Economic Papers, 54* (1), 118–149.

Labajo, M., Soriano, C., Gaddi, R., & Fabros, M. (2006). *Beyond gender parity in Philippine education: Achieving gender equality in and through education in the Philippines.* Retrieved from http://e-netphil.org/main/images/stories/research_materials/genderparity_education.pdf

Lorgelly, P.K., & Owen, P.D. (1999). The effect of female and male schooling on economic growth in the Barro-Lee Model. *Empirical Economics, 24*(3), 537–557.

Maligalig, D.S., & Albert, J.R.G.(2008). *Ensuring a more evidence-based policy for basic education. PIDS Policy Notes* (Philippine Institute for Development Studies, Discussion Paper No. 2008-03).

Manasan, R. (2007). *Risks and opportunities in securing increased resources for MDGs at the national level. PIDS Policy Notes* (Philippine Institute for Development Studies, Discussion Paper No. 2007-08).

Manasan, R.G., Cuenca, J.S., & Villanueva-Ruiz, E.C. (2007). *Benefit incidence of public spending on education in the Philippines.* Philippine Institute for Development Studies, Discussion Paper No. 2008-08. Retrieved from http://www.eaber.org/sites/default/files/documents/PIDS_Manasan_2008_02.pdf

Martino, W., & Pallota-Chiarolli, M. (2003). *So what's a boy: Addressing issues of masculinity and schooling.* Maidenhead, UK: Open University Press.

National Statistics Office, Philippines. (2008). *2008 annual poverty indicators survey.*

Nava, F.J.G. (2009). Factors in school leaving: Variations across gender groups, school levels and locations. *Education Quarterly* (U.P. College of Education), *67*, 62–78.

Orbeta, Jr.,A. (2005). *Number of children and their education in Philippine households.* East Asian Bureau of Economic Research, Development Economics Working Papers No. 22669.

Orbeta, Jr., A. (2010). A glimpse of the school dropout problem. *The Filipino Child.* Philippine Institute of Development Studies, Policy Brief No. 4.

Pollack, W. (1999). *Real boys: Rescuing our sons from the myths of boyhood.* New York: Henry Holt.

Tyre, P. (2008). *The trouble with boys.* New York: Crown Publishers.

United Nations. (2009, September 15). *Committee on Rights of Child examines report of the Philippines.* Press Release. Retrieved from http://www.unhchr.ch/huricane/huricane.nsf/view 01/38FCCB7A51169DACC1257632005BBF1B?opendocument

United Nations. Committee on the Rights of the Child (UNCRC). (2008a). *Consideration of reports submitted by states parties under Article 44 of the convention —Third and fourth periodic reports of states parties due in 2007: The Philippines* (CRC/C/PHL/CO/3-4 – 20 March 2009).

United Nations. Committee on the Rights of the Child. (UNCRC). (2008b). *Consideration of reports submitted by states parties under Article 44 of the convention —Concluding observations: The Philippines* (CRC/C/PHL/CO/3-4 – 22 October 2009).

United Nations. Department of Economic and Social Affairs, Population Division. (2003). *Population, education and development: The concise report* (ST/ESA/SER.S/226). Retrieved from http://www.un.org/esa/population/publications/concise2003/Concisereport2003.pdf

United Nations Educational, Scientific and Cultural Organization (UNESCO). (n.d.). *Right to education.* Retrieved from http://www.unesco.org/new/en/education/themes/ leading-the-international-agenda/right-to-education/

Ward, J., Lee, B., Baptist, S., & Jackson, H. (2010). *Evidence for action: Gender equality and economic growth.* Chatham House. Retrieved from http://www.chathamhouse.org/publications/ papers/view/109478

Intersections of Education and Freedom of Religion Rights in the UNCRC and in Practice

Janette Habashi

The key to the United Nations Convention on the Rights of the Child (UNCRC) is the assumption that signatory nation-states are obligated to uphold children's rights. The reason that this is an assumption is that not all signatory nation-states have implemented or even totally agreed on every article of the UNCRC. The UNCRC document delineates core rights that pertain to children's life experiences, which encompass the foundation of children's development and interactions with the adult world. As this volume has emphasized, one of the essential rights that implicitly enables a child to engage and develop is the right of education. The right of education within the UNCRC is not considered a luxury that is accessible to the few, but a right of *all* children. This impeccable concept entails the process and meaning of education to every child. To safeguard education as a fundamental right of every child is, one assumes, to ensure children's welfare and development now and in the future. Indeed, the attainment of such a right is through the achievement of other rights entailed in the CRC.

The right of education is intertwined with other rights in the CRC and should be examined in light of this interdependence. However, for the purpose of this chapter, the focus is on the relationship between children's right of education and right of freedom of thought and expression, especially since the right of education encourages tolerance, world harmony, and respect for all cultures and religions. Ensuring children's educational rights is not only essential to children's development but also to the larger global community, as children will shape the future.

The right of education in this context pertains to formal/structured education in which children have access to school, quality learning, and education that respects all other rights, and in which elementary education for children is compulsory. Indeed, the emphasis on education rights by the UNCRC is equally supported by different nation-states, although perhaps for differing reasons (Habashi, Driskill, Lang, & DeFalco, 2010). Some nation-states have focused on elements that pertain to prevention and provision of children's rights, while others have looked at the implementation of the entire UNCRC.

The purpose of educational rights as articulated in Article 29 of the UNCRC is to "develop each child's personality, talents and abilities to the fullest. It should encourage children to respect others, human rights and their own and other cultures…help them learn to live peacefully, protect the environment and respect others" (UNCRC, 1989). Education in this conceptualization is not only inclusive of arithmetic, literacy, or science; it serves also to educate children to live in harmony and tolerance. The expectation is that these ideas about education found within the UNCRC are achievable. Although the assumption is that every one of the UNCRC's articles is interdependent and intertwined with the others, this is not necessarily the case. For example, some articles bestow independence on children, while others place more importance on the guidance of parents or the state (Scolnicov, 2007).

Given this, are educational considerations attainable on their own, without upholding other UNCRC articles that might jeopardize educational rights? Is it possible to achieve educational rights without considering other rights? Could we accomplish Article 29 as a separate entity without considering the impact of Article 14, which encourages the child's right of freedom of expression, religion and thought? Is it appropriate to conceptualize the implications of denying one right—in this context, freedom of religion and thought—to allow for the realization of the right to education, or denying religious education in order to uphold the right to secular education? Of course, the underlying thrust of Article 29 is that each child should have the educational opportunity to reach his or her full potential, which is considered a stepping-stone to tolerance and world harmony. The right of education is not only a provision to train a child in a skill, but also a tool to achieve communications across cultures and religions.

Meanwhile, to understand such an interrelationship between a child's right of education and that child's right of freedom of thought and expression is to recognize the multifaceted features of Articles 28 and 29, wherein the right of education is categorized in terms of rights *to* education, rights *within* education, and rights *through* education. The right *to* education involves the right for children to access education. It is not enough for education to be available; rather, children must be able to access this education. Rights *within* education are to ensure that children's rights are respected while they attain education. Rights *through* education entail the fact that education is the basic framework for ensuring other rights (Tomaševski, 2001). The challenge of this goal is in the distribution of the rights, which requires an unequal effort across the three categories. The focus of rights to education is mainly on the right *to* education, because access to education facilitates children's development and survival and therefore, according to most nation-states (Habashi et al., 2010), has priority over the others. Nevertheless, this focus on the right *to* education should be correlated with the rights *within* education, especially if the right of the child regarding freedom of religion and thought (Article 14 of the UNCRC) is weakened because of compulsory religious education.

Therefore, the aim of this chapter is to analyze the questions about the relationship between the achievement of the right of education and the right to express religion, as well as how these two articles of the UNCRC contribute to children's embrace of tolerance and world harmony. These questions are important the right of education and the right to religious freedom are contradictory at times, specifically in respect to compulsory religious education. Thus it is important to deconstruct two segments in this relationship: (1) religious education models that enhance or undermine Articles 14 and 29, and (2) the current response on the interaction between religious education and its violation of children's right of education and the UNCRC.

Religious Education

In many secular, post-modern societies, religious education in public schools is proscribed by an assumed doctrine of separation of state and religion, whereby religious discourse is not part of the public school curriculum. In fact, this secularist stance does not eliminate the currently mandated religious education that is explicitly incorporated into public schools in certain nation-states (Skeie & Weisse, 2008). The main purpose of religious education is manifest in two main goals: one that emphasizes national identity and therefore the element of state indoctrination, and another that views the purpose of religious education to provide the individual with a moral compass and character. The two notions are inextricably tied to each other, as values are ingrained in the national doctrine and infused in the public discourse.

It is religious education that enables state ideology to continue while being framed in love, peace, and other virtues. The sheer ubiquity of the effect of religious education is found in its style of transmission, akin to indoctrination, from a state to the people (Hull, 1993; Kaymakcan, 2009). This doctrinaire aspect does not necessarily coincide with tolerance or harmony, as

> even to indoctrinate belief in a god of love is a contradiction in terms, and is harmful to the growth of the student. Love can only exist in freedom, and the whole point of the indoctrination process is to deprive the pupil of freedom through a process of dogmatic deception" (Hull, 2004, pp. 13–14).

Religious education does not usually encourage inclusiveness but rather explicitly alienates other cultures and people by highlighting only one's belief system (Jawoniyi, 2012;Van der Walt, Potgieter, & Wolhuter, 2010). Most religious education holds that the religion being taught is the ultimate virtue, and people who are not part of the community are considered less worthy. This exclusivity does not encourage communication across belief systems. Furthermore, the practice of compulsory religious education is, at best, contrary to the discourse of separation of religion and state and the notion of freedom that is embedded in Article 14(1) of the UNCRC, which states: "States Parties shall respect the right of the child to freedom of thought, conscience and religion" (UNCRC, 1989). Moreover, this practice of mandated religious education also violates Article 29(2), which states that education should encourage "The development of respect for human rights and fundamental freedoms, and for the principles enshrined in the Charter of the United Nations" (UNCRC, 1989). The lack of freedom and the ethnocentrism in religious education are not enough to offset the notions articulated in UNCRC Articles 14 and 29. Indeed, numerous international court cases have shown that such critiques of religious education as these are not sufficient to prevent its mandate in public schools (Evans, 2008).

Models of Religious Education

Compulsory religious education is not restricted to the school curricula of developed or developing countries, or Western or non-Western nation-states. Its supporters cross borders (Skeie, 2006) and ignore the mandate of the UNCRC of separation of state and religion, and freedom of expression (Article 14) and respect for all religions (Article 29). This imposition of religious education into school curricula generally manifests in one of three models and does not adhere to children's rights. It is important to examine these three models in order to analyze how religious education either undermines or validates Article 29, especially in terms of world harmony and tolerance.

The first model could be labeled *separate but equal* in religious education, as it is a response to the specific student population of a country. For example, some countries have a diverse religious population, and religious courses are organized according to the students' affiliations: Christian students attend Christian religious classes, Muslim students attend Islamic religious classes, and so forth (Benavot & Resh, 2003; Leirvik, 2010). It is argued that this model benefits students' cultural identity in that every student learns about his/her religion without learning about other religions. On the other hand, this model could be perceived as proselytizing or coercive by encouraging students to commit to a faith without being educated about other belief systems (Kaymakcan, 2009). Furthermore, this practice of *separate but equal* in religious education accommodates students' cultures but does not necessarily support the goals of harmony and tolerance detailed in Article 29 of the UNCRC. This model denies children the freedom to explore different ideas and limits the discussion of religion to an ideology that is supported by religious institutions and the state's religious agenda (Hull, 1993). Therefore, this approach does not provide an opportunity for all students to learn about other religions but rather restricts the freedom to acquire knowledge and thereby reduce social prejudice (Kilkelly, 2009).

The second model of religious education could be labeled *allegiance to one religion*, in which the mandated religious education is explicitly narrowed to one religious doctrine for all students. Under this model, a country will declare one religion—to which the majority of the population is affiliated—to be the official religion of the country, and religious education is designed to educate children in this dominant or "state" religion (Hull, 1993; Jawoniyi, 2012). In some cases, for example in Germany, different religious institutions are responsible for designing public school religious education, although the curriculum should be guided by specifics of state constitutions. All students, regardless of their belief system, must attend the classes; however, some regions have offered alternative religious classes for minorities (Skeie & Weisse, 2008).

Another instance of *allegiance to one religion* occurs when religious education is organized by the state. This is seen in Italy, where schools teach Catholicism and their curriculum is designed by the state. This approach to religious education, which promotes the religion of the majority, is a response to a country's historical tradition (Fineman & Worthington, 2009). However, the customizing of this model might vary, depending on a country's debates and policies. Nonetheless, the practice of *allegiance to one religion* limits the freedom or opportunity to learn about other religions outside the dominant state religion and therefore does not promote tolerance and the reduction of prejudice. Article 29 states in part "that the education of the child shall be directed to the development of respect for human rights and fundamental freedoms..." (UNCRC, 1989). In view of this, the imposition of a single-faith, state-designed religious education is denying the fundamental freedom of children to choose their own religion.

The fact that children, according to the UNCRC, have the right to an education—and that such an education should encapsulate respect for freedom—implies that enforcing a state-sanctioned religious education is in fact not in accordance with Articles 28 and 29 of the UNCRC. In addition, this model of religious education, which denies children freedom of religion and expression, is in opposition to Article 14 of the UNCRC (Kilkelly, 2009). Overall, this model aims to perpetuate the state ideology and produce a desired social and political outcome.

The third model of religious education is *all in one*, which exemplifies the multi-religion approach. In this model, pluralism in religious education curriculum embraces the learning of more than one religion and aims to present different religions without the goal of conversion (Evans, 2008). This approach has been promoted in the United Kingdom as an opportunity to teach all religions equally. The model was even strengthened after September 11, 2001, through teaching about Islam in the school system in a manner that eschews prejudice and stereotype (Moulin, 2012). This approach has also been encouraged in South Africa, where the society celebrates different belief systems (Chidester, 2003). The curriculum in this model is based on a common spirituality among religions and on non-confessional learning, as opposed to the confessional framework of the other two models. The non-confessional approach aims to move the instruction of religious education from a religious and state doctrine to learning and appreciating all religions, so that students learn to achieve tolerance and world harmony.

Religious pluralism is encouraged in most European countries because it meets the goals of Article 29 of the UNCRC but does not violate the secular ideology and the separation of state and religion. However, not all children enjoy this opportunity, as some children (occasionally at their parents' behest) may opt out of certain courses, or possibly be excused from public schooling. While it may seem as though an educational system that upholds religious coursework is granting children the right to a choice in whether or not to take the courses, in fact their exclusion from certain courses and/or schools altogether denies children the right to an education and the aims of Article 29 (Evans, 2008).

While these three models of religious education are used to validate mandated religious curricula in schools, they all fall short in fulfilling the mandates found in Articles 14, 28, and 29 of the UNCRC. The above-described three models are the dominant approaches to religious education around the globe. Religion is part of national ideology (Habashi, 2008) and indoctrination as it continues to be practiced within education, especially according to the first two models. However, the UNCRC refocused the religious education discussion from a national to a global debate, whereby religion is not only an exercise of community but is part of individual liberty. This is more challenging when it comes to the question of children's rights, as documented in the discussion between freedom of religion and religious education.

Religious Freedom and Religious Education

The freedom of thought, conscience, and religion articulated in Article 14 of the UNCRC is a concept about which many countries have voiced reservations (Bielefeldt, 1995), mainly because the article implies that children have a choice about their religious affiliation. For example, several Islamic countries have expressed reservations about the CRC as being incompatible with Shari'a law (UNICEF, 2007). In particular, countries such as Bangladesh have reservations about Article 14, paragraph 1, because of the seeming autonomy of children to choose their own religion. Such reservations usually are noted without consideration of the next two paragraphs. The entirety of Article 14 of the UNCRC (1989) states:

> 1. States Parties shall respect the right of the child to freedom of thought, conscience and religion. 2. States Parties shall respect the rights and duties of the parents and, when applicable, legal guardians, to provide direction to the child in the exercise of his or her right in a manner consistent with the evolving capacities of the child. 3. Freedom to manifest one's religion or beliefs may be subject only to such limitations as are prescribed by law and are necessary to protect public safety, order, health or morals, or the fundamental rights and freedoms of others.

Article 14 delineates the understanding of children's autonomy and the parents' and nation-states' role in children's freedom of religion and thought, which are essential to the discussion of religious education. At the same time that Islamic nation-states hold reservations about paragraph 1 of Article 14, many European countries have voiced objections to these reservations (UNICEF, 2007). For example, countries such as Norway, Sweden, and Austria hold that these reservations to Article 14 are at odds with the general premise of the CRC. In fact, even Muslim countries such as Pakistan have withdrawn their reservations based on Islamic law and have taken exception to reservations about Article 14 (Nyazee, 2003).

Nation-states that have voiced objections to Article 14 have not always exemplified its ideals. In Norway, at least two cases involving religious education have been brought before international tribunals. These cases involved an initiative on the part of Norway to mandate "a single class in comparative religion and philosophy that all students could study" (Evans, 2008, p. 462) that allows children to learn multi-religious perspectives. However, the focus of the course is on Lutheranism, the state religion (Relaño, 2010). The focus on one religion did not deter the courts from finding in Norway's favor, because they found this particular religious course, which encompasses multi-religious perspectives, to be neutral and objective. Paradoxically, these cases show that even though Western nation-states did not state reservations about Article 14, and in fact voiced objections to reservations, religious education in public schools is very much an issue, even in Western countries.

Moreover, the issue of religious freedom found in Article 14 is important in relation to Article 29 and the right of education. Keeping in mind Article 29, discourse and reservations involving Article 14 beg these questions: (1) Is it possible to achieve rights of education while accomplishing world harmony and tolerance without violating the freedom of expression and religion of the child? and (2) Could the right *to* education be treated equally to the right *through* education, especially when discussing religious education? Considering that the right *to* education is an access issue and the right *through* education is a content issue, nation-states and parents should not violate children's right through education while providing public education. To understand this possible relationship (right *to* education and the right *through* education), it is crucial to deconstruct the roles of parents and nation-states in freedom of religion and the assumption that children have an opportunity to express freedom of thought. Article 14 creates apprehension because it could offer an opportunity for children to opt for a religion that might be in opposition to the family or the dominant cultural values.

The element of children's independence and what might be perceived as acclaimed child autonomy is the main concern of this article. The central premise is that a child has the ability for self-determination (Freeman, 1995). However, for some scholars, children do not have the opportunity to exercise full independence in regard to religious affiliation, especially when it is compared to the individual's rights entailed in Article 18 of the International Covenant on Civil and Political Rights (ICCPR), which states that individuals have not only freedom of religion but also the right to choose and practice religion in both private and public spaces (Veerman & Sand, 1999). The element of choice and the promise of protection in exercising one's religion are not clear in the CRC, and this is considered a weakness. Even though there was some movement toward making the CRC parallel to the ICCPR on this particular right (the right to religious freedom), it was rejected during the drafting process of the Convention of the Rights of the Child (Kilkelly, 2009). This limitation on children's right to freedom of expression and religion still continues to generate concern, as the article gives parents some power over their child(ren) but denies nation-states' agenda in the process (Hull, 2004; Jawoniyi, 2012). This would account for the tensions between children and parents, as well as children/parents and nation-states, regarding religious education.

Parents have a role within the freedom of religion and thought realm, yet it is not clear where children's rights end and parents' rights begin. The parents' role is to provide guidance in religious matters as the child gains maturity. In this sense, a child has autonomy over his/her religion (Veerman & Sand, 1999). However, in case there is a conflict between children and parents, the parents' wishes take precedence, as prescribed by Article 5 of the UNCRC. Therefore, the exercise of children's autonomy and independence is the parents' prerogative. Furthermore, parents and children join together at times against nation-states to advocate for the children's right to religious freedom. Parents have defended this right of children against nation-states' mandatory religious education, although they have not always been successful. Woodhouse (2012) describes a court case in which a parent in Italy sued the government over the lack of freedom of religion in school, because Christian symbols dominated the school spaces. The court issued an order in which it requested that public schools remove all signs of Christianity. However, this order was not fully implemented. Another example of parents' advocacy of children's freedom of religion is offered by the Norwegian cases described above, in which parents brought before the United Nations Human Rights Committee

(UNHRC) a case claiming that religious education in Norway was neither objective nor neutral (Evans, 2008).

What Should Religious Education Be?

The right of education detailed in the UNCRC is undoubtedly connected with other rights, and it is important to link the right of education with the consideration of other rights. All are connected *through* education as much as *to* education, as is the case with Article 14 and the right to freedom of religion and thought. The public school approach to religious education has experimented with multiple models, some of which, it has been argued, are not complementary to the goals listed in the right of education found in the UNCRC.

The first model of *separate but equal* and the second model of *allegiance to one religion* do not provide freedom to religion and do not necessarily achieve tolerance and harmony (Hull, 2004). The third model of *all in one* (the pluralistic argument) is complex in its presentation and creates many challenges and opportunities. On the one hand, it provides the opportunity to discuss most world religions—on the assumption, that is, that the curriculum entailed is not biased toward one religion. On the other hand, this model is problematic, as some students may opt out of these courses because of their religious beliefs, and their educational rights would therefore be limited. To avoid this outcome, one should build on the possibilities provided in the pluralistic approach. The advantage of this model is that it encourages the presentation of all religions equally in its curriculum, wherein the content is demonstrated in terms of historical knowledge. This curriculum would minimize the moral argument that is continually being made for religious education in the first two models and would leave it in the hands of the parents, as is encouraged by the UNCRC. Therefore, this development would take the discussion of religious education, especially in its third model, to another level where its presence in the school curriculum does not need to be separate but *part of the social sciences*.

In a way, the new approach of including multi-religious studies as part of the social sciences would provide an opportunity to encourage the separation of state and religion and, at the same time, would enable children to engage in a world that provides tolerance for all. Indeed, this approach to world tolerance is essential for our globalized, post-modern world, especially since the planet is shrinking, and traditional borders are becoming blurry in terms of cultures and ideas. Therefore, the concept of multi-religion learning is integral to developing tolerance within the world community, especially as most nation-states are providing access to education as part of children's rights. In considering the multi-faceted aspects of the right of education and freedom of religion, it is time to revisit the UNCRC with a fresh perspective that will encourage these rights to empower each other.

This is especially the case because all of the articles of the UNCRC are inter-twined, though some appreciate the autonomy of the child and others require that this right be supervised by parents or the state. Examining the right of education together with the right to religious freedom is one way to shed light on the inter-connection of these rights, and this mode of investigation should take place for other rights embodied in the UNCRC. The right of education is so complex that focusing only on access to education might negate or delay the achievement of the right within and through education, as seen in the several examples presented in this book. The international experiences of Western and Global South nation-states discussed in the previous chapters showcase the importance of the right of education and the different ways in which to achieve this right. These examples also show how the right of education is interrelated with other rights. Shier and his colleagues' work presented the challenges of children's right of education, es-pecially when children themselves are deprived from economic security rights. Another example is how the right of education in South Africa can be achieved if it is not focused on all children. The right of treating all children equally is a key element of CRC, and if this right is not effective, the right of education is fundamentally challenged.

Therefore, this volume has not only addressed the question of why the right of education is significant to children, but has also shown how this right is inter-connected with other rights. The exercise of focusing on children's right of educa-tion and its relationship with other rights will enable us to enhance the well-being of children and empower the community to develop and to cross boundaries.

References

Benavot, A., & Resh, N. (2003). Education governance, school autonomy, and curriculum imple-mentation: A comparative study of Arab and Jewish schools in Israel. *Journal of Curriculum Studies, 35*(2), 171–196.

Bielefeldt, H. (1995). Muslim voices in the human rights debates. *Human Rights Quarterly, 17*(4), 588–617.

Chidester, D. (2003). Religion education in South Africa: Teaching and learning about religion, religions, and religious diversity. *British Journal of Religious Education, 25*(4), 261–278.

Evans, C. (2008). Religious education in public schools: An international human rights perspective. *Human Rights Law Review, 8*(3), 449–471.

Fineman, A., & Worthington, K. (2009). *What is right for children? The competing paradigms of religion and human rights.* London: Ashgate.

Freeman, M. (1995). Children's rights in a land of rites. In B. Franklin (Ed.), *Handbook of children's rights* (pp. 70–88). London: Routledge.

Habashi, J. (2008). Palestinian children crafting national identity. *Childhood: A Journal of Global Child Research, 15*(1), 12–29.

Habashi, J., Driskill, S.T., Lang, J.H., & Defalco, P.L. (2010). Constitutional analysis: A procla-mation of children's right to protection, provision, and participation. *International Journal of Children's Rights, 18*(2), 267–290.

Hull, J.M. (1993). The nature of religious education. In N. Hooshang & S. Vickers (Eds.), *Distinctive aspects of Baha'i education: Proceedings of the Third Symposium on Baha'i Education* (pp. 13–19). Birmingham, UK: The Baha'i Publishing Trust.

Hull, J.M. (2004). Practical theology and religious education in a pluralist Europe. *British Journal of Religious Education, 26*(1), 7–19.

Jawoniyi, O. (2012). Children's rights and religious education in state-funded schools: An international human rights perspective. *International Journal of Human Rights, 16*(2), 337–357.

Kaymakcan, R. (2009). Religious education culture in modern Turkey. In M. de Souza et al. (Eds.), *International handbook of the religious, moral and spiritual dimensions in education* (pp. 449–460). Dordrecht and London: Springer Science & Business Media.

Kilkelly, U. (2009). The child's right to religious freedom in international law: The search for meaning. In M.A. Fineman & K. Worthington (Eds.), *What is right for children? The competing paradigms of religion and human rights* (pp. 243–267). Burlington, VT: Ashgate.

Leirvik, O. (2010). Religious education, communal identity and national politics in the Muslim world. *British Journal of Religious Education, 23*(3), 223–236.

Lundy, L. (2006). Mainstreaming children's rights in, to and through education in a society emerging from conflict. *International Journal of Children's Rights, 14*(4), 339–362.

Moulin, D. (2012). Religious education in England after 9/11. *Religious Education, 107*(2), 158–173.

Nyazee, I.A. (2003). Islamic law and the CRC (Convention on the Rights of the Child). *Islamabad Law Review, 1*(1/2), 65–121.

Relaño, E. (2010). Educational pluralism and freedom of religion: Recent decisions of the European Court of Human Rights. *British Journal of Religious Education, 32*(1), 19–29.

Scolnicov, A. (2007). The child's right to religious freedom and formation of identity. *International Journal of Children's Rights, 15*, 1–17.

Skeie, G. (2006). Plurality and pluralism in religious education. In M. de Souza et al. (Eds.), *International handbook of the religious, moral and spiritual dimensions in education* (pp. 307–319). Dordrecht, The Netherlands: Springer.

Skeie, G., & Weisse, W. (2008). Religion, education, dialogue and conflict: Positions and perspectives of students in Germany and Norway. In T. Knauth, D.P. Jozsa, G. Bertram-Troost, & J. Ipgrave (Eds.), *Encountering religious pluralism in school and society: A qualitative study of teenage perspectives in Europe* (pp. 327–338). Berlin: Waxmann.

Tomaševski, K. 2001. *Human rights in education as a prerequisite for human rights education.* (Right to Education Primers No. 4). Stockholm: Raoul Wallenberg Institute/Swedish International Development Agency.

UNICEF. (2007). *Law reform and implementation of the Convention on the Rights of the Child.* Florence, Italy: UNICEF Innocenti Research Centre.

United Nations. (1989). *United Nations Convention on the Rights of the Child.* Geneva: United Nations.

Van der Walt, J.L., Potgieter, F.J., & Wolhuter, C.C. (2010). The road to religious tolerance in education in South Africa (and elsewhere): A possible "Martian perspective." *Religion, State, and Society, 38*(1), 29–52.

Veerman, P., & Sand, C. (1999). Religion and children's rights. *International Journal of Children's Rights, 7*, 385–393.

Woodhouse, B. (2012). Religion and children's rights. In J. Witte & C. Green (Eds.), *Religion and human rights: An introduction* (pp. 299–315). New York: Oxford University Press.

Contributors

Karen Alicia Ortiz Alvarado, from La Dalia, Nicaragua, is a qualified primary teacher and currently Community Education Worker on CESESMA's *Safe, Quality Schools* project.

Martha Baiyee is a professor of early childhood education in the Department of Teacher Education at Eastern Michigan University, where she is a former Acting Director of the Center for Child and Family Program at the Institute for the Study of Children, Families and Communities (ISCFC). In this role, Dr. Baiyee conducted research with area community agencies on preschool expulsion prevention that investigated the perspectives of both parents and providers and their experiences with intervention programs in southeast Michigan. Dr. Baiyee's research, beyond preschool expulsions, focuses on cross cultural issues of child development, learner-centered teaching, teacher education, assessment and program evaluation. As a former early childhood educator in the US and Africa, Dr. Baiyee has a unique perspective on the daily experiences of teachers who work with young children.

Natasha Blanchet-Cohen is Assistant Professor in the Department of Applied Human Sciences at Concordia University, in Canada. She has worked extensively on children's rights issues in Canada and abroad, including Venezuela and Colombia. She is an associate of the International Institute for Child Rights and

Development where she was research director from 2000 to 2009. Her applied research and publications center on issues around child agency and child protection, the creation of child-youth friendly cities, bridge-building across cultures and practices, and developmental approaches to monitoring and evaluation.

Leodinito Yongco Cañete is the Secretary of the Board of Regents and the University Secretary of Cebu Normal University (CNU), a chartered state university of the Philippines. He is also its chief planning officer. At CNU, Dr. Cañete handles graduate courses in theory development, research process, and current pedagogical issues, and serves as editor-in-chief of CNU's *Journal of Higher Education*. Dr. Cañete has published and presented research projects in demography and basic education development, gender-responsive governance and community development. He has long been interested in education institutions and their knowledge management systems, having been a teacher and educational administrator in the Philippines. His dissertation, completed at Aristotle University of Thessaloniki, defined the relationships of Filipino immigrant communities in Greece within the Greek education framework.

Zorayda Castillo from Waslala in Nicaragua's autonomous Caribbean region joined CESESMA in 2009 where she is currently Education Worker on the *Safe, Quality Schools* project. She was formerly a teacher.

Lesley Emerson is Lecturer in Education and Deputy Director of the Centre for Children's Rights, Queen's University Belfast (www.qub.ac.uk/ccr). Her research focuses primarily on education in conflicted affected societies, children's rights and children's rights-based approaches to research. She has particular expertise in relation to the role of former combatants in educating young people about conflict, its legacy and transition to peace. She is involved actively in the promotion of effective citizenship education and is co-country lead of the Five Nations Citizenship Network (www.fivenations.net).

Janette Habashi, an Associate Professor in the Department of Human Relations at the University of Oklahoma, teaches graduate- and undergraduate-level courses with concentrations in the areas of local and global human diversity issues and educational developmental theories. She is committed to advocating for social policy that reflects her passion for children and the betterment of the community. Her research with children and Indigenous populations examine socialization, national identity, political participation/resistance, and children's rights-based approaches in policy and research. Janette has published several peer-reviewed articles in prestigious social science, cultural, and childhood journals, as well as contributed book chapters and refereed conference papers to the academic community. Janette is also the founder of A Child Cup Full organization that empower women and children's educational opportunity (www.childscupfull.org).

Celeste Hawkins is a doctoral candidate in the Educational Studies program at Eastern Michigan University. She is a former Director of Family and Community Services at Avalon Housing, Inc. which provides housing support services to vulnerable and oppressed populations in Washtenaw County. She holds a B.S. in Psychology and a master's degree in Social Work and was honored as the recipient of the *Distinguished Alumni of the Year Award* from the College of Health and Human Services from Eastern Michigan University in 2011. She was recently appointed to serve on the local transitional school board in her hometown community of Ypsilanti, Michigan. Celeste's research interests include African American Vernacular English, social stigma and educational equity in K–12 public schools.

Panagiota Karagianni is an assistant professor at the Department of Primary Education at Aristotle University of Thessaloniki, Greece. Her research and publications focus on education policy, social justice and disability studies. Her teaching experience covers a wide age range from preschool to graduate school students. She has also worked at the Universities of Birmingham and Cyprus at undergraduate and postgraduate level.

Leonilda Barrera López, from Waslala in Nicaragua's autonomous Caribbean region, joined CESESMA in 2009, where she is currently Education Worker on the *Safe, Quality Schools* project. She was formerly a social worker.

Lisa Marie Lacy is a Ph.D. student of Curriculum and Instruction, with Special Education concentration, at Arizona State University. She has been a special education teacher in a public school setting, working with students aged 5 to 12 years old. Her tenure in the classroom inspired her to become a student/family advocate. Lisa uses research to uncover the multiple identities that teachers and students possess, which are often at odds with the prevailing notion of schooling. Her current interests are children's lived experiences and how these experiences shape school identities.

Laura Lundy is a professor of education law and children's rights in the School of Education, Queen's University, Belfast and a Barrister at Law. She is the director of the Children's Rights Centre at Queen's (www.qub.ac.uk/ccr), an interdisciplinary research collaboration in children's rights. Her expertise is in law and children's rights, with a particular focus on education rights and the implementation of the UNCRC. She has been a principal investigator or co-researcher in large interdisciplinary research projects funded by the UK Social and Economic Research

Council, public bodies such as the Northern Ireland Commissioner for Children and Young People and leading charitable foundations such as The Wellcome Trust and Barnardo's. She was the Chair of the Northern Ireland Human Rights Commission's working party on education rights for the Northern Ireland Bill of Rights and is a former Equal Opportunities Commissioner for Northern Ireland.

Soula Mitakidou is an associate professor of cross-cultural education at the Department of Primary Education at Aristotle University of Thessaloniki, Greece. Her research interests and publications address many aspects of diversity, including the teaching of Greek as a second language for marginalized learners, inclusive education and literacy development through children's literature. She has published a number of children's books, including bilingual Greek and English volumes, and has long worked in the area of social inclusion of minority groups.

Mokgadi (neé Kekae) Moletsane is Associate Professor in the Department of Educational Psychology at the University of the Western Cape. She is an Educational Psychologist registered with Health Professional Council of South Africa. Mokgadi obtained her PhD in Educational Psychology from the University of Pretoria. She is an alumnus of HERS –USA Bryn Mawr College, where she attended the Women in Higher Education Training Program. She publishes and presents papers at international and national conferences in the field of psychology and education. Her research interests include child development, learning and behavioral difficulties, inclusive education, psychological assessments and intervention, indigenous knowledge in psychology and education.

Bekisizwe S. Ndimande is Assistant Professor of Curriculum and Instruction in the Department of Interdisciplinary Learning and Teaching at the University of Texas at San Antonio. His research interests span the fields of curriculum studies, education policy, children's rights, and immigrant education. He has published several book chapters and many journal articles, including *Pedagogy of the Township*, in Sonia Nieto (Ed.), *Dear Paulo: Letters from Those who Dare Teach*; *Race and Resources, Race Ethnicity and Education;* and *Lutas Docentes nas Escolas Públicas para negros na África do Sul pós-apartheid, Cadernos de Educação*. Ndimande has collaborated with scholars from Brazil, South Africa, and Northern Ireland.

Martha Lidia Padilla from Samulalí, Nicaragua, came to CESESMA in 1999 where she is coordinator of the *Participation of Child Workers in the Prevention of Economic Exploitation* project. She has a degree in sociology and previously worked as a primary school teacher.

Lacey Peters is an assistant professor of early childhood education in the Department of Curriculum and Teaching at Hunter College, CUNY. She earned her PhD from the Arizona State University Mary Lou Fulton Teachers College. In addition, she has been a preschool teacher, working primarily with children aged 3 to 5-years old. Her time in the classroom served as a catalyst for becoming an advocate for children's rights and participation. Lacey uses research to promote the voices and perspectives of members of the early childhood community that are often subverted or excluded from research and policy in the United States, including children, parents (or other family members), and early childhood care and education professionals. Her current interests are primarily focused on examining children and parents' perspectives on their experiences during the pre-kindergarten to kindergarten transition.

Nkidi Phatudi is a member of the Faculty of Education at the University of Pretoria, where she has served as founder and Head of the Department of Early Childhood Education and teaches early years literacy pedagogy in first and second languages to undergraduate and postgraduate students. She is a leading researcher of the mother tongue learning group in the University of Pretoria consortia, conducting research on the value and place of mother tongue instruction (African Languages) at higher education institution and her chapter draws, in part, from that work. Phatudi has written a number of books in African languages, most of which are storybooks. She is an editor of a forthcoming second language teaching book, *Introducing English as a First Additional Language in the Foundation Phase.* Her research focus includes transitions of children from home and preschool into Grade 1, and the impacts of children's transition when their schools do not offer, or neglect their home languages.

Valerie Polakow is a professor of educational psychology and early childhood, and teaches in the Educational Studies Doctoral Program in the Department of Teacher Education at Eastern Michigan University. Her scholarship encompasses the impact of public policies on children in poverty, women and welfare, and access to child care and post-secondary education in national and international contexts. In her writings she has attempted to document the lived realities of those who have been *shut out*— from early childhood education, from K–12 education, and from post-secondary education; and to give voice to those whose rights have been violated by poverty, race, and gender discrimination. She was a Fulbright scholar in Denmark, and is the recipient of several awards for scholarship including the 2010 *Distinguished Contributions to Gender Equity in Education Research* by the American Educational Research Association. She is the author/editor of seven books including *Lives on the Edge: Single Mothers and Their Children in the*

Other America (which won the Kappa Delta Pi book of the year award in 1994) and *Who Cares for Our Children: The Child Care Crisis in the Other America.*

Cheryl Rau is of Tainui, Kahungungu and Rangitane descent and is currently the Central Regional Manager for Te Tari Puna Ora o Aotearoa/New Zealand Childcare Association. Her educational and research focus has centred on Te Tiriti o Waitangi partnerships in Aotearoa, with Māori educators articulating strategies which nurture tamariki Māori potentiality across the early childhood community and support indigenous children's rights to quality early childhood education. Cheryl's thirty-year background in education has been across multiple sectora, including primary, secondary, tertiary and community and she was previously involved in early childhood professional learning programs as the coordinator/director of Ngāhihi.

Jenny Ritchie has a background as a child-care educator and kindergarten teacher, followed by 23 years of experience in early childhood teacher education. She is an Associate Professor in early childhood teacher education at Te Whare Wānanga o Wairaka–Unitec Institute of Technology, Auckland, New Zealand. Her teaching, research, and writing has focused on supporting early childhood educators and teacher educators to enhance their praxis in terms of cultural, environmental and social justice issues. She has recently led three consecutive 2-year studies funded by the New Zealand Teaching and Learning Research Initiative. Her recent publications include "Caring for Ourselves, Others, and the Environment: Applying an Indigenous Paradigm in Early Childhood Education in Aotearoa, New Zealand" (2011) in J. Lin & R. Oxford (Eds.), *Transformative Eco-Education for Human and Planetary Survival* and "Early Childhood Education as a Site of Ecocentric Counter-Colonial Endeavour in Aotearoa New Zealand" (2012) in the journal *Contemporary Issues in Early Childhood.*

Harry Shier, from Ireland, is Education Adviser at CESESMA in Nicaragua, where he has lived since 2001. He is also a writer, trainer and researcher specializing in participation rights and the child's right to play, and is currently (2013) undertaking doctoral research at the Centre for Children's Rights at Queen's University Belfast. His published work includes *Pathways to Participation* (2001), a globally influential model for assessing adult engagement with children's participation processes.

Kylie Smith is Research Fellow and Senior Lecturer at the Youth Research Centre in the Melbourne Graduate School of Education at the University of Melbourne. In the past 10 years in her research work, Kylie has been actively involved in leading consultations with young children in curriculum and policy making in the early years. She has built partnerships with a number of local governments leading consultations with children to feed into the development of local government children's plans and policies. Kylie's research examines how theory and practice can challenge the operation of equity in the early childhood classroom and she has worked with children, parents and teachers to build safe and respectful communities.

Beth Blue Swadener is Professor of Justice and Social Inquiry and Associate Director of the School of Social Transformation at Arizona State University. Her research focuses on internationally comparative social policy, with focus on sub-Saharan Africa, and children's rights and voices. She has published nine books, including *Reconceptualizing the Early Childhood Curriculum; Children and Families "At Promise"; Does the Village Still Raise the Child?; Decolonizing Research in Cross-Cultural Context,* and *Power and Voice in Research with Children* and serves as Associate Editor of the *American Educational Research Journal.* She is a co-founder of the Jirani Project (www.jiraniproject.org), serving children in Kenya and Local to Global Justice, and is a founder of Reconceptualizing Early Childhood Education (RECE) (www.receinternational.org).

Moisés Molina Torres from La Reyna, Nicaragua, came to CESESMA in 2001 as a driver and subsequently qualified as an agronomist. He is a development worker specializing in organic farming and environmental education on the *Participation of Child Workers in the Prevention of Economic Exploitation* project.

Nohemí Molina Torres from La Reyna, Nicaragua, was one of the founders of CESESMA in 1992, and is currently coordinator of the *Safe, Quality Schools* project. She has a degree in sociology and previously worked as a primary school teacher.

Evangelia Tressou is a professor of pedagogy with emphasis on the education of marginalized groups and on mathematics teaching, at the Primary Education Department of Aristotle University, in Thessaloniki Greece. Her main research interests and many publications focus on the education of marginalized students, the problems they face with mathematics and the relation of gender with mathematics.

Index

RETHINKING CHILDHOOD

GAILE S. CANNELLA, *General Editor*

Researchers in a range of fields have acknowledged that childhood is a construct emerging from modernist perspectives that have not always benefited those who are younger. The purpose of the Rethinking Childhood Series is to provide a critical location for scholarship that challenges the universalization of childhood and introduces new, reconceptualized, and critical spaces from which opportunities and possibilities are generated for children. Diverse histories and cultures are considered of major importance as well as issues of critical social justice.

We are particularly interested in manuscripts that provide insight into the contemporary neoliberal conditions experienced by those who are labeled "children" as well as authored and edited volumes that illustrate life and educational experiences that challenge present conditions. Rethinking childhood work related to critical education and care, childhood public policy, family and community voices, and critical social activism is encouraged.

For more information about this series or for submission of manuscripts, please contact:

Gaile S. Cannella
Gaile.Cannella@unt.edu

To order other books in this series, please contact our Customer Service Department at:

(800) 770-LANG (within the U.S.)
(212) 647-7706 (outside the U.S.)
(212) 647-7707 FAX

Or browse online by series at:
www.peterlang.com